CURSED DAYS

Ivan Bunin in 1918

Ivan Bunin

CURSED DAYS

A Diary of Revolution

■:■:■

TRANSLATED FROM THE RUSSIAN,
WITH AN INTRODUCTION AND NOTES, BY
Thomas Gaiton Marullo

CHICAGO · *Ivan R. Dee* · 1998

Library of Congress Cataloging-in-Publication Data:
Bunin, Ivan Alekseevich, 1870–1953.
[Okaiannye dni. English]
Cursed days : a diary of Revolution / Ivan Bunin ; translated from the Russian, with an introduction and notes, by Thomas Gaiton Marullo.
p. cm.
Includes bibliographical references and index.
ISBN 1-56663-186-6 (alk. paper)
1. Bunin, Ivan Alekseevich, 1870–1953—Diaries.   2. Authors, Russian—20th century—Diaries.   3. Soviet Union—History—Revolution, 1917–1921—Personal narratives, Russian.   I. Marullo, Thomas Gaiton.   II. Title.
PG3453.B9Z4713   1998
891.7'8303—dc21

[B]   97-52822

To Julia Gauchman, friend and colleague

CONTENTS

PREFACE

ON JULY 30, 1925, Vera Muromtseva-Bunina, the wife of the Russian writer Ivan Bunin, wrote in her diary: "Ian [her name for her husband] has torn up and burned all his diary manuscripts. I am very angry. 'I don't want to be seen in my underwear,' he told me." Seeing Vera so upset, Bunin confided to her: "I have another diary in the form of a notebook. After I die you can do with it what you like."[1]

At the time of this incident, Bunin was fifty-six, Vera was forty-five. They had been living in exile in France for six years, having fled their country in the wake of the Russian Revolution and civil war. Although Bunin had been nominated for the Nobel Prize in Literature almost immediately upon his arrival in the West, it was not until 1933 that he would receive this award, the first Russian writer and the first writer in exile ever to be accorded such an honor. As for the diary, Bunin himself published it in 1936 with the title *Cursed Days* (*Okaiannye dni*).

Set against the backdrop of Moscow and Odessa in 1918 and 1919, *Cursed Days* is Bunin's scathing account of his last days in

1. M. Grin, *Ustami Buninykh*, vol. 2 (Frankfurt, 1981), 145–146.

Russia. Although banned during the years of Soviet power, it is en-
joying a stunning revival in the homeland today. By 1991 no fewer
than fifteen separate editions of *Cursed Days* had been published
in the former Soviet Union, including its appearance in a new six-
volume edition of Bunin's works in 1994.

The work is important for several reasons. *Cursed Days* is one
of the very few anti-Bolshevik diaries to be preserved from the time
of the Russian Revolution and civil war. It recreates events with
graphic and gripping immediacy. Unlike the works of early Soviets and emigrés and their self-censoring backdrop of memory,
myth, and political expediency, Bunin's truth reads almost like an
aberration.[2]

Cursed Days also links Russian anti-utopian writing of the
nineteenth century to its counterpart in the twentieth. Reminiscent
of the fiction of Dostoevsky, it features an "underground man"
who does not wish to be an "organ stop" or to affirm "crystal
palaces." Bunin's diary foreshadowed such "libelous" memoirs as
Evgenia Ginsberg's *Journey into the Whirlwind* (1967) and *Within
the Whirlwind* (1981), and Nadezhda Mandelstam's *Hope Against
Hope* (1970) and *Hope Abandoned* (1974), the accounts of two
courageous women caught up in the Stalinist terror of the 1930s.
Cursed Days also preceded the "rebellious" anti-Soviet tradition
that began with Evgeny Zamyatin and Yury Olesha, moved on to
Mikhail Bulgakov, and reached an apex with Boris Pasternak
and Alexander Solzhenitsyn. One can argue that, in its painful
exposés of political and social utopias, *Cursed Days*, together
with Zamyatin's *We* (1924), heralded the anti-utopian writing of
George Orwell and Aldous Huxley. Bunin and Zamyatin had cor-
rectly understood that the Soviet experiment was destined to self-
destruct.

2. On June 21, 1952, Bunin wrote to Mark Aldanov: "[A friend] once told
me that *Cursed Days* was the one book that had something to say about the Bolsheviks." See R. Fedoulova, "Lettres d'Ivan Bunin à Mark Aldanov (1948–1953),"
Cahiers du monde russe et sovietique, vol. 23, Nos. 3–4 (1982), 490.

PREFACE

Cursed Days was Bunin's only work to feature him in his "underwear." For a singular moment in his almost seventy years as a writer, he relinquished his classical and aristocratic stance, and, hauntingly, like Edvard Munch's tormented figure in "The Scream" (1893), tried to articulate the near despair that was flowing just beneath the surface of his personal, professional, and political poise.

In publishing this first English translation of *Cursed Days*, I wish to make Bunin's account accessible to Western readers so that this gifted writer may also be seen as a perceptive social critic. Unless readers can comprehend his wrenching struggle to make sense of his shattered world, they cannot appreciate his vacillation between hope and despair. To this edition of *Cursed Days* I also add a "coda"—selections from 1919 articles written by Bunin in Odessa, in which he elaborated certain insights into the Russian Revolution and civil war.[3] With these pieces I hope to complete an otherwise unavailable picture of Bunin's last days in his homeland. Bunin himself requested that "nothing be forgotten" about the trials and horrors of newly bolshevized Russia; and, as Santayana once warned, those who cannot remember the mistakes of the past are condemned to repeat them.

For their invaluable assistance at various stages in the preparation of this book, I wish to thank Linda Gregory and the staffs of the Departments of Reference, Interlibrary Loan, and Microtexts of the Theodore M. Hesburgh Library at the University of Notre Dame for obtaining many needed materials, for researching footnotes, and for photocopying texts, and to Margaret Jasiewicz, Sherry Reichold, and especially Nancy McMahon for typing correspondence and preparing the manuscript.

3. The citations from Bunin's articles in *The Southern Word* are found in *Skorb' zemli rodnoi. Sbornik statei 1919 goda* (New York, 1920), 44–50; B. Lipin, "Bunin v 'Iuzhnom slove'," *Zvezda*, No. 9 (1993), 125–141; and P. Shirmakov, "Vozvrashenie Bunina," *Svetskaia priroda i chelovek*, No. 3 (1991), 62–66. The text for *Cursed Days* is taken from the 1935–1936 eleven-volume edition of Bunin's collected works published in Berlin.

PREFACE

Several individuals deserve a special note of gratitude. Truly this book would not have come into being without Professor Klaus Lanzinger, former chairman of the Department of German and Russian Languages and Literatures at the University of Notre Dame; Professor Harry Attridge, former dean of the College of Arts and Letters; Professor Jennifer Warlick, former director of the Institute for Scholarship in the Liberal Arts; and Professor Roger Skurski, associate dean of the college, who allowed me to devote a good part of my energy to this project and who provided technical and financial assistance. I am also grateful to Professors Marc Raeff, Andrew Wachtel, and Gary Hamburg for their meticulous reading of the text; Helen Sullivan, who, along with others of the staff of the library of the University of Illinois at Urbana-Champaign, unearthed sources, researched additional footnotes, and answered myriad questions; Steven Bordenkircher, Bethany Thomas, and Matthew Welsh, who proved to be quick and ready research assistants; Vladimir Khmelkov, who helped with additional research and who translated many of the articles as well as passages involving the speech of Russian peasants and workers; and finally, my publisher, Ivan Dee, who believed in this project from the beginning and who taught me much about the publishing and scholarly worlds.

I also wish to recognize my wife, Gloria Gibbs Marullo, and my longtime colleague and friend, Sister Mary Colleen Dillon, S.N.D., of the Sisters of Notre Dame of Covington, Kentucky, both of whom read the manuscript innumerable times, kept me physically and spiritually whole during its writing, and learned more about Ivan Bunin than they really cared to. My cats, Gonzaga ("Gonzo"), Bernadette Marie, and Margaret Mary, and my other felines, Ignatius and Augustine, who both departed this life in spring 1997, provided affection and support when Bunin and I had exhausted the goodwill and cheer of everyone else.

Finally, I wish to express my gratitude to Julia Gauchman, also on the staff of the library at the University of Illinois, for her generous and expert assistance not only in the preparation of this

PREFACE

volume but also in my other works on Bunin. She has been a supporting force in my growth as a scholar, and it is to her that I dedicate this work as a token of my heartfelt affection and esteem.

T. G. M.

Notre Dame, Indiana
February 1998

CURSED DAYS

INTRODUCTION

ON JUNE 9, 1918, Ivan Bunin and his wife, Vera Muromtseva-Bunina, arrived in German-occupied Orsha, a small town directly southwest of Smolensk, en route to Odessa. "We are . . . 'abroad,'" Muromtseva-Bunina wrote in her diary. "With tears in his eyes, Ian said, 'Never have I crossed into a [foreign] country with such a feeling of the border. I am shaking all over! Can it be that I am finally safe from the power of the people, from those pigs!'" Muromtseva-Bunina continued: "Ian was deliriously happy when a German punched a Bolshevik in the face. . . ."[1]

The unfortunate Bolshevik aside, Bunin had more profound causes for relief. Only three days before, he and his wife had escaped the Revolution and civil war that was ravaging Moscow. In Odessa, in the newly established republic of the Ukraine, they hoped to find safety and rest. There they planned to wait out events, hoping to return to Moscow when the Bolsheviks were overthrown and Russia returned to its imperial status.

For Bunin, leaving his country was particularly bittersweet. He realized that whatever trials he had suffered in the twilight of im-

---

1. Grin, *Ustami*, vol. 1, 173.

perial Russia, he also had much to be grateful for. He had established himself as the last "nobleman" in Russian fiction. His works emerged from a literary tradition which, in less than a century, had moved the national written expression to the forefront of world literature and culture. In his own mind and that of many citizens and critics, Bunin was linked irrevocably to Pushkin, Turgenev, and Tolstoy. Works such as *The Village* (1909–1910) and *Dry Valley* (1911) were a fitting coda to a corpus that had begun with Pushkin's *Eugene Onegin* (1823–1831), embraced Turgenev's *Fathers and Sons* (1862), and seemed to reach near perfection with Tolstoy's *War and Peace* (1865–1869) and *Anna Karenina* (1875–1877).

For his thirty-year career as a writer in Russia, Bunin was also thankful. On several occasions he had discussed life with Tolstoy, and he enjoyed a close friendship with Chekhov; as early as 1903 he had won the Pushkin Prize for Literature, an award he would receive twice more before he left Russia; and in 1909 he had been elected to the Academy of Sciences in Saint Petersburg with the title of "honored academician." In pieces like "The Brothers" (1914), "The Gentleman from San Francisco" (1915), "Nooselike Ears" (1916), and "Chang's Dreams" (1916), Bunin had shown that he could incisively portray Russian life while plumbing the depths of universal human passions and struggles.

In these pre-Revolutionary years, however, Bunin had also endured enormous suffering and pain from which he bore deep scars. Born in 1870, he had grown up in the diminished circumstances of the post-Emancipation gentry, without a close-knit family, advanced education, or assured career. By age thirty he complained to his brother Yuly that his life was a "joke,"[2] and that existence was nothing but a daily and desperate struggle for survival. Blow followed upon blow. His marriage to Anna Nikolaevna Tsakni in 1898 failed in eighteen months; his only son, Kolya, died at the age

2. See Bunin's letter to Yuly Bunin, written in February 1900, as quoted in A. Baboreko, *I. A. Bunin. Materialy dlia biografii (s 1870 po 1917)* (Moscow, 1983), 78.

of five; Chekhov passed away in 1904 and Tolstoy in 1910, leaving Bunin alone to carry on the legacy of "aristocratic" writing in a culture that increasingly rejected "gentry" values.

Most wrenching of all for Bunin, no doubt, was that readers and reviewers misconstrued the meaning of his life and art. He wrote in 1915: "The critics rushed to brand me with labels, to establish the parameters of my talent once and for all. . . . In their view, there was never a writer who was more quiet and fixed in his views than I. . . . I was the 'singer of fall, of sadness, of noblemen's nests.' . . . Later they assigned me tags that were diametrically opposed. First I was a 'Decadent,' then a 'Parnassian' and a 'cold master.' . . . I was a Symbolist, a mystic, a realist, a neorealist, a god-seeker, a naturalist, and God knows what else. The critics plastered me with so many labels that I felt like a suitcase that had traveled the world. . . . The truth, however, was that I was very far from being fixed in my views, and that I was living a life a hundred times more complicated and more penetrating than anything I had yet published."[3]

All the pain that Bunin had suffered in his early years was merely a prelude to the anguish brought on by the emerging chaos in his land. Bunin saw that Russia was entering a cataclysmic cycle of reaction, upheaval, and reform, and was rushing headlong toward the "abyss" and the "apocalypse" he had already discovered in civilization.[4] There was ample evidence for his rising fears. In 1905 and 1906 Bunin witnessed the peasant revolts near Tula and Oryol and the devastation of his brother's, Evgeny's, estate at Ognevka. In some cosmic sense, he feared for the end of "patriarchal" Russia when in 1914 his country entered World War I.

3. I. Bunin, "Avtobiograficheskaia zametka," *Sobranie sochinenii v deviati tomakh*, vol. 9 (Moscow, 1965), 264–265.

4. See, for instance, Bunin's letter to N. Cheremnov, written on October 15, 1914, as quoted in V. Afanas'ev, "Ot 'Derevni' k 'Gospodinu iz San-Frantsisko' (Proza I. A. Bunina 1910–14 gg.)," *Uchenye zapiski Moskovskogo gosudarstvennogo pedagogicheskogo instituta*, No. 222 (1964), 137. Also see I. Bunin, "Iz predisloviia k frantsuzskomu izdaniiu 'Gospodina iz San-Frantsisko'," in I. Bunin, *Sobranie sochenii v odinadtsati tomakh*, vol. 1 (Paris, 1936), 78.

Under the weight of mounting calamities, he wrote to a friend in March 1914: "I am firmly convinced that this Christmas will not be the last bloody one, for I know that people are beasts. . . . But there are thousands of 'buts' which are joyful and comforting: the voice of the human heart." Bunin ended his letter with two visions of hope for a new society. In one, a "great idol" seemingly protects humankind from harm; in the other, the Lamb of God bids his subjects "to rise up and look around."[5]

The essential tragedy in Bunin's life was that his nation elected to follow a demagogue, not God, and that no one cared to hear about the dark side of the Bolshevik victory. Having fled peasant unrest in the provinces, Bunin and his wife arrived at Vera's parents' apartment in Moscow (just off the famed Arbat) on October 26, 1917.[6] Scarcely ten days later, during the Bolshevik revolt of November 7, Bunin had to stand guard at the apartment for a week with scarcely any sleep or food, behind locked doors, shuttered windows, and gates barricaded by huge beams of wood. This fortress, however, did not insulate him from the anarchy outside: the fires and fighting in the streets; the guns, bombs, and flying shrapnel all assaulted his acute sensibilities. Red Army soldiers finally broke through the door and demanded weapons, though there were none.

It seems almost incredible that no sooner had the chaos in Moscow subsided than Bunin sought to resume his literary life. He attended meetings of the Writers' Publishing House, the literary circle Wednesday, and the Moscow Artists' Circle. There he debated the nature of the folk and of contemporary art with such writers as Bely, Bal'mont, Ehrenburg, and Alexei Tolstoy.

Such pretenses at normalcy could not, however, alleviate the increasing difficulties of the Bunins' situation. That terrible winter of 1917–1918, together with Lenin's arrival at the Kremlin in March 1918, deepened Bunin's hatred of bolshevism. Matters did not come

5. I. Gazer, "Pis'ma L. Andreeva i. I. Bunina," *Voprosy literatury*, No. 7 (1969), 192.
6. A plaque now marks the building where the Bunins stayed.

to a head, though, until two months later, when he traveled to the provincial cities of Kozlov and Tambov (roughly 260 miles southeast of Moscow) to give a series of literary readings and to procure food and staples that were in short supply in the capital.

Of this trip Muromtseva-Bunina wrote in her diary on May 23, 1918: "Bunin's journey [to Tambov and Kozlov] gave him a genuine sense of the bolshevism that is spreading throughout Russia, a sense of hopelessness . . . of terror and the abyss. . . . He is firmly convinced that we have to go to the south as soon as possible."[7]

On the following day Bunin appealed to Vladimir Friche, who would later become a leading literary critic but who at this time was serving in the Ministry of Foreign Affairs for the new Soviet government, for passports to leave the city. Bunin told Friche that he would agree to "all kinds of cooperation"[8] with the Bolsheviks if he and his wife were allowed to depart. Friche agreed, possibly because Bunin had earlier interceded on his behalf with the mayor of Moscow, who had wished to banish Friche for distributing underground revolutionary pamphlets.[9]

Bunin's victory, though, was a Pyrrhic one. Overjoyed that he was free to leave Moscow, he suddenly realized that he might never again see the city or its cultural and religious landmarks. "Yesterday I passed by the Church of Saint Nikola," he wrote in his diary on May 21, 1918, "and [having taken in] the still unravaged beauty of this island-type refuge . . . the radiance of the words and music that issued forth from its doors . . . and the lively, shimmering gold of the vestments and candles, [I realized] that all these wonders are the stuff of the human soul, the only things that it lives for. . . . And, having realized this, I cried for a full fifteen minutes . . . shedding tears that were terrible, bitter and sweet."[1]

7. Grin, Ustami, 170–171.
8. See Bunin's diary excerpt dated May 19, 1918, in A. Baboreko, "Novoe o Bunine," Problemy realizma, No. 7 (Vologda, 1980), 157.
9. See I. Bunin, "Tretii Tolstoi," Vospominaniia (Paris, 1950), 223.
1. Baboreko, "Novoe," 157–158.

CURSED DAYS

After emotional farewells to Yuly Bunin and to Gorky's wife, Ekaterina Peshkova, the Bunins left Moscow on June 3, 1918. Their journey was difficult—traveling by hospital train through Orsha, Minsk, and Kiev before reaching Odessa on June 16. "What a terrible trip it was!" Bunin recalled in his *Memoirs*. "The train was accompanied by an armed guard—in case any new 'Scythians' escaping from the front would attack it. During the nights we passed through total darkness; all the stations were unlighted. Indeed, the only thing we met there was streams of vomit and other types of uncleanliness, together with the resounding sounds of cries and songs that were savage, hysterical, and drunken, that is, the 'music of the Revolution'!"[2]

Odessa was not new to Bunin. He had visited the city several times in the 1890s and from 1898 to 1900 had lived there with Tsakni. He enjoyed Odessa's exquisite setting on the northwestern shore of the Black Sea, where he had come to know Chekhov and such other writers as Alexander Kuprin. But in that city he had also experienced sadness and grief. It was there that his little boy had died. It was also in Odessa that, in the wake of the Revolution of 1905, Bunin had witnessed a series of pogroms against the Jews; and it was there that Tsakni had continued to reside after their separation. (The couple was formally divorced only in 1922.) The city had in fact fallen upon hard times even before the outbreak of revolution and civil war, so it scarcely beckoned to the Bunins as a promised land.

Indeed, when the Bunins arrived in Odessa in 1918 they were aghast to see how the city had declined since their earlier visits. Throughout the nineteenth century Odessa had been a bustling center of industry and commerce, almost unrivaled in growth.[3] The expansion of Russia's foreign trade, together with Odessa's harbor, port, and railroads, made the city second only to Saint Petersburg in the transport of freight. At the turn of the century it was home to nearly five hundred enterprises, employing more than

2. Bunin, "Tretii Tolstoi," 223.
3. P. Herlihy, *Odessa: A History, 1794–1914* (Cambridge, 1986), 1.

twenty thousand workers in such areas as mining, metallurgy, and food processing.[4]

Not surprisingly, Odessa's manufacturing and commercial power also attracted restless workers, students, and sailors. For instance, it became a regional center for the terrorist group "The People's Will," whose members ultimately claimed responsibility for the 1881 murder of Tsar Alexander II. Odessa's workers took part in the 1903 strike that paralyzed southern Russia; and two years later it was the site of pogroms as well as strikes and armed clashes with the police and tsarist troops. During this time, too, Russian sailors mutinied aboard the battleship *Potemkin*, an event that would become immortalized (with some poetic license) in Sergei Eisenstein's famous 1925 film. These internal disruptions, the competition of the American grain trade, the poor quality, marketing, and distribution of Odessa's goods, and, finally, the deterioration of the city's harbor facilities caused Odessa to be bypassed for other ports on the Black Sea. At best, by 1918 Odessa had become a political refuge to frenzied souls like the Bunins.

When the Bunins arrived there in mid-June, the city had already changed hands twice that year. The Soviets had established power there on January 30, 1918; but German and Austrian troops occupied the city in March, holding it until November. In the ensuing months the Bunins would see Odessa become a "political Babel."[5] The city fell to the Ukrainian nationalist Petlyura, who controlled the city from December 11 to 18, 1918; to British and French troops, who held it until April 6, 1919; to Bolshevik forces, who occupied it for five months; and to General Denikin's White antirevolutionary forces, who entered Odessa on August 24, 1919. The beleaguered city was ultimately retaken by the Soviets on February 7, 1920; and the Bunins, having signed passage on a boat in the city's port a day earlier, left Russia forever on February 9, 1920. (Ironically, they were issued passports that allowed them to return to the homeland.) Although the couple knew that the "terrible

4. *Ibid.*, 195.
5. E. Mawdsley, *The Russian Civil War* (Boston, 1987), 129.

times [in their homeland] were far from over," their own suffering of a "thousand days and a thousand nights" had come to an end.[6]

It is testimony to the Bunins' resourcefulness and resilience that despite severe political, economic, and social hardships, their life in Odessa exhibited a modicum of civility and grace. The writer Valentin Kataev recalled that Bunin cultivated an affluent and urbane image. He struck one as a "vacationer from the capital, intellectual, refined, and dressed in expensive summer sandals, foreign-made socks, and an ample well-ironed, canvas-like shirt . . . which was girded with a simple but evidently rather expensive leather belt, behind which he sometimes tucked in his hands, in the manner of Tolstoy. . . . If it grew hot, he would suddenly don a splendid panama hat which he had brought back from some distant land, or a linen peaked cap like those that Fet, Polonsky, or perhaps even Tolstoy himself used to wear."[7]

Despite the challenging circumstances, Bunin extended this aristocratic aura to his domestic surroundings. The three ground-floor rooms in which he and Vera lived provided a haven from social and political chaos and served as a live-in museum in which the couple sought to preserve the way of life that the Bolsheviks were ruthlessly extirpating. "Our apartment is very beautiful," Muromtseva-Bunina wrote to her parents in Moscow on December 4, 1918. "It is tastefully furnished, with many antiques. The rooms are large and bright . . . and have many conveniences. . . . I am living in comfort . . . such as I have never enjoyed in peaceful times."[8]

6. See Ivan and Vera Bunin's diary excerpts, written in early February 1920, in Grin, *Ustami*, 336–348. Also see Bunin's 1923 story, "The End" ("*Konets*"), in I. Bunin, *Sobranie sochinenii*, vol. 5 (1966), 59–67.

The Bunins had to face the distinct possibility that only one of them would be able to leave for the West. Muromtseva-Bunina wrote in her diary on June 16, 1925: "I recalled that when we were in Odessa, I had told Ian that if we both couldn't get on a boat, he should save himself without me. . . . But he said firmly that he would go nowhere without me, even if he were threatened by death." See Grin, *Ustami*, vol. 2, 143.

7. V. Kataev, *Sviatoi kolodets. Trava zabven'ia* (Moscow, 1969), 166–167.
8. Baboreko, "Novoe," 161.

Others agreed. As Kataev recalled, visitors to the Bunins' home saw the house on Knyazheskaya Street as "a striking contrast to the situation in Odessa, in Russia, and in the world." Ordinarily they were greeted at the door by "a very elegantly dressed maid in French heels, a starched cap, and a small cambric apron with doll-like pockets." They were then ushered into "lordly rooms which featured massive shining doors, high clean ceilings, exquisitely polished parquet floors, Venetian windows with warm marble sills and brightly gleaming iron latches . . . and a small quantity of the most essential, but very good furniture . . . [all of which] was totally appropriate . . . to an aristocrat, a long-established nobleman, a Russian academician, a man of impeccable taste."[9]

This domestic arrangement thus became a physical and spiritual refuge not only for the Bunins but for other Russian writers, professionals, and intellectuals who had fled the Bolsheviks. In Odessa Bunin enjoyed a singular spirit of community and camaraderie which he had not known as a citizen of Russia, nor would he later experience it as an emigré in France. "Never before," Kataev recalled, "had Odessa attracted such a brilliant society."[1] Bunin's home was frequented by such White generals as Wrangel, of whom Muromtseva-Bunina wrote in her diary on February 4, 1919, "the more I know him, the better I like him."[2] Others among the elite who came to socialize and to find respite at Bunin's included politicians such as Kerensky, Rudnyov, Rodzyanko, and Fondaminsky-Bunakov; writers such as Kataev, Voloshin, Teffi, Inber, Olesha, Bagritsky, Paustovsky, Vertinsky, and Alexei Tolstoy; scholars such as Ovsyaniko-Kulikovsky and Leonid Grossman; artists such as Nilus; and actors and actresses such as Olga Knipper (Chekhov's widow).[3]

9. Kataev, *Sviatoi*, 183.
1. *Ibid.*, 168.
2. Grin, *Ustami*, vol. 1, 207.
3. About Knipper, Muromtseva-Bunina wrote in her diary on November 13, 1919: "Yesterday Knipper visited us. She made a strange impression. She was very sweet and friendly; she spoke intelligently, but I got the idea that she had nothing in her soul, that she was like a house without a foundation . . . without a

CURSED DAYS

At times the ambience of the gatherings in the Bunins' home was highly charged and political. Participants debated who had lost Russia, how the Revolution would be defeated, what would be the future of post-Soviet Russia. At other times they held a wake for their homeland. As relatives of the deceased, they paid their respects to the corpse and gathered in small groups to console themselves for their loss, to recall happier times, and to shake their heads over the "traitors" who had laid their homeland low. They lamented the plight of family or friends who had remained in the new Soviet state, or committed suicide, or fallen victim to starvation, drugs, despair, and the "Red terror."

At other times the atmosphere of the gatherings in the Bunin household was strictly academic, out of touch with the mounting anarchy outside. In this case it was not unlike the ambience of the famous Tower, a 1905 Moscow literary salon whose mentor, Vyacheslav Ivanov, tried to disconnect from time and space with his thick carpets and boarded-up windows. The *intelligenty* of all backgrounds who regularly gathered at Bunin's read their works and discussed philosophy, literature, and art. Recalling these almost surreal events, Kataev wrote: "It may seem strange, almost incredible that at a time when civil war raged all around . . . there continued in Bunin's house, behind the mirrorlike windows, a life more imagined than real, a life in which a quite small circle of people discussed questions of literature, poetry, criticism, the reading of the Goncourt brothers in the original . . . the eternal arguments about Tolstoy and Dostoevsky. . . ."[4]

Bunin's nineteen months in Odessa was the last time he would ever be so public. He gave readings and lectures, and published a series of articles in which he commented, boldly and insightfully, on the ideas and issues of the time. He advised novice writers about the nature of their craft. He contributed to several

---

cellar stocked with provisions and good wine. . . . The Bolsheviks have been very courteous to her, so she does not see them as we do." See Grin, *Ustami*, 319.
4. Kataev, *Sviatoi*, 193.

newspapers, including *Southern Word*, a publication founded by members of the White Volunteer Army in Odessa, and for which Bunin served as coeditor for a short period.

When he was not occupied with public literary and political matters, he would roam the streets of Odessa. There, unfailingly, he found stimulation and relief. In the city he could observe a microcosm of the world: the customs and speech of more than one million inhabitants, of whom 39 percent were Russians, 36 percent Jews, 17 percent Ukrainians, and the remainder Greeks, Armenians, and Poles.[5] In Odessa Bunin mingled with shopkeepers, peasants, and professionals as he strolled down the city's tree-lined streets and boulevards, taking in its sweeping vistas and marveling at its churches, buildings, and monuments.

Although Bunin was undeniably a class-conscious aristocrat, he sought out motley crowds whose appearance, sounds, and smells provided stimuli and rich sensory detail for his writing. "Almost every day, in any weather," Kataev wrote, "Bunin would walk about Odessa for several hours at a time. . . . I once observed Bunin at a soldiers' street market where he stood in a crowd, notebook in hand, calmly and unhurriedly writing down . . . the ditties that two brothers of the Black Sea fleet were reciting as they did a lively dance, their arms on each other's shoulders, swinging their wide bell-bottoms. . . . I almost fainted with the sickening smells of sesame oil and garlic; but Bunin paid no attention whatsoever to these and worked calmly, covering page after page with notes. . . . He was incredibly curious, and he always had to know the life about him in all its details, and to see everything with his mercilessly sharp eyes."[6]

Apart from these quiet moments, the storms of revolution and war relentlessly pounded the city. Anxiety, hunger, and disease; frequent searches; inflation and financial woes; arrests, executions,

---

5. At this time Odessa had one of the largest concentrations of urban Jews in the world. See Herlihy, *Odessa*, 124. Also see P. Kenez, *Civil War in South Russia, 1919–1920* (Berkeley, 1977), 180.
6. Kataev, *Sviatoi*, 195–196.

and "terrors"; ignorance of events in both Russia and the world; and the anarchy caused by the endless procession of armies into the city made the Bunins' experience a mental state of "siege" and of "captivity by Hottentots."[7] Terrifying rumors, mostly false, seeped into their otherwise secure home and mind, forcing them to hide money and manuscripts, and spreading a contagion of despair.

The most shattering experience in Odessa, however, was the random bloodlust that Bunin called the "Satan of Cain's anger": Russians and others began to annihilate one another with abandon. The Bunins recognized that even Odessa had become a Sodom and Gomorrah; if they were not to succumb to its evil, they must flee the city, never turning back. "Odessa was like an individual who was feverish and infected with typhus," I. Solokov-Mikitov wrote in his memoirs of the period. "The routed armies of General Denikin were leaving the city in disarray, pillaging and ravaging as they went. . . . Speculators yelled and argued in crowded cafés. . . . Random victims, washed up on the city's banks by waves of civil war . . . hid in cold attics and cellars. . . . Taverns and dens were filled with deserters and pickpockets. . . . Military patrols roamed through the city, looking like street thieves. . . . People openly sold stolen goods in noisy bazaars."[8]

Throughout his stay in Odessa Bunin repeatedly expressed his anguish with a characteristic penchant for drama and self-pity. Memoirists of the time confirmed the rapid decline in his physical and spiritual health. "The first time I saw Bunin in Odessa," Alexeev wrote, "I was stunned by his drawn and tortured face. His sallow complexion and his flaccid, lifeless cheeks had taken on the hue of an old, fading cypress tree. Bushy eyebrows overhung his eyes from the top; grey swollen bags (the consequence of insomnia) rimmed them from below."[9]

He still dressed and played the part of an aristocrat; but, in a manner not unlike that of Uncle Pavel, the obdurate *barin* in Tur-

7. See Bunin's diary excerpt dated August 8, 1919, in Grin, *Ustami*, 295.
8. Baboreko, "Novoe," 168–169.
9. G. Alexeev, "Zhivye vstrechi," *Vremia* (August 22, 1921), 2.

genev's *Fathers and Sons,* Bunin seemed to be dying from within. As the Soviets gained the upper hand in the final months of 1919, he realized that exile was now the only option for himself and his wife. They had experienced Soviet rule briefly in Moscow and now Odessa; they dared not continue to lead lives at risk. The Soviet press had attacked Bunin for his pro-White leanings; he had suffered several run-ins with local commissars and mobs; and rumors of his impending arrest were common. The Bunins knew that a Soviet "paradise" could never materialize, and that they could not endure a third period of physical and spiritual suffocation. "I always feel that 'airlessness' which attends the Bolsheviks," Muromtseva-Bunina wrote in her diary on April 7, 1919. "I felt it during the first five moments we were in Moscow, when the Bolsheviks were not nearly as savage and bloodthirsty as they were after our departure, but even then I could not breathe. I remember, when we rushed out of their sweet paradise, the great gladness, the joy of light breathing that seized us right away."[1] A modern-day Adam and Eve, they chose to be banished from the Soviet Eden.

Whenever Bunin put pen to paper in Moscow and Odessa in 1918 and 1919, it was to indict his countrymen for their failings and to recall them to their senses before their country self-destructed. In *Cursed Days* it was one of Bunin's primary objectives to use the images and ideals of the past to comment insightfully on the issues and problems of the present. The book is thus an artful mix of old and new. It bears an affinity to several medieval genres from Russian literature, and at times recalls historical chronicles whose authors recorded momentous events as they condemned internecine strife, lamented the divine wrath visited upon sins, and begged for mercy and deliverance from pestilence, invaders, and the like. *Cursed Days* also brings to mind medieval Russian *slova* or "sermons of solemn narration," in which homilists extolled virtue and condemned vice, riveting their listeners' attention with dazzling discourse and rhetoric, and borrowing from the Bible, the

1. Grin, *Ustami,* 225.

teachings of church fathers, and excerpts from literature and secular works. In still other ways *Cursed Days* recalls the "stamplike"
structure of Russian icons in which the depicted individual is
starkly situated amidst miniatures that depict episodes from his or
her life.

The book also resurrects motifs from nineteenth-century Russian realism, especially the fiction of the Russian Natural School
of the late 1830s and 1840s which depicted "slices" of unvarnished
city life by means of type, daguerreotype, and exposé. In *Cursed
Days*, Bunin, like the writers of the Natural School, boldly takes
to the street. He talks to friends and strangers, eavesdrops on conversations, records data, and seeks to present an exhaustive picture
of his subjects and surroundings. Like the nineteenth-century Russian novel, *Cursed Days* is also epic and encyclopedic: numerous
characters, subplots, and "voices"; reflections on timely and eternal questions; the merging of public and private lives; and intrigue
rooted in "lacerating" rumors, incessant scandal, and bored and
fearful citizens from all social classes and walks of life. Indeed,
Cursed Days often appears as the work of a Gogolian or Dosto-
evskian "madman" who writes "anything that comes to mind." Internal dialogues and freewheeling digressions on literature, history,
and philosophy find expression in a style that is chaotic and high-
strung, often defying the rules of grammar and taste, and devolv-
ing into sentence fragments punctuated with numerous question
marks and exclamation points.

Despite these suggestions of earlier literary styles, *Cursed Days*
has a contemporary feel. The work follows upon Russian revolutionary fiction in espousing a literature of fact. Bunin sidesteps em-
pirical time and space by shattering the linear and logical
narratives of Pushkin, Tolstoy, and Chekhov into shardlike fragments, and by interspersing these shreds with selections from ver-
bal, pictorial, musical, and dramatic modern art. He crisscrosses
his tale with snatches of conversations, clippings from newspapers,
and snippets from songs and hymns, ditties and doggerel. To these
fragments he adds jottings from diaries, memories of village and

urban life, and citations from writers, intellectuals, military men, and political figures—Russian and non-Russian, present and past. To complete his pictures of social and national life, Bunin uses smatterings of sketches from posters, placards, and banners, intimate dramatic tableaux, scenes of music and dance, the "mass spectacles" of parades, funerals, and revolts, and village and urban flashbacks to the February and October revolutions of 1917.

Cursed Days and Bunin's writings in *Southern Word* drive home this theme: Revolutions must be viewed with "genuinely savage hatred" and "genuinely savage contempt." They promise much, but destroy. To the untrained eye, the Russian Revolution may seem a salvific event. For the first time in memory, Russians appear to be happy, purposeful, and content. They dramatize the "national surge" in parades, banners, and songs. They shout slogans, bidding workers and peasants to throw off their shackles and unite as one. In one fell swoop, newly bolshevized Russians have changed their time and space: they update calendars, introduce time zones, and rename buildings, cities, and streets after Lenin, Trotsky, and others. Nothing, it seems, eludes their reformist touch, even Russian orthography.

And revolutionary Russians are buoyant about the future, certain that prosperity is just over the horizon. Indeed, post-1917 Russians are so enthusiastic about their newfound Soviet beliefs that they invite enemies and nonbelievers alike to join the proletariat. With the brashness that comes with assumed success, they thumb their nose at the West and vow to have their "Bolshevik belly" crush the world.

Bunin records these impressions, but he does not accept them. The key message in both *Cursed Days* and his writings for *Southern Word* is that Lenin, Trotsky, and their cohorts are nurturing a perverse dynamic just below the appearance of revolutionary sweetness and light. Metaphorically Bunin believes that the Bolsheviks are lunatics who have taken over the asylum, and who have seized control of Russia for the sole purpose of asserting a Nietzschean "will to power." Impudent and arrogant, they have cut short a "magnificent, centuries-old life" and replaced it with a "be-wildering existence," destroying all systems of morality and law and advancing their own interests under the guise of the Revolution and of the proletariat they claim to represent.

Before the Revolution, Bunin charges, Bolshevik leaders were pitiful, dull, mangy-looking creatures; since their coup, they de-mand respect as social engineers and "people of substance." They have become "commissars" whose vulgar penchant for wine, women, and palaces underscores the chameleonlike quality of their values and beliefs. They vaunt communal ownership but feather their nests; they curse the past but speak incoherently of the future. They pose as saviors but murder their own countrymen and panic at any sign of danger. Like hirelings, they are the first to flee from other predators, abandoning Russia to its fate.

Bunin takes every opportunity to refute Bolshevik claims of a new, so-called "Soviet man" by showing Russian citizens as disor-dered and diseased. Their eyes are cloudy and drugged; their bod-ies recall those of skeletons and chickens; their faces are, variously, glossy, wizened, or sallow. The citizens in *Cursed Days* appear so regressed, physically and spiritually, that they seem "reborn" to lower forms of life. One group, with its slanted eyes, wooden faces, and wild hair, appears to be heir to "Mongol atavism." A second group recalls ghosts and ghouls—their visages are painted and pow-dered, their bodies "look all white in the twilight," and their voices give off plaintive wails. A third group resembles dogs, monkeys, and other animals; a fourth has severe genetic difficulties: vacuous expressions and idiotic smiles.

Collectively these citizens of Moscow and Odessa are the modern-day "humiliated and injured," who have given up on themselves and life. Despite their newly "empowered" status, they seem even less politically astute than before 1917. Indeed, they bear a haunting resemblance to their medieval ancestors who, also un-able to take control of their affairs, invited Viking Varangians to restore order to their land. Bunin charges that contemporary Rus-sians cannot distinguish between friends and foes, nor have they

INTRODUCTION

talent or inclination for democratic unions. The new soviets are vicious and inept; commissars mismanage armies, ruin the culture, and dispossess citizens. The smaller, more informal assemblies are also ineffective, bordering on chaotic. Although village communes and workers' and soldiers' groups fancy themselves as new "collective societies," they dispense justice with old-fashioned mob-style cruelty. Illiterate manifestos proliferate, and trivia ignites mob anger. The "legislative bodies" of citizens spit and shove as they utter curses and threats. Hopelessly unable to govern themselves, they do not even try to help their country in an effective, democratic way.

Bunin sees this generalized, brutish ineptitude extended quite naturally from politics to art. He condemns the inability of most Russians to see showmanship as serious art. In his view, modernists and proletarian writers lack integrity and bend with political winds. Bores and masters of scandal, they champion pornography and mock the very best in Russian history, religion, and art. Their "revolutionary" works also play to the Soviet penchant for bread and circuses. An aura of entertainment—"orgies," "repulsive theatrics," and "clownish stunts," Bunin writes—allows the mob to dress up cruel reality in vaudevilles, comedies, and mock high style. The celebrating of revolutionary anniversaries and milestones pillory honor as murderers, hypocrites, and sexually diseased youth become heroes of socialism, proclaiming Soviet salvation to the world.

Such public displays, however, cannot conceal from a thinking person the growing emptiness and horror of bolshevized life. In its vulgarity and sham, Bunin sees that the only forward movement of the new Soviet existence is toward the grave. People are paralyzed and wearied not only by physical deprivation and duress but by a spiritual stress rooted in the expectation of disaster at every turn. In *Cursed Days* the people yearn for their own end and envy those who have departed this world. "Why bother living?" Bunin asks. "In truth, we should have hanged ourselves a long time ago."

In the dire plight of his homeland Bunin finds precedents in the ancient, medieval, and modern histories of both Russia and the world. He derides Bolshevik views that Russia is undergoing a "seismic shift to something new and unprecedented." Rather, he sees his country only as repeating the tragedies of the past. In Bunin's view, post-1917 Russia resembles ancient Egypt and Israel: Russians are like Pharaoh's people who endure plagues for their obstinacy, and like faithless Hebrews who, having worshiped false gods, are condemned to "live outside the walls of a destroyed and profaned Zion."

Bunin also shows revolutionary Russia returning to its tortured medieval past. As he sees it, the new Soviet homeland has refitted itself for the Mongol yoke. Lenin is a new Mamai, his followers modern Tatars who soak the earth in blood and force the homeland to regress to a pagan (read: Asian) bazaar filled with "loathsome dark faces" and "Eastern cries and speech." For Bunin, the new sedition and strife has allowed the dark side of *l'âme russe* to resurface and renew its reign, entrenching the national penchant for "savagery and tears" and for "always moving forward in circles."

Bunin believes that "revolutionary" Russia also bears the scars of more modern times. It mirrors, for example, the "glorious revolution" of Cromwell, and the French upheaval of 1789. Then as now, he decries the cruelty of "idealists and dreamers," the "animal self-satisfaction" of its citizens, the heavy hand of its institutions, the lying of its literary "charlatans" and "degenerates," the "absolute absurdity" implicit in its demand for "freedom, brotherhood, equality—and death!"

"Who is the enemy?" Bunin asks, and more often than not he replies, "It is us." He is particularly harsh with three groups: professionals, gentry and youth, and the folk themselves. The first group, the Russian writers, intellectuals, and professionals who often lived abroad or divorced themselves from reality, Bunin accuses of looking slavishly to the West as a panacea for their country's ills. At home they did little but complain about Russia's backwardness, rouse anger among its citizens, and "kick the government for the umpteenth time." Even when they posed as champions of enlightenment, Bunin claims, this group only pretended to represent the people. Publicly they acclaimed the folk and the masses; privately they scorned them. They knew the "people" only from legend, literature, or fleeting conversation, and praised them in the abstract—as "icons" who inexplicably exhibited "great grace, novelty, and originality of future forms." Most Russian writers, intellectuals, and professionals, Bunin charges, regarded their purported "radicalism" not as food for thought but as sustenance to assuage their own inner emptiness. The *modus operandi* of this group was to look vacuously upon national existence with "muddled mysticism," even as they closed their eyes to "smashed skulls" and placed "laurel wreaths on lice-covered heads."

Bunin's second group guilty of the homeland's fall is the educated Russian public, in particular its gentry and youth. Russians have refused to admit the flaws of their national character and to see post-Emancipatory Russia in the throes of death. The reasons for such blindness, he believes, are inertia, self-interest, fear, and a juvenile unwillingness to confront the challenges and complexities of their situation. Before the Revolution, Bunin asserts, the gentry lived lives of genteel abandon: frivolous and haphazard, cheerful and carefree. An "old Russian disease" infected the gentry's minds and hearts: they despised work and routine, and hid from life in the "depths" of their souls. They paid only lip service to their heritage and sought their well-being in money, not memory. Russian noblemen, Bunin insists, were so stirred by the romantic wish to do something special that they never did anything at all. They longed and languished, seeking rescue from "frogs with magic rings."

It pained Bunin that the gentry scorned the literature of their "grandfathers" and "fathers," and that only the output of "declassé" and "professional" writers captured their imagination. Such writers, he charges, did considerable damage to their readers. They distanced themselves from the folk and projected only "ideas" and bitterness at life. They were creatures of fashion and ideology. It was nothing to them to extol the peasant rebels of the past and the "heroic" Russian people of the present in pulp fiction or "puff pieces." When it suited, they illustrated their "love of the folk" with stories and clichés that were illiterate and false.

Russian adolescents too had espoused a literary approach to life. In Bunin's view they had identified too comfortably with such fictional heroes as Pushkin's Onegin, Lermontov's Pechorin, and Turgenev's Bazarov. Forgetting that these youthful characters were frozen in time and space, the youth adopted their self-styled superfluousness as their own. Russian novels were, however, not the only items that had captured their adolescent minds and hearts. Pre-1917 Russian youth also used songs about Sten'ka Razin and readings from Marx and other radicals to concoct a sham faith in the folk and a genuine hatred for all groups but their own indulgent one.

Finally, Bunin indicts the folk themselves for his country's ills. The Russian masses, Bunin asserts, are not the "Christ-loving peasants" who peopled the fiction of Turgenev and Tolstoy, with their messianic message for the world and their thirst for beauty, justice, and good. They are instead the spiritual brothers of Rasputin who view both life and death as cheap. However unfairly, Bunin saw the "masses" as anti-Semitic, spiteful, and coarse. Without the slightest hesitation they might murder, rape, and carouse one day, and on the next bow before icons and journey to monasteries in "bouts of frenzied sentimentality." For such behavior, Bunin asserts, the folk deserved not a revolution but hangings, beatings, or, at the very least, a "swift kick in the pants."

Despite his torment, Bunin does not succumb to total despair. The darkness of his outlook in *Cursed Days* is infused with periodic rays of light. Bunin believes he is one of a few Russians whom the new Soviet state has tried unsuccessfully to destroy. Everyone else, Bunin claims, is a robot or a zombie who has crossed a fatal line into nonexistence. But his soul still transcends time and space and joins family and loved ones from afar, expressing agony and fear, love and hope for their fate. He not only hopes against hope for a Bolshevik defeat, and for someone to put an end to his "cursed days"; he also believes he has sufficient passion and courage to fight the Soviets with a time-honored weapon—the pen, which he, as an "old world" Russian writer, wields in behalf of tradition and truth.

Bright spots in nature and in humankind are balm to Bunin's soul and revive his faith in miracles. Such signs, he believes, point to the cyclic, broad, and enduring nature of Russian life. He never tires of repeating that the history of his homeland has been violent and bleak; but in moments of crisis his country has invariably drawn on its spiritual and cultural riches to rise like a phoenix from the ashes. Yes, Bunin is anxious for the fate of Russia, but he does not consign his patriarchal homeland to oblivion. Like the prophet Isaiah centuries before, he believes that new shoots will sprout from its charred stump. "I will never accept that Russia has been destroyed," he told Muromtseva-Bunina several weeks before they emigrated.[2] Bunin never doubted that the Bolshevik experiment in his homeland would meet an ignoble end. He was firmly convinced that "socialism contradicts and is completely unsuited to the human soul." "In twenty-five years," he predicted, ". . . Russia would be host to a powerful surge of religious feeling, and . . . the passion for individualism would rise from the ashes of communism."[3] He was wrong only in his timing.

For all his suffering in Moscow and Odessa in 1918 and 1919, Bunin always took satisfaction in having been an intimate witness to the Russian Revolution and the civil war, and in possessing the talent to record events for posterity. Similar "recording" would be repeated by writers who remained in Russia under Soviet rule. Nothing could have stopped Bunin from seeking and telling the truth. Indeed, writing Cursed Days and for Southern Word, he could have claimed spiritual kinship with Zamyatin's hero, D-503,

2. See Muromtseva-Bunina's diary excerpt of December 26, 1919, in Grin, Ustami, 325.
3. See Muromtseva-Bunina's diary excerpt of January 28, 1919, in Grin, Ustami, 207.

in his 1924 diary-novel We, when D-503 continues to record his impressions of a new utopian state even after he is strapped to a hospital bed and undergoes the "great operation" targeted for enemies of the regime. Bunin would have agreed with the last and prophetic lines of his fictional successor: "And I hope that we win. More than that, I am certain we shall win. For Reason must prevail."[4]

4. E. Zamyatin, We (New York, 1952), 218.

MOSCOW 1918

January 1 / 14, 1918[1]

This damn year is finally over. But what will be next? Perhaps things will get worse. And that seems even likely.

But something remarkable is happening: almost everyone is unusually happy for some reason—no matter whom you meet on the street, you see a simply radiant face.

"Enough moping around, old boy! In two or three weeks you'll be ashamed of how you're feeling. . . ."

Hale and hearty, he squeezes my hand tenderly but firmly (he pities me for my stupidity), and takes off at a trot.

---

1. During the years between 1917 and 1920, Russia used two different systems of dating simultaneously. The official calendar of the Russian Empire had been the Julian, which in the twentieth century is thirteen days behind the Gregorian, used in the West. (Russian animosity toward the papacy was a key reason why Moscow refused to accept the Gregorian calendar when it was created by Pope Gregory XIII in 1582.)

On January 26, 1918, the Soviet government announced that Russia would adopt the Gregorian calendar on February 1, 1918—which then became February 14 in the so-called "new style." Anti-Bolshevik forces, though, continued to adhere to the old calendar throughout the Russian civil war. For this reason, all dates for the text of *Cursed Days* and Bunin's articles in *Southern Word* are given in both old and new styles. All other dates are rendered in new style, when this can be ascertained.

CURSED DAYS

Today I again met with Speransky from *Russian News*.[2] Then I ran into an old woman on Merzlyakovsky Street.[3] She stopped, and with shaking hands, leaned on her crutch as she burst out crying:

"Good sir, tell me what's going on! Just where are we heading? Everyone is saying that Russia has perished, that it's been going downhill for thirteen years!"[4]

January 7 / 20, 1918

At a meeting of the Writers' Publishing House[5] I heard stunning news: the Constituent Assembly[6] has been disbanded!

I also heard about Bryusov: he keeps going more and more to the left and is now "almost a regular Bolshevik." I'm not surprised. In 1904 he hailed autocracy, demanding (a regular Tyutchev!)[7] that Constantinople be seized without delay. But in 1905 he published his poem "The Dagger" in Gorky's newspaper *Struggle*. Then, when war broke out with the Germans, he became an ultrapatriot. Now he's a Bolshevik.[8]

2. *Russian News* (*Russkie vedomosti*) was a liberal newspaper of public and political affairs published in Moscow from 1863 to 1918.

3. In general, Bunin's travels in this section are all in the vicinity of Red Square in the center of Moscow.

4. That is, since the Revolution of 1905.

5. The Writers' Publishing House in Moscow (*Knigoizdatel'stvo pisatelei v Moskve*) was a cooperative publishing company that existed from 1912 to 1919. It published works by Bunin, Maxim Gorky, and Alexander Serafimovich, as well as several literary series. Bunin was one of its founders and also its chief editor until November 1914.

6. The Constituent Assembly (*Uchreditel'noe Sobranie*) was a popularly elected group of representatives from throughout the Russian Empire. It sought to determine the course of Russian political life after the March and October revolutions of 1917. The Assembly was short-lived, however, meeting only for thirteen hours. It was closed by the Bolsheviks on January 6, 1918.

7. Bunin is referring to the Slavophile views of the poet Fyodor Tyutchev.

8. Bryusov's highly romantic "The Dagger" ("*Kinzhal*") was actually published in October 1904. Bryusov formally joined the Communist party in July 1920. *Struggle* (*Bor'ba*) was a Bolshevik newspaper published from December 10 to December 19, 1905.

RUSSIA, 1918–1919

BARENTS
SEA

Petsamo

Murmansk

NORWAY

SWEDEN

WHITE
SEA

Archangel

N

Ural Mountains

Finland

Gulf of Bothnia

Lake
Onega

Northern Dvina

Helsinki
Vyborg
Stockholm
Petrograd
Lake
Ladoga
Revel
(Tallinn)
Tsarskoe Selo
Sukhona

Perm
Ekaterinburg
(Sverdlovsk)

Dorpat
Novgorod
Vologda

BALTIC SEA

Riga
Pskov
Livonia

Courland

Volga
Iaroslavl
Nizhnii
Novgorod
Kazan

Ufa

GERMANY

Königsberg
East
Prussia
Vilno
Smolensk
MOSCOW
Murom
Ufa

Silesia

Vitebsk
Tula
Simbirsk

Minsk
Mogilev
R U S S I A
Orel
Samara
Orenburg

Poland

Warsaw
Brest-
Litovsk
Gomel
Tambov

Cracow
Chernigov
Voronezh
Saratov
Ural

Lwow (Lemberg)
Kiev
Berdychev
Kharkov
Volga

Galicia
Dnieper
Poltava
Donets
Don
Tsaritsyn (Volgograd)

AUSTRIA-
HUNGARY
Dniester
Bug

Kishinev
ODESSA
Rostov
Astrakhan

ROMANIA
Bucharest
SEA
OF AZOV
Kuban
Stavropol
CASPIAN SEA

SERBIA

Crimea

Sofia

BULGARIA
Sevastopol
BLACK SEA
Caucasus Mountains

Constantinople
Tiflis

0   100   200   300   400   500 Miles

OTTOMAN
EMPIRE
PERSIA

MEDITERRANEAN
SEA

February 5 / 18, 1918
Beginning February 1st we have been ordered to observe new style [to keep track of calendar time]. So, according to the Soviets, it is now February 18th.

Yesterday there was meeting of [the literary group] "Wednesday."[9] Many "young people" were there. Mayakovsky behaved rather decently most of the time, though he kept acting like a lout, strutting about and shooting off his mouth. He was wearing a shirt without a tie. The collar of his jacket was raised up for some reason, just like those poorly shaven people who live in wretched hotel rooms and use public latrines in the mornings.

[At the meeting] Ehrenburg and Vera Inber read from their works. Sasha Koiransky said about them:

> Ehrenburg howls
> And Inber follows in tow—
> But Moscow and Petersburg
> Wouldn't give up Berdichev[1]
> For all their collective woe.

February 6 / 19, 1918
The newspapers report that the Germans have begun their attack.[2] Everyone says: "Oh, if it were only so!"

9. Wednesday (*Sreda*) was a literary circle that existed in Moscow from 1899 to 1916. Its members included such writers as Bunin, Gorky, Alexander Kuprin, and Leonid Andreev; such actors and musicians as Vasily Kachalov and Fyodor Chaliapin; and such artists as Isaak Levitan and Alexander Golovin.

1. At this time Berdichev was the fourth largest city in the Ukraine, and a major commercial and industrial city. It was also an important Hasidic center, with Jews comprising between 80 and 90 percent of the population. From 1917 to 1920 Berdichev was, for the most part, under Ukrainian rule but suffered terribly in the revolution and the civil war. For instance, in 1914 Berdichev counted more than eighty thousand inhabitants, but by 1920 it had less than half that number. Even more darkly, Berdichev was a site of the Holocaust on Soviet soil during World War II. See John and Carol Garrard, *The Bones of Berdichev: The Life and Fate of Vasily Grossman* (New York, 1996).

2. After the Central Powers concluded a separate peace with the independent Ukrainian government on February 9, 1918, Leon Trotsky, the negotiator for the Bolsheviks, walked out of the talks and began negotiating with the Allies. The

We took a walk to Lubyanka. There were "meetings" every-where. [In one of them] a red-haired fellow talked on and on about the injustices of the old regime. He was wearing a coat with a round, dark-brown collar. His face was freshly powdered and shaven; he had red curly eyebrows and gold fillings in his mouth. A snub-nosed gentleman with bulging eyes kept objecting hotly to what the red-haired fellow was saying. Women were fervidly adding their two cents' worth, but always at the wrong time. They kept breaking into the argument (one that was based on "principle," so the red-haired fellow said) with details and hurried stories from their own lives, by which they felt compelled to prove God-knows-what. Several soldiers were also there. They acted as though they understood nothing; but, as always, they had their doubts about something (or more accurately, everything) and kept shaking their heads suspiciously.

A peasant approached the crowd. He was an old man with pale, swollen cheeks and a grey triangular beard, which he curi-ously kept sticking into the mob as he approached, finally driving it in between the sleeves of two gentlemen who had kept silent but were listening to all that was going on. The peasant also began to listen attentively, but it was apparent that he too understood noth-ing and that he didn't believe anyone or anything. A tall blue-eyed worker likewise made his way into the crowd along with two more soldiers who were carrying sunflowers in their hands. Both of the soldiers were short-legged, chewing sunflower seeds and looking at everything in a gloomy and mistrustful way. The worker's face had a look of scorn on it and also a smile that was lighthearted but evil. He stood to the side of the crowd, pretending that he had stopped only for a minute to amuse himself, as if to say, "I know, even be-fore I get there, that everyone is talking nonsense."

A lady complained hurriedly that now she didn't have a piece of bread to her name, even though once she had had a school.

German response, a major offensive into Russia which began on February 18, 1918, met with no resistance.

She had had to let all her students go because she had nothing to feed them.

"Whose life has gotten better with the Bolsheviks?" she asked. "Everyone's worse off and we, the people, most of all!"

A heavily made-up little bitch interrupted her, breaking in with naive remarks. She started to say that the Germans were about to arrive and that everyone would pay through the nose for what they had done.

"Before the Germans get here, we'll kill you all," a worker said coldly and took off.

The soldiers nodded in agreement: "If that isn't true!" they said, and they also left.

In another group a worker was arguing with an ensign of the tsarist army. The ensign tried to speak as softly as possible, attempting to be logical and choosing the most inoffensive expressions to make his point. He almost had won the crowd to his side when a worker started screaming at him.

"Your brother should put a bigger lock on your mouth, that's what he should do! You shouldn't be spreading propaganda among the people!"

K. said that R. had come to visit them again. He was there for four hours; and for no reason at all he kept reading a small book on magnetic waves, which had been lying on the table. He then drank some tea and ate up an entire loaf of bread which had been given to K. and his family. By nature, R. is a gentle, quiet, and utterly polite type of individual; but now he comes to visit, sits, and without any conscience eats an entire loaf of bread and doesn't give a damn about his hosts. How quickly he is falling apart!

Blok has openly joined with the Bolsheviks. He has published an article which Kogan (P. S.) has praised.[3] I still haven't read it,

3. The article in question is "The Intellectual and the Revolution" ("*Intelligent i revoliutsiia*"), which Blok wrote on January 8, 1918. Kogan's article, entitled "Voice of a Poet" ("*Golos poeta*"), was published on February 15, 1918, and hailed Blok's piece as a "requiem to the old world, an exultant hymn of greeting to socialism and democracy."

but I guessed at its contents and told them to Ehrenburg—it turned out I was correct. In general, Blok's tunes aren't all that complicated; he's a very stupid man.[4]

From Gorky's newspaper *New Life:*[5]

"Today even the most naive simpleton knows that he must not talk about the [Soviet of] People's Commissars,[6] and, in particular, not about their lack of courage and revolutionary merit or the basic integrity of their politics. Before us stand a group of political adventurers who, in order to advance their own personal interests and to prolong the agonies of a dying autocracy for several weeks more, are ready to commit the most shameful treachery and to betray the interests of the homeland, the Revolution, and the Russian proletariat in whose name they commit all types of excesses on the vacant throne of the Romanovs."

From the newspaper *Power of the People:*[7]

"As it is our persistent observation that, every night, people under arrest are meeting their end when being interrogated by the Soviet of Workers' Deputies,[8] we ask that the Soviet of People's

4. The dislike was mutual, Blok disdaining what he saw as the dryness, monotony, and tendentiousness of Bunin's writing. "It is a sin," Blok wrote of Bunin in 1908, "to force the soul to sing when it does not want to sing." See A. Blok, "Stikhi Bunina," *Zolotoe runo,* No. 10 (1908), 50.

5. *New Life* (*Novaia zhizn'*) was a daily newspaper with Menshevik leanings which began publication on May 1, 1917. Openly hostile to the Bolshevik Revolution and the Soviet state, it was closed by the new regime in July 1918.

6. The Soviet of People's Commissars (*Sovet nardonykh komissarov*) (1917–1922) succeeded the Soviet of Ministers that had functioned during both the Imperial Regime and the Provisional Government. Its purpose was to take over the existing government and implement Bolshevik policy. From the very beginning, the Soviet of People's Commissars aroused controversy because of the vast political powers it assumed and maintained. (Lenin was its chairman.) By late November 1918 it was a regularly functioning body, and by early 1919 it effectively controlled all administrative operations, ending whatever hopes Russians may have had for democracy in their country. For more on the Soviet of People's Commissars, see W. B. Lincoln, *Red Victory: A History of the Russian Civil War* (New York, 1989), 103–105.

7. *Power of the People* (*Vlast' naroda*) was a newspaper published by the Social Revolutionaries from April 28, 1917, to April 2, 1918.

8. The Soviets of Workers' Deputies (*Sovety Rabochikh Deputatov*) were elected political organizations that first appeared in Russia during the Revolution

Commissars step in and prevent similar hooliganlike actions and escapades in the future. . . ."

This complaint [is from someone] from Borovichi.[9]

From the newspaper *Russian Word*:[1]

"Tambov peasants from the village of Pokrovskoye[2] have put together this protocol:

'On January 30th, we as a collective society prosecuted two thieves, the citizens Nikita Alexandrovich Bulkin and Adrian Alexandrovich Kudinov. And by the agreement of our collective society, they were indicted and immediately put to death.'"

Here is the personal legal code that [Pokrovskoye] "collective society" drew up as regards punishments for various crimes.

"If someone strikes someone else, then the one who has been struck must hit the offender ten times."

"If someone strikes someone else and causes injury or a bone to be broken, then the offender shall lose his life."

"If someone commits theft or accepts stolen goods, then this person shall lose his life."

"If someone commits arson and is observed doing so, then this person shall lose his life."

Soon after this "code" was accepted, two thieves were caught red-handed. They were quickly "judged" and sentenced to be executed. One was killed right off: his head was bashed in with a steel bar, his side was pierced with a pitchfork, and his body was

---

of 1905–1907. They attempted to take control of the strike movement in Russia and to win gains for the working class. In 1917 they reappeared in industrial areas and included military personnel, creating soviets of deputies in these two classes. The complaints against the Soviets of Workers' Deputies were legitimate. See V. Brovkin, ed., *Dear Comrades: Menshevik Reports on the Bolshevik Revolution and the Civil War* (Stanford, 1991), 117.

9. Borovichi is a manufacturing city about 175 miles southeast of Saint Petersburg.

1. *Russian Word* (*Russkoe slovo*) was a liberal daily, published in Moscow from 1894 to 1917, which contained extensive information on the Russian Empire and foreign countries.

2. Tambov is both a city and a province, approximately 260 miles southeast of Moscow. It is a major agricultural and industrial center in western Russia.

thrown out stark naked onto the highway. Then they took care of the other one. . . .

One reads things like this every day:

Monks [have been sentenced to] break up ice over on Petrovka Street. Passersby are exultant, gloating: "Aha! So you've been chased out! Now, pal, they'll make you work!"

In the courtyard of a house on Povarskaya Street, a soldier in a leather jacket is cutting wood. A peasant passerby stops and looks for a long time. He then shakes his head and says sadly:

"Ah! You should go fuck yourself! Ah, you dizzerter, you should go fuck yourself! Ras'sia has perished!"[3]

February 7 / 20, 1918

The lead article from *Power of the People*: "The fateful hour has come—Russia and the Revolution will perish. Everyone to the defense of the revolution which has only recently begun to shine radiantly over the entire world!"—When did it shine? I ask. When did your shameless eyes see it shine?

From *Russian Word*: "General Yanushkevich, former head of staff, has been executed. He was arrested in Chernigov and, by order of the local revolutionary tribunal, was to be moved to Petrograd to the Peter-and-Paul Fortress.[4] Two soldiers of the Red Army were to accompany him there. But one night, one of them

3. The peasant uses the word *dezelter* instead of *dezerter* (deserter), and *Rassiya* for *Rossiya* (Russia).

More than two million men had deserted the Russian army by November 1917. See N. Golovine, *The Russian Army in the World War* (New Haven, 1931), 124; and Lincoln, *Red Victory*, 40.

4. Chernigov is both a city and an administrative region, northeast of Kiev in the Ukraine. Saint Petersburg was renamed Petrograd after August 1914, when Russia entered World War I. The Peter-and-Paul Fortress was built in 1703 in Saint Petersburg and is best known as the prison in which such political offenders as Dostoevsky, Gorky, and Alexander Ul'yanov, the older brother of Lenin, were detained.

shot him four times when the train pulled up at the station at Ore-byozh."[5]

It is still winter; snow glistens about. But, like spring, the sky shines brightly through clouds of luminous steam.

Over on Strastnaya Street, people are advertising that Yavorskaya will give a benefit performance. An old woman, fat, rosy-red, mean-spirited, and coarse, cries out:

"Just take a look at that! They're smearing paste all over the place! And who's going to clean up the mess? And the bourgeois will be going to the theaters. They shouldn't be allowed to go. After all, we don't go. And everyone's afraid of the Germans; 'They're coming, they're coming!' people say, but somehow they never get here!"

A woman in a pince-nez walks down Tverskaya Street. She wears a soldier's sheepcoat, a red, plush jacket, a torn skirt, and a pair of galoshes in absolutely wretched condition.

A crowd of ladies, high school girls, and officers stand on the street corners, selling things.

A young officer gets into a tram, and, his face red with embarrassment, he says that unfortunately he cannot pay for a ticket.

It was just before evening. A blinding sun lay low on Red Square; smooth, well-trodden snow was all around. It was sleeting. We stopped by the Kremlin. The sky had a moon and rose-colored clouds. It was quiet; there were huge snowdrifts. Near an artillery base, a soldier in a sheepskin coat was making crunching noises with his boots; his face seemed as if hacked from wood; but how pointless this guard now seems!

We walked out of the Kremlin—little boys were running about all excited, crying out in unnatural tones:

"The Germans have taken Mogilyov!"[6]

5. The name of the city is actually Oredyosh, a town about ninety miles directly south of Saint Petersburg.
6. German forces actually reached Mogilyov, a city located in western Belarus, on February 27, 1918.

MOSCOW 1918

February 8 / 21, 1918
Andrei (my brother Yuly's servant) is acting more and more insane.
It is even horrifying to watch.

He has served my brother for almost twenty years, and he has
always been simple, kind, reasonable, polite, and devoted to us.
Now he's gone completely crazy. He still does his job carefully,
but it is apparent that he's forcing himself to do so. He cannot look
at us and shies away from our conversations. His whole body in-
wardly shakes from anger; and when he can keep silent no longer,
he lets loose with wild nonsense.

For instance, this morning, when we were visiting Yuly, N. N.
said, as always, that everything has perished and that Russia was
flying into an abyss. Andrei was setting the table for tea. He suddenly began waving his arms, his face aflame:

"Yes, yes, Russia's flying into an abyss, all right! But who's to
blame, who? The bourgeois, that's who! Just you wait, you'll see
how they'll be cut to pieces! Remember what happened to your
General Alexeev!"[7]

Yuly asked:

"Please, Andrei, tell us once and for all, why is it that you
hate precisely him more than anyone else?"

Not looking at us, Andrei whispered:

"I cannot explain why. . . . You yourselves can understand. . . .

"But it was just a week ago that you were firmly on his side.
What in God's name happened?"

"What happened?" he said. "Just you wait, you'll understand
soon enough."

Derman came by—he had just escaped from Simferopol'.
There, he says, "indescribable horror" is going on. Soldiers and

7. At this time, General Mikhail Alexeev was a founder of the new White
Volunteer Army in Rostov in southern Russia. In late February, Bolshevik troops
forced Alexeev and his troops to abandon the city and to retreat southward down
the Don River into the Kuban region. For more on General Alexeev, see Lincoln, *Red Victory*, 76–78.

workers are "walking up to their knees in blood." An old colonel was roasted alive in the furnace of a locomotive.[8]

February 9 / 22, 1918
Yesterday we visited B. There were quite a number of people there—and everyone was unanimous in saying that, thank God, the Germans were advancing and that they had taken Smolensk and Bologoye.[9]

This morning I took a trip into the city.

There was a crowd on Strastnaya Street.

I approached and listened. There was a lady with her hands in a muff and an old peasant woman with a snub nose. The lady was speaking hurriedly, turning red, and getting confused from excitement.

"No way is it a stone about my neck," the lady said hastily. "This monastery[1] is for me a sacred place, but you're trying to tell me that . . ."

8. Simferopol' is the capital of the Crimea, about fifty miles northeast of Yalta. At the time the city was a place of ongoing violence, including pogroms against Jews and the murders of wounded officers. It was captured by Soviet forces on January 26, 1918, and again on November 13, 1920. See D. Pasmanik, *Revoliutsionnye gody v Krymu* (Paris, 1926), 79.

Derman's story was based in fact. Raw cruelty and fanaticism marked the Russian civil war from the beginning. For instance, Red soldiers chained White officers to planks and slowly pushed them into furnaces or boiling water. They also blinded and/or disemboweled their enemies, subjecting them to sexual mutilation, severing their tongues, ears, and noses, and cutting off their arms, legs, and heads.

The barbarism was mutual. For instance, White troops placed the frozen corpses of Red soldiers in obscene positions, packed them on freight cars, and returned them to their comrades with labels that said, "fresh meat, destination Petrograd." See Lincoln, *Red Victory*, 48–49, 383–385.

9. Smolensk is an administrative and cultural center, 350 miles south of Saint Petersburg; Bologoye, a town, roughly 210 miles southeast. Although the Germans were literally "on the doorstep" of Smolensk, they did not capture the city; Bologoye was not even inside their line of fire.

1. The religious edifice in question is the Strastnoi or "Passion" Monastery, which was built in Moscow during the 1640s and which commemorated the arrival of the miraculous icon of the Mother of God to that city. After the civil war the Soviets dissolved the religious community living at Strastnoi and turned the

"I'm not telling you anything," the peasant woman interrupted in an insolent way. "For you it's sacred, but for us it's a stone that gets bigger and bigger. We know. We saw these monasteries in Vladimir![2] A painter takes a board, smears something on it, and there you have it—God. So go pray to him."

"After what you said, I don't want to talk to you anymore."

"So don't talk!"

An old man with yellow teeth and grey stubble on his cheeks was arguing with a worker:

"You've got nothing left now, neither God, nor conscience," the old man said.

"Yes, you're right, there's nothing left."

"And you've gone and shot a fifth of all law-abiding people!"

"Oh, you should talk! As if *you* didn't go about shooting people for three hundred years?"

On Tverskaya Street a poor old general wearing silver glasses and a black fur cap was selling something. He stood timidly, meekly, like a beggar. . . .

It is simply amazing how everyone has given up, how they have all lost heart!

There are rumors about some Polish legions who are supposedly coming to save us.[3] By the way—why precisely the word "legion"? What a wealth of new and increasingly highfalutin words! Everything is a game, a puppet show, "high" style and pompous lies. . . .

The wives of all these sons of bitches who live in the Kremlin now use all the direct lines to talk just as if they were their personal telephones.

---

monastery into a museum under the aegis of the League of Militant Atheists. The entire complex was torn down during urban renewal projects in Moscow during the 1930s.

2. Vladimir is a city located about 110 miles northeast of Moscow.

3. A so-called Polish Corps of Legionnaires (founded by the Russian Provisional Government in July 1917) had captured Minsk on February 19, 1918. They remained in Belarus, though, until they were disbanded by the German military command in May 1918.

February 10 / 23, 1918
"Peace, peace, but there is no peace. Dishonest ones live among
My people. They keep watch like bird-catchers. They appear on
earth, setting traps and capturing people. But My people love this.
Listen, O Earth, for I will bring this people to their destruction,
the fruit of their thoughts."

This is from Jeremiah[4]—I've been reading the Bible all morning long. It is amazing. Especially the words: "But My people love
this. . . . I will bring this people to their destruction, *the fruit of
their thoughts.*"

I am also reading the galleys for my *Village* for Gorky's publishing house, The Sail.[5] The devil got me involved with this institution! Nonetheless *The Village* is a remarkable thing; but only
those who know Russia understand it. But who [outside of Russia]
knows it?

I then looked through my verse from '16 (also for The Sail).

The master has died, the home's in ruins,
The windows flash hot like iron,
Fields with manure, nettles and more,
And the pot, long empty, not fryin' . . .
Heat and toil all around
And through the estate runs a mad hound.[6]

I wrote this in the summer of '16, while at Vasilevskoye,[7] fear-

---

4. Bunin is paraphrasing excerpts from Jeremiah, e.g., 5:26, 31, and 6:14, 19.
5. Bunin's *The Village* (*Derevnia*) had already appeared in book form in
Russia in 1910 and 1912. Gorky's The Sail (*Parus*), 1915–1918, sought to put forth
such "proletarian" writers as Mayakovsky (hence Bunin's antipathy toward the institution). Although Gorky had advanced Bunin seventeen thousand rubles for a
planned collection of his works, The Sail for some reason published only the
tenth volume, taking in works written only in 1915 and 1916. *The Village* was thus
not included in this volume, nor was it ever printed by The Sail at a later date.
6. From Bunin's poem "The Vigil" ("*Kanun*").
7. Vasilevskoye was an estate that belonged to Bunin's cousin, Sofya Nikolaevna Pusheshnikova. Bunin often spent his summers at Vasilevskoye, and wrote
many stories there, including "The Gentleman from San Francisco" in 1915.

ing what many likely feared in those days, especially those who lived in the village close to the people.

And in the summer of last year, our fears were fully realized:

The rye's on fire, the seed's all dead,
But who will save it and risk his head?
The smoke wafts high, the alarm bell shames,
But who will try to put out the flames?
An army of madmen has broken loose,
And like Mamai, they'll score all Rus'. . . .[8]

Until now I did not understand how we could bring ourselves to sit out the entire summer of '17 in the village and how and why we didn't lose our heads in the bargain![9]

"The time has not yet come for us to understand the Russian Revolution impartially, objectively. . . ." This you now hear every minute. Impartially! All the same, there will never be any genuine impartiality. But the main thing is that our "partiality" will one day be very, very valuable for the future historian. After all, are the "passions" of "revolutionaries" the only important ones? And who the hell are "we" if not also the people?

Yesterday at a gathering of [the group] Wednesday, Auslender read some wretched thing, in the style of Oscar Wilde. Auslender's entire body was somehow sickly-looking; but his dark, wizened eyes had a golden gleam, like dried violet ink.

The Germans are apparently not acting as they usually do in a war. They are not fighting and conquering but "simply coming

8. Bunin is continuing to quote from "The Vigil." "Rus'," or more accurately, "Kievan Rus'," was the name of the first state into which the various East Slavic tribes of the forest steppe and forest zones united during the pre-Mongol period. "Kievan Rus'" is also used as the collective term for the autonomous principalities that converged after the disintegration of the Kievan state, beginning from about 1150 and ending with the Mongol conquest of these territories between 1236 and 1240.

9. For more information on Bunin's "summer of '17," see Grin, *Ustami*, 160–162.

by train"—to occupy Petersburg. And all this is supposed to happen in the next forty-eight hours, neither more nor less.[1]

An article in *Izvestia* compares the "Soviet councils"[2] to Kutuzov. The world has never seen more brazen rogues [than these "councils"].

February 14 / 27, 1918

There's a warm snow out.

But hell is going on in the trams. Swarms of soldiers with knapsacks on their backs are fleeing Moscow, fearing that they'll be sent to defend Petersburg against the Germans.

Everyone is certain the Germans have already begun to occupy Russia. About this the people say: "Well, let the Germans come. They'll restore order to our land."[3]

As always, a frightful number of people gathers around the movie houses and greedily reads the posters. Evenings they cram the places full. And it's been like that all winter long.

---

1. Bunin's comment that the Germans were entering Russia "by train" was true. Russians were aghast that the Germans were conducting an *Eisenbahnfeldzug*, or "Railway War," and that they were using Russian roads and railways as if they were "tourists" and "pilgrims." "It is the most comical war I have ever known," the German Max Hoffmann wrote in his diary on February 22, 1918. "We put a handful of infantrymen with machine guns . . . on a train and rush them off to the next station. They take it, make prisoners of the Bolsheviks, pick up a few more troops, and go on. This procedure has, at any rate, the charm of novelty."

German troops pushed to a depth of 125 miles or more along a front stretching from the Baltic to the Carpathians, during what Lenin called "The Eleven Days War." (The main fighting actually lasted fourteen days, but the Soviet delegation arrived at Brest to sue for peace on the eleventh day.) The Germans, though they never entered Saint Petersburg, got as far as Narva, the easternmost city in Estonia, eighty-five miles from their goal. See Mawdsley, *Civil War*, 35.

2. Generally speaking, the "soviets" ("*sovety*") were representative institutions of authority and self-government that came into being as a result of the Revolution of 1905, and that sought to direct strike activities among workers. By the fall of 1917 the soviets became Bolshevized, with more than half of their members becoming Communists or Communist sympathizers.

3. Such sentiments were common. Even Lenin felt compelled to tell his followers: "Learn discipline from the Germans. We must produce order." See Lincoln, *Red Victory*, 52.

At Nikitsky Gates[4] a cabby crashes into an automobile and dents its fender. The cabby, a giant with a red beard, is completely beside himself:

"Forgive me, for God's sake, I'll get down on my knees before you!"

The driver is pockmarked, sallow, stern-looking but merciful: "Why on your knees! You're a worker just like me. Only next time, take care you don't run into me!"

The driver behaves as though he were the boss, and not without reason. These are the new masters.

Newspapers have empty columns—the result of censors.[5] Muralov "has slipped away" from Moscow.[6]

A cabby alongside the Prague restaurant[7] says with laughter and joy: "What the hell, let the Germans come. After all, it's all the same. They've ruled us before.[8] People say that there, in their own country, they've already arrested some thirty key Jews.[9]

4. The Nikitsky Gates (*Nikitskie vorota*) were one of several defense barriers built into the wall of the White City (*Belyi gorod*) section of Moscow in the sixteenth century. They were destroyed when city planners rehabilitated the center of Moscow during the reign of Catherine the Great. The square upon which the gates opened, though, still retains its name.

5. Censorship was abolished in the wake of the February Revolution; but on November 7, 1917, the Bolsheviks reinstated strictures on publishing with the famous "Decree Concerning the Press."

6. This was not true. Nikolai Muralov had commanded the Moscow Military District since the October Revolution; but he left the city in March 1919, on assignment, to serve on the eastern front in the Russian civil war.

7. The Prague restaurant on Arbat Street was one of the most famous eating establishments in Moscow.

8. The Germans entered into Russia's political life on several occasions. For instance, in the thirteenth century, German (Teutonic) knights occupied the area around Pskov until they were routed by Alexander Nevsky in 1242. In the 1730s Germans were active in all spheres of Russian political and social life. Ernst Biron was a grand chamberlain and favorite in the court of Empress Anna Ivanovna. After Anna's death, for three weeks he was also regent for the child tsar, Ivan VI.

9. Bunin may be referring to the fact that, early in 1918, Germany was rocked by strikes from workers demanding higher wages for their labor. Russian revolutionary propaganda, unprecedented profits in German iron and steel industries, and civil disturbances in Vienna and in other industrial centers of the Austro-Hungarian Empire were causes for their unrest. For more information, see G. Feldman, *Army, Industry, and Labor in Germany, 1914–1918* (Princeton, 1966), 407–518.

So what the hell, why not the same thing here? We're a grue-some bunch. Tell one of us to 'get going' and the others will fol-low."

February 15 / 28, 1918
After yesterday evening's news alleging that the Germans have al-ready taken Petersburg, the newspapers are all in despair. All the same, though, the newspapers issue calls "to stand as one in the struggle with the German members of the White Guard."[1]

Lunacharsky is even calling up high school students to enlist with the Red Guard, "to fight Hindenburg."[2]

So far we are surrendering thirty-five provinces to the Ger-mans and have lost millions of cannons, armored cars, trains, and shells. . . .[3]

Again there's a heavy snow. High school coeds walk about, covered with it—all beauty and joy. One of them is especially beautiful, with charming blue eyes that peek out from under a raised fur collar. . . . What lies ahead for these youth?

Toward evening everything is springlike, aflame from the sun; golden clouds hang in the west. There are also puddles and soft, white snow that has not yet melted.

---

1. The panic was justified. On February 27 a German airplane dropped bombs on the Fontanka Embankment inside the city.
2. In an appeal entitled, "To Student Youth" ("*K uchashchieisia molodezhi*"), published in *Izvestia* on February 27, 1918, Lunacharsky wrote: "We, the mem-bers of the Committee for Enlightenment, know that there exist many passion-ate hearts who beat with radiant love for the workers' cause, and that they can be found amidst student youth, those of the upper classes of high-schools . . . uni-versities . . . and other educational institutions. And we call upon these to walk alongside working youth and to act as a bulwark against the imperialist beast. Women among student youth can supplement the ranks of the army with med-ical and hospital assistance."

The Red Guard (*Krasnaia gvardiia*) were armed bands of factory workers who came into being with the February Revolution of 1917. Their members sought to maintain public safety and to spread the revolution throughout Russia. For individuals like Bunin, the Red Guard represented disorder, anarchy, and menace to people and property.

3. Bunin's count is somewhat exaggerated. By late February the Germans controlled between 20 and 25 Russian provinces, and by one count had captured

February 16 / March 1, 1918
Yesterday evening I was at T.'s. Of course, everyone kept talking about one and the same thing: what is going on. Everyone is horrified, except for Shmelyov who has not given into despair and keeps exclaiming:

"No, I believe in the Russian people!"

All morning long I wandered through the city. I came across two soldiers who were passing by; their conversation was hale and hearty:

"Moscow's now worth sh-t, pal."

"The provinces are also sh-t."

"Well, the Germans will come; they'll bring order."

"Of course, and we won't object. People are gettin' screwed everywhere."

"And if you and I weren't gettin' fucked here, we'd have perished in the trenches."

In Belov's store,[4] a young soldier with a fat, drunken face orders almost a ton of butter and loudly says:

"We ain't ashamed to buy anything. After all, our present commander-in-chief Muralov is a soldier just like me, and just the other day his men polished off twenty thousand rubles' worth of vodka."

Twenty thousand! Most likely this guy is suffering from his own grand delusions, his own boorish fantasies. But God knows— perhaps it's true.

At four o'clock a group of journalists met at the Artists' Circle[5] "to draft a protest against censorship by the Bolsheviks." Mel'gunov presided. Kuskova urged that publishers stop printing newspapers as a sign of protest. Imagine, that would really scare the Bolsheviks! Then everyone passionately assured each other that

---

63,000 Russian prisoners, 2,600 pieces of artillery, and 5,000 machine guns. See M. Gilbert, *The First World War: A Complete History* (New York, 1994), 401.

4. Belov's was a specialty foodstore in Moscow.

5. The Literary-Artistic Circle (*Literaturno-khudozhestvennyi kruzhok*) was founded in 1899 in Moscow and brought together authors, playwrights, and artists.

the Bolsheviks were on their last legs. They're already evacuating their families from Moscow. Friche, for example, has moved [his loved ones out].

People were talking about Salikovsky:

"Wouldn't you know it! He was a lousy journalist and now you have this crazy Rada making him the governor general of Kiev!"[6]

We came back with Chirikov, who told me the latest and highly trustworthy news: General [Mikhail] Kamenev has shot himself;[7] the main German headquarters are over on Povarskaya Street;[8] it's dangerous to live there because that's where the most heated fighting will take place; the Bolsheviks are in contact with the monarchists and big-shot merchants; and, with Mirbach's consent, it has been decided to elect Samarin as the new tsar.[9] . . . But if that's so, who's all this heated fighting going to be with?

Nighttime, the same day
I said goodbye to Chirikov and ran into a very young soldier on Povarskaya Street. He was in rags, scraggly, filthy, and dead drunk. He first stuck his mug into my chest, but then having stepped back a bit, spat at me and said:

"Despot, son of a bitch!"

I've been sitting at my desk and going through my manuscripts and notes—it's time to get ready to head south—and I've

---

It was in the Circle that Bunin launched his savage attack on the Modernists on October 8, 1913.

6. "Rada" is the Ukrainian term (equivalent to "council") for any representative governing body. After the Revolution of 1917, the Central Rada and the Ukrainian National Rada were the highest ruling organizations in the Ukraine. Kiev, the capital of the Ukraine, changed hands no less than sixteen times in thirty-six months. See Lincoln, *Red Victory*, 303.

7. Bunin is misinformed on some of these points. It was General Kaledin, not Kamenev who committed suicide on January 28, 1918. See D. Lehovich, *White Against Red: The Life of General Anton Denikin* (New York, 1974), 189; and Lincoln, *Red Victory*, 82.

8. The German embassy in Moscow was located in the Berg Palace, the former home of a sugar industrialist, and was one of the most sumptuously furnished dwellings in Moscow.

9. The rumor was not true.

just run across some proof of my "despotism." Here's a note that I made on February 22 / March 7, 1915:

"Our maid Tanya apparently loves to read a great deal. She goes under my desk, takes out my basket with all my torn papers in it, selects a couple of things, folds them, and whenever she has a free moment, reads them—slowly, and with a slight smile on her face. But she's afraid to ask me for one of my books, she's shy. . . . How cruelly, repulsively we live now!"

Here's another one that I wrote in Vasilevskoye during the winter of '16:

"It's late evening, I'm sitting and reading in the study, in an old easy chair, in comfort and warmth, and next to a marvelous old lamp. Maria Petrovna walks in and gives me an envelope made of dirty-grey paper:

"They're raising the prices again. The people have become absolutely shameful."

As always, the person at the Izmalkovo telegraph office[1] has written, "Pay the courier 70 kopecks," in a flamboyant way and with purple-colored ink. And, again as always, this "courier"—the old peasant woman, Maxotochka, who also brings us our telegrams—had a kid who took a pencil and changed the number 7 to 8, but in a crude way. I got up and went through the dark dining room and the hall into the foyer. There stood a small peasant woman wrapped in a shawl that was covered with snow, a whip in her hand. The air was rife with the smells of a sheepskin coat, along with those of a hut and the cold.

"Maxotochka," I said, "was it you who marked up the price? Are you again asking for more money?"

"Master," Maxotochka replied in a voice made wooden by the weather outside, "just take a look how bad the road is. It's one pothole after another. It knocks the wind out of you. You should be ashamed of yourself again. It's so cold that it knocks the stuffin' out of you. After all, it's twenty miles this way and back."

1. The village of Izmalkovo was several miles immediately west of Elets, about two hundred miles directly south of Moscow.

I shook my head, and, with a reproachful look, I thrust a ruble into Maxotochka's hand. Going back through the dining room, I look through the windows: an icy, moonlit night shines very brightly out on the snowy yard. And all of a sudden I see a bright boundless field, a shining road filled with potholes, frost-covered sleds noisily making their way down it, and a nag hitched to the side of one of them, running at a light trot, all covered with frost, and with huge eyelashes grey with rime. . . . What was Maxotochka thinking about as she shrank from the cold and the fiery wind and leaned on the corner of her carriage?

Back in my study, I opened the telegram: "Together with everyone in Strel'na,[2] we drink to the glory and pride of Russian literature!" For this Maxotochka had to make her way over twenty miles of potholes.

February 17 / March 2, 1918
Yesterday the journalists unanimously affirmed that they did not believe that peace had really been signed with the Germans.

"I can't imagine," A. A. Yablonovsky said, "Hohenzollern's signature right next to Bronstein's!"[3]

2. Strel'na was a famous restaurant in Moscow, known for its gypsy chorus.
3. Bronstein was the real name of Leon Trotsky. As a result of the German offensive into Russia, and after serious debate, Lenin persuaded his comrades on the Council of People's Commissars to accept the harsh terms of the Treaty of Brest-Litovsk, which was signed on March 3, 1918, and ended the war between Germany and Soviet Russia. Under the treaty, Russia lost control over most of the Baltic provinces, part of Belorussia, the Ukraine, and the oil port of Batumi on the Turkish frontier. In economic terms the treaty meant the loss of over a quarter of Russia's population, agricultural land, and railways, and about three-quarters of its coal, iron, and steel. Militarily the Russian army was to be completely demobilized, and the navy was disarmed and its warships detained in Russian ports. The Soviets not only lost the Ukraine but were obliged to evacuate it, to make peace with its Rada, and to recognize the Rada's separate treaty with Germany and its allies, Estonia, Livonia, and Finland.
Lincoln elaborates: "[With the signing of the Treaty of Brest-Litovsk] three hundred years of triumphs won by Russian arms and diplomacy dissolved in a single moment. Sixty million people and two million square kilometers of territory, including land that had produced nearly a third of Imperial Russia's crops, slipped from the Bolsheviks' grasp." See Lincoln, *Red Victory*, 89.

Today I visited Zubov's place (on Povarskaya). There Kolya[4] was going through some books. Spring was everywhere: it was very bright from the sun and snow; the sky was especially lovely, light and dark blue among the branches of the birch trees.

At 4:30 Arbat Square[5] was filled with bright sun. Crowds of people were tearing copies of *Evening News*[6] from the hands of the newspaper boys: peace had been signed!

I called *Power of the People*. Was it true that peace had been signed? They answered that they themselves had just called *Izvestia* and that they had received a firm reply: "Yes, it had been signed."

So for those who said, "I can't imagine such a thing," take that.

February 18 / March 3, 1918
This morning there was a meeting at Writers' Publishing House. Before it began I kept cursing out the Bolsheviks with the worst words I could find. Klestov-Angarsky—he is some kind of commissar—didn't say a word.[7]

Someone had pasted posters up on the walls of buildings, indicting Trotsky and Lenin for their ties to the Germans, saying that the two had been bought by them.[8] I asked Klestov:

"Well, and just how much did these scoundrels get?"

---

4. Bunin's nephew, Nikolai Alexeevich Pusheshnikov.

5. Arbat Square was one of Moscow's most fashionable districts, the domain of the aristocracy and the upper middle class.

6. *Evening News* (*Vechernie izvestiia*) was the late-day edition of *Power of the People*.

7. Klestov-Angarsky recalls: "Bunin was a man 'of another time.' . . . [When I first met him] he received me with a dry and haughty air. Everything about him conveyed the impression of an impoverished aristocrat-gentryman who sought to hide his indigence with arrogance and conceit." See M. Angarskaia, *Po sledam ottsa* (Moscow, 1992), 152.

8. The rumor was true. The Bolsheviks did, in fact, use German subsidies for purposes of party organization and propaganda. See R. Pipes, *The Russian Revolution* (New York, 1990), 411. One diplomat of the time remarked that although Trotsky was for him "the greatest Jew since Christ," the Germans had bought a "lemon," if Trotsky indeed was on their payroll. See Lincoln, *Red Victory*, 166.

"Don't you worry," he answered with a confused grin, "I'm sure it was plenty."

One hears one and the same thing all over town:

"Only Russia has signed the peace; the Germans have refused to do so. . . ."[9]

A foolish self-delusion.

Toward evening the crosses of the churches give off a matted rose-gold light.

February 19 / March 4, 1918

Kogan told me about Steinberg, the commissar of justice: He's an old-fashioned, devout Jew; he does not eat nonkosher food, and he keeps the Sabbath holy. . . . Then Kogan spoke about Blok: he's in Moscow now, a passionate Bolshevik, and Lunacharsky's personal secretary.[1] Kogan's wife says with emotion:

"But don't judge him so harshly! After all, he's still just a kid!"[2]

At five o'clock this evening I learned that some drunken soldiers threw a bomb at the Officers' Economic Society on Vozdvizhenka Street. People say that somewhere between sixty and eighty people were killed.

I have just read a document that came from Sevastopol':[3] "A Resolution Endorsed by the Crew of the Battleship *Liberated Russia*."

"To everyone both here and abroad who takes pointless and foolish fire at Sevastopol'!

"Comrades! You're wasting your fire and to your own peril. Soon you'll have nothing to hit, but you'll keep firing all the same and get nothing for your pains; and then, dear ones, we'll come and kill you with our bare hands.

"Comrades! The bourgeois are swallowing those who now lie in coffins and graves. You traitors and shooters, you have lost your

9. This was not true.
1. Blok was never Lunacharsky's personal secretary.
2. Blok was thirty-eight years old at the time.
3. Sevastopol' is an important port on the Black Sea in the Ukraine. At this time it was under Soviet control.

cartridges; so you are helping the bourgeois to swallow everyone around. We call on all comrades to join with us and forbid the shooting of all those who wear the hats of enlisted men.

"Comrades! Let us agree on the following, that from today on any firing we hear will say to us: 'One less bourgeois, one less socialist among the living!' Every bullet you shoot must hit a fat belly; it must not raise foam on the shore.

"Comrades! Take care of your cartridges more than your eyes. You can still live with one eye, but you can't live without cartridges.

"If people resume shooting close to funerals taking place either in town or on the shore, then remember that we, too, the sailors of the battleship *Liberated Russia*, will fire one round. Only don't blame us if your eardrums break, and the glass in your windows shatters to boot.

"And so, comrades, let there be no more foolish or pointless firing in Sevastopol'. Let the firing have only one purpose: to shoot the counterrevolution and the bourgeois, not at the water or in the air; for no one can live without these even for a minute!"

February 20 / March 5, 1918
I went to Nikolaevsky Station.[4]

It was very sunny out, almost too much so, with a light frost. From the hill behind Myasnitsky Gates[5]—I saw a blue-grey haze, clusters of homes, and the golden cupolas of churches. Ah, Moscow! Snow was melting on the square in front of the station. The entire place shone like gold, mirrorlike. I was taken by the massive, powerful sight of carts with boxes on them. Can it really be that all this power, this wealth is coming to an end? There were a great many peasants, soldiers in many kinds of old overcoats,

---

4. Nikolaevsky Station (*Nikolaevskii vokzal*), renamed Leningrad Station (*Leningradskii vokzal*), is located northeast of Red Square.
5. The Myasnitsky Gates (*Miasnitskie vorota*), also known as the Red Gates (*Krasnye vorota*), were removed in the 1928 reconstruction of Lermontov Square in the northeast quarter of Moscow.

wearing them any old way, and with various types of weapons—one had a saber at his side, another had a rifle, another had a huge revolver in his belt. . . . These are now the masters of everything, the heirs of a colossal heritage. . . .

Of course, there's all kinds of pushing and shoving going on in the tram.

Two old ladies savagely curse out the "government":

"They should all drop dead. They give you a few crumbs that I'm sure have been sitting around somewhere for a year. You chew on them—and the smell is so bad that it really burns you up!"

Next to them stands a peasant. With an idiotic smile on his lips, he looks and listens in a strange, dull, and dead way. The dirty remains of a white Manchurian hat hang down on his brown face. His eyes are pale.

A giant soldier looms over the other people who are sitting and standing there. He's a full head taller than anyone else, in a magnificent grey overcoat drawn in tightly with a handsome belt at the waist, and wearing a grey round hat like Alexander III used to wear. Everything about him is massive. He's a genuine thoroughbred, with a full triangular brown beard and a Bible in his gloved hand. He is so unlike anyone else there, the last of the Mohicans.[6]

The street that I take on the way back is so blinding that it seems to go directly into the sun. Suddenly everyone makes an appearance and takes a good look: a scene of ancient Moscow, like a picture by Surikov. A crowd of peasant men and women in sheepskin coats surround another peasant who wears a red calfskin hat and an *armyak*[7] the color of rye bread. He is hurriedly unharnessing a horse that is lying down and thrashing about on the pavement. The animal was pulling a huge sleigh filled with straw. When the horse fell to the ground, it dislocated the shaft and the

6. A designation that Bunin later also used to describe himself as the last "gentry" writer of Russia.

7. An *armyak* is a peasant's coat of heavy cloth, with no collar or buttons, worn with a sash.

sleigh ran up on the sidewalk. The peasant cries out at the top of his voice: "Hey lads, give me a hand!" but no one moves to help him.

We went out again at 6 p.m. We met M. He said he had just heard that the Kremlin was being mined and that people wanted to blow it up if the Germans came.[8] At that very moment I looked into the magnificent green sky over the Kremlin, at the aged gold of its ancient cupolas . . . the Great Princes, the Terem Palace, the Church of the Savior in the Forest, Archangel Cathedral[9]—all so native and intimate; only now do I understand them as I should! Blow it up? Anything is possible now.

Rumors: In two weeks there will be a monarchy and a government made up of Adrianov, Sandetsky, and Mishchenko. All the best hotels are being prepared for the Germans.[1]

The Social Revolutionaries[2] are said to be preparing for a revolt. The soldiers are allegedly on their side.

February 21 / March 6, 1918
Kamenskaya was here. Like hundreds of others, she and her family are being evicted from their homes. They were given a dead-

---

8. The rumor had no basis in fact.
9. The Terem Palace (*Teremnoi Dvorets*) is a palace in the Kremlin. The Church of the Savior in the Forest (*Spas na Boru*), also known as the Cathedral of the Transformation (*Preobrazhenskii Sobor*), and the Archangel Cathedral (*Arkhangel'skii Sobor*) are among the religious edifices there.
1. These rumors were untrue.
2. The Social Revolutionaries, a political party founded in 1901, represented the older populist tradition of Russian radicalism. Their program was to transform Russia's agricultural life along socialistic lines. In 1917 the Socialist Revolutionary party (with the exception of its left wing) declared its hostility to the October Revolution and to the Bolshevik seizure of power. Their movement received widespread support from the Russian public. For instance, in the elections for the Constituent Assembly held in November of that year, the Socialist Revolutionary party received more than 50 percent of the popular vote, and counted 440 of the Assembly's approximately 700 delegates. From January 1918 on the Social Revolutionaries sought to restore the Constituent Assembly; and when the Bolsheviks signed the Treaty of Brest-Litovsk, they decided on armed resistance against the Soviet government.

line of only forty-eight hours to get out, but it will take more than a week to pack up their apartment.

I met Speransky. He said that, according to *Russian News*, a German commission is coming to Saint Petersburg to count the losses suffered by German nationals there, and that the German police will keep a presence in the city. [He also said] that the German police will also be in Moscow; that the German military staff is already there; and that Lenin is in Moscow, sitting inside the Kremlin. That is why the Kremlin has announced that it is in a state of siege.[3]

February 22 / March 7, 1918
This morning, a sad job: we are going through our books, deciding which ones to keep and which ones to sell. (I am getting money together for our departure.) . . .

[My brother] Yuly told me the "most reliable news" from *Power of the People*: Petersburg has been declared a free city, and Lunacharsky has been designated its mayor. (Mayor Lunacharsky!)[4] Also: tomorrow all banks in Moscow will be transferred to the Germans;[5] and the German attack continues. . . . In general, the whole place is going to the devil!

This evening we were at the Bolshoi Theater. As always now, the streets are dark; but the square in front of the theater has several lights on it, making the gloom in the sky seem even thicker. The façade of the building is dark and funereally sad. The car-

3. None of these stories had any basis in fact. For instance, Lenin was not in Moscow on March 6; the new Soviet government did not move there until March 11.
4. Both rumors were false. For instance, in the spring of 1917 Lunacharsky was named *tovarishch gorodskoi golovy*, or, loosely translated, "assistant to the mayor" of Petrograd.
5. The rumor was not true. In fact, though, financial exchanges in Moscow and Petrograd were responding to the German advance by raising the exchange rate for securities, thereby causing the public to believe that the Germans would restore private ownership of land and capital. See I. Ksenofontov, *Mir, kotorogo khoteli i kotoryi nenavideli* (Moscow, 1991), 364–365.

riages and cars that used to park in front of it are no longer there. The theater was empty inside, only a few boxes were taken. A Jew, with a brownish-looking bald spot and a grey clipped beard, was wearing golden spectacles. He kept pulling back his daughter, who insisted upon sitting on the barrier in front of her. Her blue dress made her look like a black ram. People told me that he's some kind of "emissary."

When we left the theater I looked between the columns of the theater and saw a blue-black sky with two or three dusky-blue patches of stars. A cold wind was blowing sharply. Driving was difficult. Nikitskaya Street was without lights, sepulchrally dark. Four homes rose in the dark green sky. They seemed to be very big, as if making their presence known for the first time. There were almost no passersby, and whoever was around was walking almost at a trot.

It was like the Middle Ages! But then, at least, everyone was armed and the homes were almost impregnable. . . .

Two soldiers were standing on the corner of Povarskaya and Merzlyakovskaya streets. Were they patrolmen or robbers? Probably both.

February 23 / March 8, 1918
"Bourgeois newspapers" are again being published—but with large empty [censored] columns in each issue.

I met K. "The Germans will be in Moscow in a few days," he says. "But it's a terrible thing. People say that Russians will be sent to the front to fight against the allies."[6] Yes, everything is the same. Everything is still the same: anxious, tedious, and unresolved waiting.

We keep talking about where to go. This evening I was at Yuly's, and on the way home we came under fire. People were madly shooting from rifles somewhere above Povarskaya Street.

P. was having the floors of his house cleaned. One of the

6. Neither rumor was true.

workers was stooped, with black greasy hair and wearing a wine-colored shirt. Another was pockmarked and had wild curly hair. They began dancing about and pulling each other by the hair. Their faces were glossy, their foreheads sweaty. We asked them:

"Well, tell us, gentlemen, how's it going? Good?"

"What can you say? It's all bad."

"What do you think is going to happen?"

"God knows," the curly one said. "We're a gruesome bunch. What do we know? I can barely read, and he's completely blind. What will happen? Why this: criminals have been let out of prison, they're the ones who are ruling over us now. They should have never been set free; they should have been shot with a sawed-off shotgun a long time ago. They knocked the tsar off the throne; nothing like this ever happened when he was around. And you can't stew over the Bolsheviks now. The people have gotten weak. I couldn't skin a chicken, but I could easily give the folk a good swift kick in the pants. No, the people have gotten weak. There's only about a hundred thousand Bolsheviks in all; and we're so many millions and can't do nothin'. They can now open a state liquor store, or they could give us our freedom, but we could drag them all from their apartments and tear them to shreds."

"They're all kikes," the black one said.

"And Polacks to boot. People say that this Lenin we got now is not the real one—that the real one was killed a long time ago."

"And what do you think about peace with the Germans?"

"There won't be no peace. The Germans will end it soon enough, though. But the Polacks will again be ours.[7] The main problem is that there's no bread. Yesterday my friend here bought himself a small doughnut for three rubles, and I had to get along on some thin soup. . . ."

7. The Russian Provisional Government had recognized Poland's right to independence on March 30, 1917; but it was not until early October 1918 that the Polish Regency Council announced the formation of an independent government for the country.

MOSCOW 1918

February 24 / March 9, 1918

The other day I bought a pound of tobacco; I hung it on a rope between the window frames and the *fortochka*[8] so that it wouldn't dry out. The window looked out onto a courtyard. Today about 6 a.m. something went flying through the glass. I jumped up and found a rock on the floor. The glass was broken, the tobacco was gone, and someone was running away from the window—robbers everywhere!

There are featherlike clouds, sunshine every now and then, and puddles like blue patches. . . .

A prayer service is going on in the house across from us. People are carrying the icon of "Unexpected Joy"[9] and the priests are singing. How very strange all this seems now. And how very touching. Many are crying.

Again there's a rumor that the Bolsheviks have many monarchists in their ranks and that, in general, all this bolshevism is geared to bring back the monarchy. Again this is nonsense that the Bolsheviks themselves have made up, of course.

Savich and Alexeev are supposedly now in Pskov "to establish a government."[1]

I put in a call to *Power of the People*: "Give me telephone 60-42," I said. They put me through. But it seemed that the line was busy—*Power of the People* had unexpectedly eavesdropped on someone's conversation with the Kremlin:

"I have fifteen officers and Lieutenant Kaledin. What should I do with them?"

"Shoot them right away."

I have always thought that anarchists were unusually happy

---

8. The *fortochka* is a small hinged pane in the windows of Russian houses, used for ventilation.

9. The icon of "Unexpected Joy" (*"Nechaiannaia Radost'"*) depicts this story: The Virgin Mary shows a sinner the wounds on the hands and legs of the Christ Child, asserting that whenever he does evil, her Son suffers pain. The sinner begs forgiveness and begins to lead a righteous life.

1. This was a rumor—and false. Its possible source is the fact that both Savich and Alexeev actively worked to persuade Nicholas II to give up his throne.

and kind people; but the Bolshevik soviet fears them greatly. The editor, Barmash, is a completely crazy individual from the Caucasus.

In Sevastopol' the sailors have an "ataman"[2]—one Rivkin whose tattered beard is almost three feet long; he's robbed and murdered without end, but he's "a most gentle individual."

Many people now pretend they have news that no one else has.

In Filippov's coffeehouse, people supposedly saw Adrianov, the former mayor of Moscow. He's also allegedly one of the most important privy councilors in the Soviet of Workers' Deputies.

February 25 / March 10, 1918
Yurka Sablin—is commander of the armed forces! He's a twenty-year-old kid, a specialist in black American dances, and a sickeningly sweet individual. . . .

There is a rumor that the Allies—now it's their turn!—have entered into agreement with the Germans and have charged them with bringing order to Russia.[3]

Again there are demonstrations, banners, posters, music; one goes one way, one goes another, and a hundred people yell:

"Stand up, rise up, working people!"

Their voices are hollow, primitive. The women have Chuvash and Mordvinian faces;[4] and the men have criminal features that

2. Historically the ataman was a Cossack chieftain. In colloquial Russian the word means "gang leader" or "chief."

3. The rumor was not true. In a rare moment of agreement, Western leaders and their representatives in Russia agreed to support the Bolsheviks once the Russians had resumed hostilities with Germany. (Only the American government dissented from this decision.) See R. Debo, *Revolution and Survival: The Foreign Policy of Soviet Russia, 1917–1918* (Toronto, 1979), 135–136. Trotsky, though, believed just the opposite. "All of us," he wrote, "including Lenin, were of the impression that the Germans had come to an agreement with the Allies about crushing the Soviets and that a peace on the Western front was to be built on the bones of the Russian revolution." See J. Bunyan and H. Fisher, *The Bolshevik Revolution* (Stanford, 1934), 514–515.

4. Bunin displays his "Russian" and "aristocratic" biases. The Chuvash are an indigenous, Turkic-speaking people who live along the right bank of the mid-

make them look like a matched set. Some seem to have come right from Sakhalin.[5]

The Romans used to brand the faces of their prisoners with the words: "Cave furem."[6] But these Russian faces need nothing; they show it all without any branding.

And then there's the "Marsellaise," the national hymn of the French themselves, which the revolutionaries have changed in the most vulgar way![7]

February 26 / March 11, 1918
On the corner of Povarskaya Street, someone, either a worker or a peasant, reads aloud a notice about the newspaper *Evening Hour*,[8] listing the names of its staff. He finishes reading it and says:

"They're all bastards. And famous ones at that!"

The editorial officers of *Russian News* report that Trotsky is a German spy, also that he was a detective for the police in Nizhny-Novgorod.[9] Stuchka published this in *Pravda*, out of spite for Trotsky.

---

dle Volga. The Mordvinians are a Finno-Ugric group and inhabit the eastern part of the Volga basin.

5. Sakhalin is an island of Russia lying close to the mainland of northeastern Asia between the Sea of Japan and the Sea of Okhotsk. From 1869 to 1906 Sakhalin was a penal colony. More than thirty thousand individuals served terms there, enduring corporal punishment and forced labor in forests and mines. Revolts were common, the largest occurring in 1888. Chekhov visited Sakhalin in 1890 and recorded his experiences in *Sakhalin Island* (*Ostrov Sakhalin*) in 1893–1894. The exiling of prisoners to Sakhalin was curtailed by the outbreak of the Russo-Japanese War in 1904–1905 and abolished completely in 1906.

6. "Beware the Madman."

7. In July 1875 Pyotr Lavrov published a revolutionary song, entitled the "Worker's Marsellaise" (*"Rabochaia Marsel'eza"*), which had the same melody as the "Marsellaise" and which became popular with workers and intellectuals in Russia during the 1880s and 1890s.

8. *Evening Hour*, more accurately, *New Evening Hour* (*Novyi vechernii chas*), was a newspaper published in Saint Petersburg in 1917 and 1918.

9. Neither rumor was true. Trotsky never worked in Nizhny-Novgorod (a city approximately two hundred miles directly east of Moscow), though he and Lenin were often called "spies" by opposition forces.

February 27 / March 12, 1918
Today is another holiday—the anniversary of the Revolution.[1] But there are no people on the streets, and not at all because winter storms have again made their appearance. Everyone is just tired of it all.

What savage, horrible nonsense. Our phone has been ringing off the hook all day long and giving forth burning news.

"People are being dispersed all over the place! Karakhan has been named ambassador to Constantinople, and [Lev] Kamenev—to Berlin.[2] . . ."

We read a small article by Lenin. It was a trivial, dishonest piece—discussing first the international and then "the Russian national surge."

February 28 / March 13, 1918
It's winter again. There's a lot of snow out; it's sunny, and the windows of buildings shine brightly.

News from Sretenka Street—German soldiers have taken the Spassky barracks.[3]

German troops also have supposedly entered Petersburg. Tomorrow there will be a decree to denationalize the banks.[4] But I think that once again the Bolsheviks are out to make fools of us.

The telephone has been ringing all day long—it crackles, jingles, and throws off fiery red sparks!

1. Bunin is referring to the February Revolution of 1917 which began on March 8, 1917, and which, having toppled the Romanov dynasty, established the Provisional Government with a mandate to govern until the founding of a popularly elected Constituent Assembly.
2. In truth, Kamenev was sent to England and France to propagandize the revolution and to gauge the militancy of Western socialist parties. He was unsuccessful in both endeavors.
3. This was not true.
4. Red Guards and loyal Bolshevik sailors occupied Russia's banks in December 1917; a month later Lenin declared them national property. See Lincoln, *Red Victory*, 111–112.

March 1 / 14, 1918
We spent the evening at Shklyar's place.

On the way there we saw the lawyer Teslenko. He was approaching his home on Red Square. We stopped and greeted him. Hale and hearty, he said the Bolsheviks are now engaged in one thing: "To rob and get hold of as much money as possible, since they themselves know very well that their end is near."

Besides us, Derman and Gruzinsky were also at Shklyar's place. When they were in a tram, a soldier told Gruzinsky this story:

"I was going around without any work, so I went to the Council of Deputies to ask for a job—they said they didn't have anything for me; but they gave me two search warrants so that I could rip off others. I really cursed them out, though, for I'm an honest type. . . ."

Derman has received news from Rostov:[5] the Kornilov movement[6] is weak there. Gruzinsky objected that just the reverse was true—the movement was strong and growing. Derman added: "The Bolsheviks are committing horrible atrocities in Rostov. They've dug up Kaledin's grave and have shot six hundred nurses. . . ." Well, if not six hundred—and that most likely—a good number of them nonetheless. This is not the first time that our Christ-loving peasants—the very ones about whom these nurses have spread so many legends—have raped and murdered them.

People say that Moscow will be in the hands of the Germans by March 17 / 30, and that Budberg will be the mayor.[7]

A cook from the Ravine restaurant[8] told me that he has been

5. Rostov, also known as Rostov the Great, is one of the oldest cities in Russia and is located roughly two hundred miles northeast of Moscow.

6. After the Bolsheviks had seized power, Kornilov joined Generals Alexeev and Kaledin to organize a resistance movement in the Don region. No such coalition could be successful, however, because the population there was unenthusiastic about an anti-Bolshevik crusade and because Kornilov and his colleagues could not agree on a common strategy and goals.

7. Neither event came to be.

8. The Ravine (*Iar*) was a restaurant in Moscow and, like the Strel'na, also known for its gypsy chorus.

robbed of everything it took him thirty years of hard work to ac-
cumulate, and that now he has been reduced to hovering by the
stove amidst ninety-degree heat. "But Orlov-Davydov," he added,
"sent a telegram to his peasants telling them—I myself read it—to
burn down the house, kill the cattle, and cut down the forests. He
told them to leave one birch tree standing, though, so that he
would have rods to beat them and something to hang them on."

There is a rumor that the Germans have organized a criminal investigation department in Moscow, and they are supposedly
watching the slightest steps of the Bolsheviks, noting everything
and writing it all down.[9]

News from our village:[1] the peasants are returning stolen
things to the landowners.[2]

The last item is absolutely true. I heard this on the streets:

"Now the soldiers are shitting in their pants. They're going out
and bragging, calm and carefree—let the Germans come, they
say, the devil with them—but now things have gotten so serious
that they're really afraid. We're going to get it good, they say, and
to tell the truth, it serves us right: we've really become like pigs!"

But if, in fact, something "serious" is in the air, then the "pri-
mordial nature of the great Russian Revolution" should have quieted down somewhat. But how wild the village got in the summer
of last year; how terrible it was to live in Vasilevskoye! But suddenly there was this rumor: Kornilov began ordering the death
penalty—and almost all during July, Vasilevskoye became stiller
than water, lower than grass. In May and June it had been terrifying to go out into the streets; and every night one would see here
and there the red glow of fire on the black horizon. One time at
dawn, near where we lived, the peasants had set a barn on fire;
and then they had run around, screaming that the "masters" them-

9. The rumor was false.
1. Most likely Glotovo, near Elets.
2. In response to Lenin's 1917 decree abolishing private ownership of the
land, peasants everywhere had looted livestock, farm implements, and valuables
from local manor houses. See Lincoln, *Red Victory*, 63.

selves had done it to burn down the entire village. But at noon on that same day a neighbor's cattle yard caught fire; and again people came running from all over, screaming that I had done it and wanting to throw me into the fire. The only thing that saved me was the fury with which I threw myself at the crowd.

March 2 / 15, 1918
People talk about: "The profligate, the drunkard Rasputin, the evil genius of Russia." He was a good peasant, of course. What about you people who have yet to crawl out of all those Bears or Stray Dogs?[3]

To all appearances, the new decline in literature could not go any lower. A Musical Snuffbox[4] has opened up in a most vile tavern. Speculators, cardsharps, and prostitutes sit, gobble up meat pies at a hundred rubles a crack, and drink moonshine from teacups, while poets and writers (Alyoshka Tolstoy,[5] Bryusov, and

---

3. The Bear (*Medved'*) was a restaurant in Saint Petersburg. The Stray Dog (*Brodiachaia sobaka*) was a nightclub also in Petersburg and a favorite of writers and artists; it closed in 1915.

About the Stray Dog, Bunin wrote in his *Memoirs* in 1950: "The Stray Dog in Petersburg, where Akhmatova said, 'We all are sinners here, we all are whores,' was also the setting for 'The Flight of the Virgin Mary with the Child into Egypt.' It was some kind of 'liturgical thing' for which Kuz'min wrote the words, Sats composed the music, and Sudeikin thought up the decorations and costumes.

"As regards the 'action' of the piece, the poet Potyomkin had a donkey that was severely swaybacked and walked along on two crutches. On its back, it carried Sudiekin's spouse who played the Mother of God. . . .

"Among the frequenters of the Stray Dog were quite a few future 'Bolsheviks': Alexei Tolstoy, then still a young and strapping individual with a huge fat face, and hair cut in a peasant style, and looking like an important *barin* in his raccoon coat and in top hat; Blok, who had the impenetrable, stonelike face of a handsome poet; and Mayakovsky, who, dressed in a yellow jacket, had lips that were crooked, pursed, and toadlike, and eyes that were extremely dark and provocative in a bold and gloomy way." See Bunin, *Vospominaniia*, 46.

"The Stray Dog," Lincoln writes, "was a cellar cabaret . . . where the stench of sweat and cheap tobacco . . . [mingled] with [the smells of] urine from a perpetually malfunctioning toilet." See Lincoln, *Red Victory*, 347. For more on these "poetry inns," see *ibid.*, 346.

4. A Musical Snuffbox (*Muzykal'naia tabakerka*) was a literary café in Moscow in 1918 and home to such poet-Imagists as Vadim Shershenevich.

5. There are three Tolstoys in Bunin's narrative: Alexei Konstantinovich Tol-

others) read their own pieces and those of others, choosing the most vile ones. Bryusov, people say, has read Pushkin's "Gavriliada,"[6] filling in the blanks with words. Alyoshka had the nerve to suggest that I also read there—"We'll pay you a big fee," he said.

"Get out of Moscow!" It's pitiful, what's going on. The city was particularly repulsive this afternoon. It was raining, everything was all wet and dirty, the sidewalks and the pavement had potholes, lumps of ice were everywhere, not to mention the crowds of people who were out walking. But the city was empty during the evening and night, and the few lit lamps made the sky seem thick, gloomy, and black. I went along an alley that was quiet and completely dark—and I immediately saw some open gates. Behind them was the splendid profile of an ancient home standing deep in the recesses of the courtyard, and looking softly dark against a night sky that was totally different from the sky I had seen on the street. In front of this house stood a hundred-year-old tree, its spreading branches looking like a huge tent.

Today I read a new story by Trenyov ("The Farmworkers").[7] It was repulsive. As is always the case now, the thing reeked of something false and pretentious. It talked about the most terrible things, but it didn't seem terrible at all because the author was not serious about what he was doing. That is, he was exhausting his "talent for observation" and using an extreme "folksy" language to boot. In fact, his entire narrative style was so bad that I wanted to throw up. But no one sees or understands this, no one even thinks like this—just the opposite, they're in raptures over what Trenyov is doing. "What juicy language, how beautiful!" they say.

---

stoy (1817–1875), poet and novelist; Alexei Nikolaevich, (Alyoshka) Tolstoy (1883–1945), the emigré (later Soviet) writer; and Leo Nikolaevich Tolstoy (1828–1910), the great novelist.

6. The "Gavriliada," a parody of the Virgin Mary's Immaculate Conception, was written by Pushkin in 1821.

7. Trenyov wrote the "Farmworkers" (*"Batraki"*) in 1912.

The Congress of Soviets.[8] A speech by Lenin. Oh, how beastly this all is!

I read in a newspaper about corpses lying at the bottom of the sea: murdered, drowned officers. And then they go put on A Musical Snuffbox.

March 3 / 16, 1918

The Germans have taken Nikolaev and Odessa.[9] And people say that Moscow will be taken on the 17th, but I don't believe it and still intend to head south.

Mayakovsky is being called "Idiot Polyfemovich"[1] in the high schools.

March 5 / 18, 1918

It's grey out with some sparse snow. There was a crowd of people alongside the banks on Il'inka Street—the smart ones were taking their money out. Generally speaking, many people are preparing to leave in secret.

Tonight's paper reported that the Germans have taken Kharkov.[2] The man who sold me the newspaper said to me: "Better the devil than Lenin."

March 7 / 20, 1918

People are saying in town:

"[The powers-to-be] have decided to kill off anyone who is seven years old and younger so that no one will remember our time."

8. The Fourth All-Russian Congress of Soviets met in Moscow from March 5 to 18, 1918. On March 16 delegates ratified the Treaty of Brest-Litovsk by a majority of 784 to 261, with 115 abstentions.

9. Nikolaev lies roughly one hundred miles northeast of Odessa. Both Odessa and Nikolaev were occupied by German and Austrian troops from mid-March to November 1918.

1. From the mythical character Polyphemus the Cyclops, whom Odysseus blinded in Book Nine of *The Odyssey*.

2. Kharkov is a major industrial, cultural, and scientific center in northeast Ukraine. It was captured by German and Austrian forces on April 8, 1918.

I asked a doorman.

"What do you think? Can it be true?"

He sighed and said, "Anything can happen, anything is possible."

"But will the people allow such a thing to happen?"

"They'll let it happen, my dear *barin*; they'll really let it happen! But what can you do with them? The Tatars, they say, ruled over us for two hundred years,[3] but could the folk really have been that weak even then?"

At night we went along Tverskaya Street: Pushkin[4] bowed his head low and sadly against a sky that was cloudy but shot through with rays of light. He seemed to be saying: "Good Lord, how sad my Russia is!"

There was not a single person around, except for occasional soldiers and Bol—viks.

March 8 / 21, 1918
Ekaterina Peshkova said about Spiridonova:

"I was never attracted to her. She's a revolutionary hypocrite, a hysterical person. Her early things merely plagiarized the dumb things that Figner wrote."

Yes, but what a heroine this Spiridonova once was.

The magnificent homes next to us (on Povarskaya Street) are being requisitioned one after another. Their owners keep moving stuff out and taking it somewhere else: furniture, rugs, paintings, flowers, plants. Today I saw a huge palm tree, all wet from the snow and rain, and looking deeply unhappy as it stood the entire day in a wagon next to the doorway. And at the same time people were carrying into those homes all the things "government" institutions must have—new office furniture and the like. . . .

3. The Tatars or Mongols ruled Russia from the thirteenth to the fifteenth century.
4. The famous statue of Pushkin in Moscow, erected in 1880.

Are these people really so sure of their jobs? Do they really think that they're going to be around for a while?

"Weariness has shattered my heart. . . ."[5]

March 9 / 22, 1918
Today Vasily Vasilievich Vyrubov—he was wearing long shoes and a light, tight-fitting coat made of fur—is still acting like a "hussar"—he again said what has become absolutely repugnant to hear or read:

"Russia was destroyed by a sluggish, self-interested power that did not heed the wishes of the people, their hopes, their dreams. . . . In light of this, the revolution was inevitable."

My answer to his:

"The people did not start the revolution; individuals like you did. The people spat on absolutely everything we wanted, on all we were dissatisfied with. I am not talking to you about the revolution—let it be inevitable, splendid, anything you like. But don't lie about the people—they need all your executive ministries, the successions of the Shcheglovitovs by the Malyantoviches, and the abolition of all kinds of censorship like they need snow during summertime. This the people showed firmly and cruelly when they abandoned, to the devil, the Provisional Government, the Constituent Assembly, and 'everything that generations of the best Russians died for,' as you yourself have expressed it, and 'including your victorious end,' to boot."

March 10 / 23, 1918
The only way that people are saving themselves is not to use the talents they have—their talents to imagine, pay attention, or think—otherwise they would not be able to live.

[Leo] Tolstoy once said about himself: "All my troubles come from the fact that my imagination is a bit more lively than those of others. . . ."

5. Bunin is paraphrasing from Psalms 55:4 and 102:4.

My troubles, too.

The weather is dirty black out; snow sometimes flies through the air.

We've been going through our books, choosing the ones to sell. I've been getting money together. I have to get out of here; I cannot physically endure such a life.

Yesterday I was at Veselovsky's. He talked about Friche, whom he saw the other day. "Yes, yes, it was not all that long that Friche was the most pitiful and unassuming creature in a worn-out jacket—but now he's a person of substance, a commissar for foreign affairs, and wearing a frock coat with satin lapels!"

Veselovsky then played on a harpsichord—Bach and Hungarian folk songs. It was charming. Then we looked through some ancient books—what vignettes, what initial letters on the pages! And all of this was from a golden age that has been destroyed forever. But this decline has been continuing for a long time already.

How spitefully and reluctantly did the doorman open the door for us today! Everyone has the most cruel revulsion to any kind of work.

March 11 / 24, 1918
The wife of the architect Malinovsky is a dull woman with a large forehead. All her life she has never had the slightest thing to do with the stage, but now she is commissar for the theaters;[6] and only because she and her husband were friends with Gorky in Nizhny. This morning we were at the Writers' Publishing House, and Gontaryov told us how Shklyar waited a full hour for Malinovskaya somewhere by the entrance when suddenly a car approached with her in it, and he rushed forward to help her out with truly abject servility.

Gruzinsky said: "With every fiber of my being, I now avoid going out on the street unless I really have to. And not at all from

6. Bunin's misgivings were correct. Elena Malinovskaya zealously sought to bring Communist ideals to theatrical art.

fear that someone is going to mug me, but merely because of the faces that I see out there now."

I understand him like never before, for I also experience the same thing, only, I think, still more sharply.

The wind scatters sparse, completely springlike clouds through the white and light blue sky; spring water glistens and runs along the sidewalks.

March 12 / 25, 1918
I met the lawyer Malyantovich. He was once a minister. Even now everything with him is a holiday, everything is like water off a duck's back. All rose-colored and lively, he told me:

"No, don't be upset. Russia cannot perish if only because Europe won't allow it. Don't forget, a European balance of power is necessary."

I visited Tikhonov (as regards an edition of my works to be published by The Sail). Tikhonov is always sponging off Gorky. Yes, this is a very strange publishing house! Why did Gorky feel compelled to get this Sail up and running, and why did it take a whole year to publish only a small book by Mayakovsky?[7] And why did Gorky buy me, pay me seventeen thousand rubles in advance, but has yet to publish a single volume of mine? What is this Sail covering up? And, in particular, how does this entire company— Gorky, Tikhonov, Gimmer-Sukhanov—get on with the Bolsheviks? I doubt if they're "fighting" with them; for when Tikhonov and Gimmer came to Moscow, they stayed at the National Hotel,[8] which the Bolsheviks took over for their own. I got in there only after I had gotten a pass from the Bolshevik who "managed" the place and then passed through an entire chain of soldiers who were sitting on the step landings with rifles in their hands. Tikhonov and Gimmer, though, see it as home. Portraits of Lenin and Trotsky

7. The work in question is Mayakovsky's forty-seven-page *War and Peace* (*Voina i mir*), published in Petrograd in 1918.
8. The National Hotel, one of the most famous hotels in Moscow, was built in 1903.

hang on the walls. But as regards the reason why I am there, Tikhonov just fidgets and says: "We're just about to publish your works. Don't worry."

Tikhonov also told me that until now the Bolsheviks have been amazed that they have managed to seize power and are still holding on to it:

"After the Revolution, Lunacharsky ran around for about two weeks with wide-open eyes: 'Just think,' he said, 'we only wanted to organize a demonstration and suddenly we had this unexpected success!'"[9]

March 13 / 26, 1918

What garbage! The patriarch and all the princes of the church are going to the Kremlin with their hats in their hands![1]

I saw Vyrubov. He passionately cursed out the allies: they have entered into negotiations with the Bolsheviks instead of coming to occupy Russia![2]

I also had dinner and spent the evening with Gorky's first wife, Ekaterina Pavlova [Peshkova]. Bakh (a well-known revolutionary and old emigré), Tikhonov, and Mirolyubov were also there. The latter kept praising the Russian people, that is, the peasants: "A merciful people, a splendid people!" he said. Bakh added (though

9. So quickly had the October Revolution succeeded that even Lenin seemed momentarily stunned. "You know," he confided to Trotsky on the evening that Kerensky's government fell, "to pass so quickly from persecutions and living in hiding to power—*es schwindelt*—it makes one's head spin!" See Lincoln, *Red Victory*, 44.

1. The Bolsheviks saw Russian Orthodoxy only as a counterrevolutionary force, and announced a formal separation of church and state in early January 1918. In response the patriarch of Moscow, Tikhon, pronounced anathema against the Soviet authorities on February 1, 1918, and encouraged the church's members to oppose the new Russian leaders. On March 14, 1918, a group of churchmen, led by Tikhon, tried to meet with Lenin to protest the church-state separation, but they were unsuccessful in their quest.

2. In early March 1918 Trotsky was conducting separate negotiations with the Allies in case the Germans ignored the Treaty of Brest-Litovsk or the Soviets failed to ratify the agreement. The Allies were willing to do anything to maintain an eastern front during the war and to prevent the Germans from focusing their efforts in the west.

he essentially does not have the slightest understanding of the people, since he has spent his entire life abroad):[3]

"But what are we arguing about, gentlemen? After all, was the French Revolution without its cruelties? The Russian people are like everyone else. They have, of course, negative features; but most of them are good. . . ."

We came home with Tikhonov. On the way he spoke for a long, long time about the Bolshevik ringleaders, as someone who was quite close to them. He said: "Lenin and Trotsky have decided to keep Russia in chaos and not to stop the terror and the civil war until the European proletariat enters upon the scene. Are they in cahoots with the Germans?[4] No, that's ridiculous. They're fanatics, they believe in universal conflagration. But they fear everything like fire and suspect plots everywhere. And up until now they have also been in trembling for their power and for their lives. They, I repeat, never expected they would succeed in October. After Moscow had fallen, they were terribly confused. They ran over to us at *New Life* and begged us to be ministers, and presented us with briefcases. . . ."

March 15 / 28, 1918
It's the same cold weather outside. There is no heat anywhere, and the cold in the apartments is terrible.

Russian News was shut down because of an article that Savinkov wrote.[5]

Many believe that Savinkov will kill Lenin.[6]

3. Bakh had lived as an emigré in France, the United States, and Switzerland. He did not return to Russia until 1917.

4. Rumors that the Germans had sided with the Bolsheviks in the Russian civil war were common.

5. *Russian News* (*Russkie vedmosti*) was closed on March 24, 1918, allegedly for publishing B. Savinkov's article "From the Road" ("S *dorogi*"), opposing the new Soviet order. The editor, P. Egorov, was sentenced to three months' solitary confinement.

6. In March 1918 Savinkov established in Moscow the Union for the Defense of the Motherland and Freedom, an underground, counterrevolutionary group which sought to overthrow Soviet power and to establish a military dictatorship. It lasted until June 1918.

"The Commissar of the Press," Podbel'sky, has closed and sued [the newspaper] *The Lantern*[7]—"for including articles that incite anxiety and panic in the population." Such concern for a population that is being robbed and murdered every minute!

March 22 / April 4, 1918
Yesterday evening, when the lights were beginning to shine behind some wet trees, I saw the first rooks.

Today it was grey and overcast, but there was a great deal of light in the clouds.

I keep reading the newspapers and I almost cry from malicious delight. Generally speaking, this past year will take no less than ten years from my life!

Tonight the dark-blue sky had plump white clouds with occasional bright stars between them. The streets were dark. The homes merge into one; they stand very tall and dark in the sky; the lighted windows in them are soft, rose-colored.

March 23 / April 5, 1918
All of Lubyanskaya Square shines in the sun. Watery mud flies from the wheels of carriages and cars. And Asia, Asia everywhere— soldiers, boys, people selling gingerbread, halvah, cookies with poppy seeds, and cigarettes. I hear Eastern cries and speech—and I see all those loathsome dark faces, their yellow and mouselike hair! Soldiers and workers, always on thundering trucks, have triumphant mugs. . . .

The old bookseller Volnukhin wears glasses and a sheepskin coat. He's a dear, intelligent man; but he has a sad, attentive look.

At a name-day party for N., people kept toasting any word that had a religious air. The "old regime" is still strong.

We also attended [a reading] of Premirov's "The Tavern."[8]

---

7. *The Lantern (Fonar')* was an illustrated weekly published in Petrograd in 1918.

8. Premirov's "The Tavern" (*"Kabak"*) was published in 1913.

Without a doubt there's talent out there. But what good is it? Literature is at an end. But *The Lower Depths* is again playing at the Art Theater. That's to be expected! And again there's that boring Luka![9]

Up until now Ekaterina Pavlovna [Peshkova] has been firmly convinced that only [Osip] Minor can save Russia.

[I've been reading] the Menshevik newspaper *Forward*.[1] Always the same thing, always the same thing!

The wives of all the commissars have also been made commissars.

[I saw] a company of the Red Guard. They were all awkwardly going along and stumbling about, one on the pavement, another on the sidewalk. The "instructor" kept crying: "Pay attention, comrades!"

A man selling newspapers, a former soldier, said to them:

"Hey, you filthy bastards! You go off to war and take the girls with you! Just look, *barin*—one's got a hooker on his arm right now!"

The night is very dark and springlike. Shafts of light coming from the clouds over the church heighten the darkness; the stars give off a playful, white light.

The house where the Tseitlins live on Povarskaya Street has been taken over by anarchists. A black sign with white letters hangs over the entranceway. Inside, behind the curtains, magnificent chandeliers bathe everything with a suffused light.

March 24 / April 6, 1918
Now people—these poor, deluded things—are talking about Japan coming to help Russia, and about a landing in the Far East.[2] They

9. Gorky wrote *The Lower Depths* (*Na dne*) in 1902. Luka is a sixty-year-old pilgrim in the play. The Moscow Art Theater, founded in 1898 by Konstantin Stanislavsky and Vladimir Nemirovich-Danchenko, championed theatrical realism in Russia.

1. The newspaper *Forward* (*Vpered*) was published in Moscow from March 1917 through April 1918.

2. The rumor was true. As the revolution moved eastward and the Bolsheviks prepared to seize Vladivostok, the Allies worried that the huge stockpile of

also say that the ruble will be worth absolutely nothing, that flour will cost a thousand rubles a pound, and that people should stock up on reserves. . . . We say we can do nothing: we'll buy two pounds of flour and stay calm.[3]

We visited N. V. [Orlov]-Davydov on Bol'shoy Levshinsky Prospekt. He lives in a small, yellowish home (it once belonged to the writer Zagoskin) with a black roof in the front and a yellow fence with black iron chalices on the gates. A turquoise sky shone from behind latticelike trees. Old Moscow, gone forever.

We also visited P. In the kitchen stood a soldier with a large fat mug and eyes that were varicolored, like a tomcat's. He said that socialism is now impossible, of course, but that the bourgeois should be cut to pieces nonetheless. "Trotsky's a great guy," he said, "he'll really give it to them."

I saw a dried-up, serious-looking lady and a youth wearing glasses. They were selling cigarettes on the street.

I also bought a book about the Bolsheviks, published by *Commune*.[4] What a terrible gallery of convicts! The young Lunacharsky has a neck more than a foot long.[5]

---

military supplies destined for the eastern front might fall into German hands. Also, the Japanese looked with apprehension upon Soviet expansionism, since Vladivostok was Russia's major trading and military center on the Pacific Coast. On April 5, 1918, a Japanese force of five hundred marines landed in Vladivostok, but withdrew several weeks later. For more on the Japanese intervention into Russia, see Lincoln, *Red Victory*, 97–99.

3. Only a month before, the daily bread ration in Moscow had fallen below a quarter of a pound, and the workers' entire daily ration produced a pitiful 306 calories, less than a tenth of what experts thought necessary for a "healthy diet." See Lincoln, *Red Victory*, 59.

4. The work in question is *The Bolsheviks: Documents in the History of Bolshevism from 1903 Through 1916, Taken from the Former Moscow Police Division* (*Bol'sheviki: Dokumenty po istorii bol'shevizma s 1903 po 1916 god byvshego Moskovskogo Okhrannogo Otdeleniia*), published in 1918. *Commune* (*Zadruga*) was a cooperative publishing venture founded in Moscow in 1911 but moved abroad in 1922.

5. Bunin was indeed justified in judging Lunacharsky and such other Bolsheviks as Kamenev, Lenin, Krupskaya, Sverdlov, and Trotsky as "convicts," since most of the pictures in the book were mug shots from police files.

ODESSA 1919

∷∷∷

April 12 / 25, 1919
Almost three weeks have passed already since our ruin.[1]

I very much regret I did not write anything down. I should have taken note of almost every minute. But it was beyond my powers to do so. But we had absolutely no idea of what was going to happen on March 21 / April 3!

On noon of that day our maid Anyuta called me to the phone. "Who's calling?" I asked. "Someone from the editorial office, it seems," i.e., from the staff of *Our Word*, the newspaper that we, the former collaborators of *Russian Word*, having gathered in Odessa, began to publish on March 19 / April 1, since we felt fully assured that we would enjoy a more or less peaceful existence "until we could return to Moscow." I picked up the receiver. "Who is it?" I asked. "Valentine Kataev. I'm rushing to tell you some unbelievable news: the French are leaving Odessa."[2] "How can this

1. Bunin is referring to the arrival of the Red Army in Odessa on April 6, 1919. It should be noted that in the month before, Odessa was on the verge of anarchy. Thousands who had fled the Bolsheviks had congregated in the city, forming mobs of homeless, hungry people. Less than one-third of the city's economic enterprises were functioning, and unemployment was widespread. The city was virtually without heat or electricity; shortages triggered a tenfold inflation of prices. *Odessa News* wrote on March 2, 1919: "Never before has Odessa passed through such a nightmarish situation. The population is succumbing . . . to starvation and cold." See G. Brinkley, *The Volunteer Army and Allied Intervention in South Russia, 1917–1921* (Notre Dame, 1966), 132.

2. Beginning in 1918, workers and other democratic groups in both Europe and the United States initiated "Hands Off Russia" movements, insisting that their

be, when are they going?" "This very minute." "Have you lost your mind?" "I swear to you, it's true. They're fleeing in panic!"[3]

---

respective governments cease "meddling" in Russian civil war. Their efforts were successful. Mounting public opinion against intervention, together with repeated reversals suffered by the Whites, prompted Western allies in March 1919 to agree that all their contingents should be withdrawn from Russian soil. Two months later the leaders of France, the United States, Great Britain, Italy, and Japan sent a note to Admiral Kolchak, the Whites' leader, declaring that they would not interfere in Russia's internal affairs.

The disaster of the French presence in Odessa aptly illustrates the failure of foreign intervention in the Russian civil war as a whole. The French expeditionary force that had landed in the city to cheering crowds in November 1918 was minimal: 6,000 French, 2,000 Greeks, and 4,000 Poles. These were later augmented by a Rumanian contingent and by new French and Greek troops, swelling the number of interventionist troops to some 45,000 soldiers and sailors in the Odessa region. Together with an additional battalion of 7,500 French and Greeks in the neighboring Crimea, French interventionists sought to take control of southern Russia and even advance to the Don.

From the beginning, though, the mission was doomed, for the French had embarked on the venture without reflecting upon the loyalties of the various conflicting groups or the goals of their own initiative. French officers led their troops into the confusion of Odessa with no more precise instructions than "to make common cause with patriotically thinking Russians." The French believed that their very presence would inspire anti-Bolshevik forces to march vigorously on Moscow. But the French also had little use for the Russian anti-Bolshevik forces. Gallic fighting men disdained the Whites of the Volunteer Army as "barbarians and villains," whose 1917 "treachery" had allowed Germany to concentrate most of its dwindling resources against the western front.

Beyond their difficulties with the Whites, French troops in Odessa suffered from a lack of discipline, organization, and military strategy. They failed to maintain law and order in the city and to supply it with provisions. In part because of French incompetence, economic conditions in Odessa deteriorated. And French troops in Odessa became the targets of Bolsheviks who, organized into special "foreign colleges" of French-speaking agitators, inspired mutiny among French soldiers and sailors.

French authorities at home, shocked by the failure of their troops and apprehensive that flagging morale would incur even greater disaster, decided to terminate the adventure. Orders from Paris to evacuate Odessa reached the city on April 2, 1919; four days later most French ships steamed away from the port. That same day Grigoriev's partisans swept into the city before moving on to the Crimea, which the French would also desert three weeks later. See J. Swettenham, *Allied Intervention in Russia, 1918–1919* (London, 1967), 248–249. See also Lincoln, *Red Victory*, 315; Lehovich, *White Against Red*, 257, 263; Kenez, *Civil War*, 178–191; and Brinkley, *Volunteer Army*, 131–134.

3. When the French government ordered its troops to evacuate Odessa on April 3, residents of the city panicked and mobbed the docks. See Brinkley, *Volunteer Army*, 133.

I ran out of the house and grabbed a cab, but I did not believe my eyes. Donkeys loaded with goods, French and Greek soldiers[4] in field dress, gigs with all kinds of military property. When I got to the editorial office I found a telegram: "Clemençeau's ministry is falling apart. Revolution and barricades in Paris. . . ."[5]

On this very day twelve years ago Vera and I came to Odessa en route to Palestine. What fantastic changes have occurred since that time! A dead, empty port; a dead, burned-out city. . . . Our children and grandchildren will not be able even to imagine the Russia in which we once lived (that is, what was it like yesterday) and which we ourselves did not value or understand—all its might, complexity, richness, and happiness. . . .

Just before I woke up this morning, I had a dream that someone was dying and that he had died. Very often now I see death in my dreams—either one of my friends is dying, or a close family member, especially my brother Yuly. I find it terrible even to think about him: how and on what is he getting along, and is he even still alive?[6] The last time I heard something about him was on December 6/19 of last year. A letter from Moscow addressed to [my wife Vera] and dated August 10 / 23 arrived only today.

Incidentally, the Russian post office has been defunct for a long time now, since the summer of '17, that is, from the very moment we followed European fashion and appointed our first minister of posts and telegraphs. It was also then that we got a minister of labor, something we also never had before—and Russia hasn't

---

4. Clemençeau had proposed that Greek soldiers accompany French troops in the Allied intervention of southern Russia. See Brinkley, *Volunteer Army*, 86.

5. At this time Clemençeau was minister of war in France, but he was out of favor with his countrymen because he had not persuaded Woodrow Wilson and other Western leaders that the industrial Saar Basin should be ceded to France, and that Germany should pay reparations for the entire cost of the war. He was also under attack for sending French troops to intervene in the Ukraine. For more information on Clemençeau at this time, see G. Dallas, *At the Heart of a Tiger: Clemençeau and His World* (New York, 1993), 578–582.

6. Yuly Bunin died in Moscow in July 1921.

done a lick of work since.[7] Then, too, it was during the summer of '17 that the Satan of Cain's anger, of bloodlust, and of the most savage cruelty wafted over Russia while its people were extolling brotherhood, equality, and freedom. Everyone immediately became crazy, deranged. For the slightest infraction, everyone began yelling at everyone else: "I'm arresting you, you son of a bitch!"[8]

At the end of March in '17 a soldier almost killed me on the Arbat because I had allowed myself a certain "freedom of speech" and cursed the newspaper *Social Democrat*[9] because one of its vendors had thrust himself upon me. That scoundrel of a soldier knew perfectly well that he could do with me whatever he liked, and with complete impunity. The vendor, along with the crowd that surrounded us, immediately took the soldier's side: "Really, comrade, are you so repulsed by a newspaper that is for the working masses? Does this mean you're against the revolution?"

How all these revolutions are the same! During the French Revolution an entire abyss of new administrative institutions suddenly appeared. A whole flood of decrees and instructions sprang forth. The number of commissars—why were they called precisely commissars?—and all kinds of other authorities in general went on without end; committees, unions, and parties grew like mushrooms; and everyone "began devouring everyone else." A completely new and special language came into being: "bombast mixed up with the coarsest abuse aimed at the *vulgar remains of a dying tyranny.* . . ."

One of the most distinguishing features of a revolution is the

7. These ministries came into being by order of the so-called First Coalition Government, which lasted only from May 5 to July 2, 1917. The individuals in question are Matvei Skobolev, minister of labor, and Irakly Tsereteli, minister of posts and telegraphs.

8. Bunin is referring to the so-called "July days," when radical soldiers, sailors, and mobs, together with the Bolsheviks, tried to seize power in Petrograd. The attempt was unsuccessful.

9. The newspaper *Social Democrat* (*Sotsial-Demokrat*) was an organ of the local Moscow soviet and of the Communist party there. It was published in 1917 and 1918, and on March 15, 1918, merged with the newspaper *Pravda*.

ravenous hunger for histrionics, dissembling, posturing, and puppet show. The ape has awakened in man.

Oh, these dreams about death? What a huge place death occupies in our short lives! And there is nothing to say about the years: day and night we live in an orgy of death. They keep talking in the name of some "bright future" that will supposedly issue forth from this satanic gloom. There have already appeared on this earth an entire legion of specialists and contractors who seek to fashion human well-being. As Ibsen's bell ringer asks, "And in what year will it, this future come?"[1] They always say: "This will be the last and decisive battle!"—The eternal fairy tale about a red bull.[2]

It poured cats and dogs last night. The day was grey, cold. The little tree that has grown green in our yard has burst into flower. But some damned spring this has been! . . . I do not *feel* like spring at all. After all, what is spring *now*?

Rumors and more rumors. We spend our lives in tense expectation (just as we did all last winter here in Odessa, and the winter before in Moscow when everyone kept expecting the Germans to come and save us). And this waiting around for something to come and resolve it all, and always in vain. But we will not go unscathed, of course; our souls will be maimed even if we survive. But what would everything be like if we did not have even these expectations, these hopes?

"Dear God, in what a time you have ordered me to be born!"[3]

---

1. Bunin's allusion is incorrect. Ibsen's "bell ringer" is, more accurately, the character Aslaksen in *An Enemy of the People*, written in 1882. Aslaksen is a printer who, in Act Four, keeps ringing a bell to maintain order at an assembly of the townspeople. But Aslaksen does not talk about the "future" anywhere in the play.

2. "This will be the last and decisive battle" is a line from the "Internationale." After the Revolution the Soviets changed it to "This *is* the last and decisive battle." The expression "the fairy tale about a red bull" in Russian is actually, "the fairy tale about a white bull" (*skazka pro belogo bychka*), i.e., "to talk endlessly about one and the same thing." Bunin is making a political statement by changing "white" to "red."

3. Bunin is paraphrasing Job 3:3: "Perish the day when I was born."

CURSED DAYS

April 13 / 26, 1919

Yesterday the poet Voloshin visited us for a long time. He had gotten into trouble because he had approached the Bolsheviks to help "decorate the city for the First of May."[4] I warned him: "Stay away from them. It would not only be stupid but also base for you to come to their aid, since they are well aware that you were in the opposing camp yesterday." But Voloshin replied only with nonsense: "Art is outside of time, it is outside of politics. I will help decorate the city but only in my capacity as a poet and an artist." Decorate what? Gallows, and his own to boot? But he took off to see them nonetheless. The next day *Izvestia* reported: "Voloshin came crawling to us; all kinds of bastards are hurrying to suck up to us. . . ." Now Voloshin wants to write a letter to the editor. He's full of righteous indignation. And he's acting even more stupidly than before.[5]

---

4. The idea of decorating Moscow and other Russian cities for the First of May came from Lenin himself, who had suggested key slogans from Marx and Engels to be hung from prominent buildings. But revolutionary artists produced creations that were quite different from what Lenin had in mind. "Demented squares battled with rhomboids on the peeling façades of colonnaded Empire buildings," Ehrenburg later wrote. "Faces with triangles for eyes popped up everywhere." (Some of Moscow's artists even went so far as to paint the trees along the Kremlin wall in vivid shades of violet, brick red, blue, and crimson.) Lenin, cursing the "decadence" that had produced such work, ordered a massive cleanup, only to find that the artists had worked with paints that no amount of scrubbing could remove. Nearly a year later some of the paintings still remained on the walls for Russians and visitors to comment upon. See Lincoln, *Red Victory*, 350.

5. According to Muromtseva-Bunina's diary excerpt of April 25, 1919, Bunin rejoiced over Voloshin's misfortune. Of this incident, Bunin later recalled: "The Bolsheviks invited Odessa artists to take part in decorating the city for the First of May. Several of them joyfully seized upon the invitation. One cannot turn away from life, you see; moreover, as these artists would often say, 'The main thing in life is art—and art lies outside of politics.' Voloshin also burned with a desire to decorate the city, and fantasized how he should do it. . . . I kept reminding him that the city he intended to decorate was without water and bread, that it was host to constant raids, searchings, arrests, and shootings, and that at night it was the sight of impenetrable darkness, pillaging, and horror. . . .

"Of course, Voloshin's 'letter to the editor' was never published. And I told him that this would happen. But he wouldn't listen. 'They couldn't print it,' he

Still more rumors and rumors. Petersburg has been taken by the Finns;[6] Kolchak has taken Syzran' and Tsaritsyn.[7] . . . Hindenburg is maybe going to Odessa, maybe to Moscow.[8] . . . All of us keep waiting for help from someone, from something, from a miracle, from nature itself! We now go out daily along Nikolaevsky Boulevard[9] to see if, God forbid, the French battleship has not left port. Mercifully it's still there. It somehow looks gloomy in its berth, but its presence makes things easier to endure.

April 15 / 28, 1919

Ten months ago an individual by the name of Shpan[1] came by to see me. He was an extremely mangy and ragged-looking individual, like a down-and-out traveling salesman. He offered to be my manager and promised that I should go with him to Nikolaev, Kharkov, and Kherson,[2] where I would give a public reading of my

---

told me, 'because they promised me that I would be on *Izvestia*'s editorial board.' *Izvestia*, however, did publish this: 'Voloshin has been dismissed from the artistic commission for the First of May.' " See Bunin, "Voloshin," *Vospominaniia*, 193–194; and, Grin, *Ustami*, 241.

6. On December 6, 1917, Finland, which had been part of the Russian Empire since 1809, declared its independence from the new Soviet state. Although Finnish troops posed a direct threat to Petrograd, advancing to within twenty-five kilometers of the city, Finnish leaders preserved a policy of "armed neutrality" with the Bolsheviks from 1917 to 1919. See Lehovich, *White Against Red*, 318–319.

7. Syzran' is a city on the middle Volga; Tsaritsyn (now Volgograd) is an important railroad and port also on the Volga River, approximately four hundred miles southwest of Syzran'. At the time of Bunin's writing, Kolchak had taken Syzran' but not Tsaritsyn.

8. The rumor was not true. Indeed, according to an article published in *The Times* on April 30, 1919, hearsay in the West was that Hindenburg was about to retire from public life.

9. Nikolaevsky Boulevard lies in the most beautiful part of Odessa. It extends for five hundred yards along the edge of the slope above the city's harbor, bounded on one side by handsome buildings and on the other by parks and four rows of trees. The boulevard also commands a superb view of the sea and in pre-Revolutionary times was a favorite promenade for Odessa's wealthy citizens.

1. Shpan was a recently appointed commissar of the theater. See Muromtseva-Bunina's diary excerpt, April 8, 1919, in Grin, *Ustami*, 227.

2. Kherson is an important commercial and industrial center in southern Ukraine.

works "every evening for a thousand rubles at a crack." Today I met him on the street: he is now a commissar for theatrical affairs and a colleague of that crazy scoundrel Professor Shchepkin. He was clean-shaven and well off—everything about him said so—and dressed in a splendid English coat, thick, soft, and with a wide half-belt in the back.

Looking out the windows we see a tramp with a rifle hanging from a rope on his shoulder—he is a "Red Policeman." The entire street trembles at the sight of him in a way they never did at the thousands of the fiercest-looking policemen who were around before. What has happened? Roughly six hundred of "Grigoriev's men"[3] blew into town, bowlegged youths led by a pack of convicts and hooligans, who somehow captured an extremely well-to-do city with a million people in it! When they entered, everyone died of fright, they ran and hid. But where, for example, where are all those who so railed against the Volunteers[4] a month ago?

3. Because of the successes of the Red Army, the Ukrainian ataman, Nikifor Grigoriev, joined with Bolshevik troops for the battle for Odessa. In early April his troops, numbering about fifteen hundred men (not the six hundred in Bunin's account) took the city and forced the French to abandon their ill-conceived intervention.

4. The Volunteer Army was the major anti-Bolshevik group in southern Russia. Founded by Generals Alexeev and Kornilov, it was led for two years by General Denikin and toward the end of the civil war by General Wrangel. Relying heavily on Cossack support, the Volunteer Army sought to establish a temporary military dictatorship and to reincorporate the borderland nationalities that had separated themselves from Russia. It also called for delaying such major decisions as agrarian reform and state reorganization until the Bolsheviks had been defeated and a new constituent assembly elected. Beyond these objectives, though, the Volunteer Army had no genuine ideology or clearly defined aims. When the Revolution and the civil war destroyed the Russia they loved, they were ill-equipped, intellectually and emotionally, to understand why the empire had collapsed or why so many Russians objected to restoring "patriarchal" Russia. For these reasons, the Volunteer Army clashed not only with Soviet forces but also with anti-Bolshevik socialists who had broad popular support, as well as with the non-Russian borderland governments that controlled large sections of southern Russia.

The fifteen hundred or so Volunteers in Odessa could not act on their own, not only because of French constraints but because Denikin had insisted on centralized authority but was too far away to provide effective leadership. As a result, Odessa's economic situation became chaotic, speculation ran wild, and com-

ODESSA 1919

April 16 / 29, 1919
Yesterday we took a walk at twilight. The heaviness in my soul is indescribable. The crowd that fills the streets is physically repulsive; I am sick to death of these animals. If only I could find some respite, if only I could hide somewhere, perhaps go to Australia! But all the highways and byways have been closed. It is an insane nightmare now to go down even Great Fountain Street: one cannot do so without permission, otherwise they'll kill you like a dog.

We met L. I. Gal'bershtadt (a former contributor to *Russian News* and *Russian Thought*).[5] He has "changed his colors." Only yesterday he was an avid member of the White Guard, who cried (literally) when the French fled. Now he's already got himself fixed up with the newspaper *Voice of the Red Army Soldier*.[6] Like a thief, he whispered to us that he is "absolutely crushed" by the news coming from Europe: it seems that the Western powers have firmly decided not to interfere in any way in Russia's internal affairs. . . . Yes, yes, this they see as "internal affairs," even though scoundrels are pillaging and killing in broad daylight next door!

Voloshin visited us again this evening. It was monstrous! He said he had spent all day with Severnyi (Yuzefovich), the head of the local Cheka,[7] who has a "soul like crystal." That's just what he said: "like crystal."

Professor Evgeny Shchepkin, "the commissar for people's education," has given the governance of the university to "seven representatives of the revolutionary student body," who, people say, are such scoundrels that one will never find others like them![8]

---

plaints grew in volume. Volunteer authorities, though, could do nothing to halt the decline.

5. *Russian Thought* (*Russkaia mysl'*) was a scholarly literary and political journal published in Moscow from 1880 to 1918.

6. *Voice of the Red Army Soldier* (*Golos Krasnoarmeitsa*) was published by the Ukrainian Soviet Army in Odessa in 1919.

7. The Cheka was the first Soviet secret police, from the Russian *Chrezvychainaia Komissiia*.

8. Shchepkin's move was somewhat belated, since the two thousand students at Odessa's New Russian University (*Novorossiskii Universitet*), founded in

Voice of the Red Army Soldier reports that "the Rumanians have penetrated deeply into Soviet Hungary."[9] We are beside ourselves with joy. Now here's noninterference in "internal" matters for you. But after all, such interference has nothing to do with Russia.

"Blok hears Russia and the Revolution like the wind. . . ."[1] O, what phrasemongers! Rivers of blood, a sea of tears, but these do not faze him.

I often remember the indignation that greeted my supposedly all-black pictures of the Russian people. People are still indignant, but who are they now? The very same individuals who were reared and nursed on that very same literature which, for a hundred years, literally discredited all classes, that is, "the priest," "the philistine," the petty bourgeois, the bureaucrat, the policeman, the nobleman, the well-to-do peasant—in a word, everyone and everything, except the "people"—who were "always without a horse," of course—as well as "youth" and tramps.

April 17 / 30, 1919
"The regime, old and rotten to the core, came crashing down, never to rise up again. . . . In a fiery, elemental surge, the people toppled the decayed throne of the Romanovs—forever."
    But if this is so, then why, from the very beginning of the

---

1865, had already taken control of the institution. They had shut down the university at least once, and expelled professors who opposed them.
    Shchepkin roused Bunin's ire for other reasons: he had closed the church at the university; he regularly informed the Cheka on professors not to his liking; and he would not defend the innocence of other teachers under attack by the Bolsheviks. Shchepkin was fired shortly after he had been appointed commissar.
    9. Hungary was a Soviet republic from March 21 to August 1, 1919. On April 16, with the support of French military leaders occupying Hungarian towns in the south and with the tacit approval of the other Great Powers, Rumanian troops crossed the demarcation line in the southeast and penetrated deep into the country.
    1. A reference to Blok's poem "The Twelve" ("Dvenadtsat' "), written in 1918.

March days, was everyone so insanely afraid that there would be a reaction, a restoration?

"All honor and glory to the madman who arouses humankind with a golden dream. . . ."[2] How Gorky loved to bark this out! But all this dream ever did was to crack open the head of a factory owner, turn his pockets inside out, and put the garbage who worked for him in an even worse condition than the owner himself did.

"Revolutions are not made by hands in white gloves. . . ."[3] So why should anyone be upset that counterrevolutions are done with an iron hand?

"Console yourselves for the sorrow of all Jerusalem!"[4]

Since breakfast I've been lying in bed with my eyes closed. I'm reading a book about Savina—simply for something to do. I'm completely indifferent to everything; my only feeling now is that this is *not life*. Then, I repeat, there is this exhausting waiting around for something to happen. It simply cannot go on like this: someone or something will save us—tomorrow, the day after, perhaps even tonight!

It's been grey since morning, all day. It rained in the afternoon, and it really let loose in the evening. I've gone out twice to look at the crowds celebrating the First of May. I had to force myself; such spectacles literally crush my soul. "I feel people physically," Tolstoy once wrote about himself. Me too. People did not understand this about Tolstoy, nor do they understand it about me; that is why they are often taken aback by my passion, "my likes and dislikes." Even now the notions "people" and "proletariat" are

2. From the poem "The Insane Ones" by Pierre Beranger, written in 1831 and declaimed by the ruined "actor" in Act Two of Gorky's play *The Lower Depths*.

3. Bunin is here citing Lenin's own paraphrasing of Jacobin revolutionary ideas.

4. Bunin is here quoting from the Apocrypha, specifically the Book of Esdras 10:20.

only words: but for me they have always had eyes, mouths, and voices. Whenever I hear someone giving a speech at a meeting, I sense his entire body in the act.

Going out at noon, I saw a fair number of people trickling out onto Cathedral Square, but those already there were standing about senselessly, looking at the entire puppet show in an unusually dull way. There were, of course, the processions with red and black banners, and the "chariots" decked out in paper flowers, ribbons, and flags. Actors and actresses dressed in operalike folk costumes stood, sang, and comforted the "proletariat." There were also "living *tableaux*" depicting the "might and beauty of the worker's world," of "brother" Communists with arms embraced, of "docile *paysans*," and of "grim-faced" workers in leather aprons. In a word, everything was the way it was supposed to be, all staged by order of Moscow, courtesy of that reptile Lunacharsky. When will the Bolsheviks end this most base mockery of the mob, this repulsive buying of their souls and bellies? And when will they begin to show the least bit of sincerity, or at the very least a passionate enthusiasm for things? For example, the way Gorky used to get all unhinged and excited! I remember one Christmas when we were at his place in Capri[5] and when he said (in the exaggerated dialect of people who live in Nizhny-Novgorod):

"Ladies and gentlemen, let's stroll over to the piazza today; the public, the devil take them, will perform the most unusual routines—the whole piazza dances, you see. The kids scream like devils, they steal cookies from under the noses of the most venerable shopkeepers, they turn somersaults, and they blow on a thousand pipes. . . . There will also be, you see, the most interesting processions in which people from the various guilds will sing the most marvelous street songs." And his green eyes welled up with tears.

I was at Catherine Square around twilight. It was gloomy and

---

5. Bunin regularly visited Gorky at Capri from 1909 to 1913.

damp. Catherine's monument[6] was wrapped and bandaged from head to toe with dirty wet rags; and it was also entwined with branches and pasted over with red wooden stars. Across from it was the office of the Cheka decked out with red flags which, extremely filthy and droopy from the rain, cast thin and bloody reflections on the wet asphalt.

This evening almost the entire city was dark: a new insult, a new decree—do not dare even think about turning on the electricity, though it is available. But candles and kerosene are not to be found anywhere, and only here and there does one see wretched, gloomy lights peeking out from behind shutters: the glimmer of smoking homemade wicks. Who is responsible for this idiocy? In the final analysis it seems that the people themselves are to blame, since the decree was issued to please them.

I remember an old worker who was standing near the gates of the building where *Odessa News*[7] used to be. It was the first day the Bolsheviks took control. Suddenly a crowd of boys jumped out from behind the gates with piles of freshly printed *Izvestias*, crying out, "The bourgeois in Odessa must contribute 500 million rubles to the government!"[8] The worker began to wheeze, choking with anger and malicious joy. "That's too little! That's way too little!" he said. Of course, for him the Bolsheviks were the genuine "worker-peasant force." They "were realizing the most cherished hopes of the people." Everyone knows what kind of "hopes" these "people" have, for they have been called upon to rule the world and to take charge of all culture, law, honor, conscience, religion, and art.

6. The statue of Catherine the Great in Odessa is thirty-five feet high and was erected in 1900. The bronze figure of the empress stands upon a granite pedestal resembling a column, which is surrounded by four bronze figures, including that of her lover, Prince Potyomkin.

7. *Odessa News* (*Odesskie novosti*) was published between 1901 and 1916.

8. As soon as the Communists took control of Kharkov, Kiev, and Odessa, they declared that the bourgeoisie in each city had to pay an indemnity. The liability against Odessa was indeed 500 million rubles. See V. Brovkin, *Behind the Front Lines of the Civil War: Political Parties and Social Movements in Russia, 1918–1922* (Princeton, 1994), 98.

"Without any annexations and contributions from Germany!"[9] "That's the way it should be!" "Five hundred million, five hundred billion from Russia!" "That's too little!" "That's way too little!"

The "left-wing," all the "excesses" of the Revolution, are blaming the old regime. The Black Hundreds[1] are pointing the finger at the Jews. But the people are not guilty! Soon this very people will blame everything on someone else—their neighbor or the Jew! "What, who me? Well if Ilya does it, so will I. After all, the Jews are always starting something. . . ."

April 19 / May 1, 1919
I went out for something to do, and also to look for food. People say that everything will be closed and that there will be nothing to buy. Sure enough, there is almost nothing in the stores that are still open. Sure enough, it has all vanished somewhere. By accident I happened to run into a pile of fish in a store on Sofiiskaya Street. But the price was outrageous—twenty-eight rubles a pound.

A. M. Fyodorov stopped by. He was very pleasant, though he kept complaining about his poverty. In reality he has lost his last asset—who will rent his summer cottage now? But then it is not his to rent out anymore since it is now the "property of the people." He has worked his entire life and somehow managed to buy a truly valuable piece of land. Then he built a small house on it (and went into debt along the way)—but now it turns out that this

9. The worker is citing Lenin's speech given at the Second All-Russian Congress of Soviets on October 26, 1917. See Lincoln, *Red Victory*, 44.
1. Initially the Black Hundreds (*Chernosotentsy*) were reactionary public organizations who opposed revolution in Russia at the beginning of the twentieth century. They believed that autocracy should remain intact and that the tsarist regime should pursue chauvinistic policies. Their political agitation, along with their anti-Semitic fervor, led to a wave of pogroms and terrorist acts against revolutionaries and progressive public figures. After the Revolution of 1905–1907, the Black Hundreds lost momentum, and their membership declined. (The group was officially banned after the February Revolution of 1917.) By 1919 the term *chernosotenets* or "member of the Black Hundreds" was applied to extreme reactionaries and militant opponents of socialism.

home "belongs to the folk," and that some "workers" will live there together with their families for the rest of their lives. One could hang oneself from outrage!

All day long there has been a persistent rumor that the Rumanians have taken Tiraspole, and that Mackensen is already in Chernovitsy, and that "Petrograd has already fallen."[2] Oh, how much everyone wants this to be true! But, of course, it's all rubbish.

This evening I was with Professor Lazursky[3] at the synagogue. Everything has been so terrifying and repulsive that one is drawn to the churches, the only havens still untouched by the flood of cruelty and dirt. Only there is too much opera going on in these places, and it is good to be there only for a while: wildly passionate wailing, sobbings which tell age-old sorrow, homelessness, the East, antiquity, wanderings—and the Divine One before Whom one can pour one's soul first in a despairing and childlike mournful complaint that overwhelms the soul with its cry, and then in a gloomy and savagely threatening roar that penetrates everything beyond it.

Now all the homes are dark. The entire city is in darkness except for the thieves' dens.[4] There one can hear balalaikas and see shining chandeliers and walls covered with black banners with white skulls and the inscription: "Death, death to the bourgeois!"

I am writing by the light of a stinking kitchen lamp, using up the last of the kerosene. How sick, how outrageous this all is. My Capri friends, the Lunacharskys and the Gorkys, the guardians of Russian culture and art, express self-righteous anger when they warn *New Life* about abetting "tsarist sympathizers." What would

2. Tiraspole is a town roughly fifty miles northwest of Odessa. Chernovitsy is the historical capital and the political, cultural, and religious center of Bukovina. It lies on the boundary between Rumania and the Ukraine. The rumors are all false.

3. Vladimir Lazursky had also taught Greek and Latin to Andrei L'vovich and Mikhail L'vovich Tolstoy, sons of the great writer.

4. Dwindling fuel supplies produced an acute shortage of electricity that plunged all Russian cities into darkness.

they do with me now if they caught me writing this criminal tract by a stinking kitchen lamp or trying to hide it in the crack of the ledge?

I remember how astute the doorman was in Moscow during the fall of '17. Someone had just said: "No, forgive me if you will! But our duty was and still is to bring a Constituent Assembly to our country!"

The doorman was sitting by the gates and heard these passionate words. People were going by him and arguing. But he just shook his head sadly and said:

"God knows where these sons of bitches have really brought us!"

First it was the Mensheviks and their trucks, then the Bolsheviks and their armored cars. . . .

The truck: what a terrible symbol it has become for us! How many trucks have been part of our most burdensome and terrible memories! From the very first day, the Revolution has been tied to this roaring and stinking animal, filled to overflowing first with hysterical people and vulgar mobs of military deserters, and then with elitist-type convicts.

All the vulgarity of contemporary culture and its "social pathos" are embodied in the truck.

A man on the street was screaming, with spit coming out of his mouth. His eyes seemed particularly frenzied; his pince-nez was all askew. A small tie stuck out from behind a dirty cotton collar; his waistcoat was splattered with mud; his jacket hung from his shoulders and was too short and tight; and his hair had dandruff and was greasy, sweaty, and disheveled. . . . And people kept assuring me that this repulsive individual was supposedly seized by a "fiery selfless love for humanity" and a "thirst for beauty, justice, and good"!

What about the people who were listening to him?

On the street, a deserter stood all day long, doing nothing

other than to mechanically wolf down the sunflower seeds in his fists. His coat was over his shoulders, his cap was perched on the back of his head. Stout, thin-legged, and quietly brazen, he just munched away, not saying anything except to ask an occasional question. But he didn't believe any of the answers he was given, thinking it was all nonsense. He was so physically repulsive that it made one sick: his huge thighs were shoved into thick winter khakis; his eyelashes were like a calf's. His lips were youthful but also beastly primitive, and milky from the seeds he was chewing.

From Tatishchev's *History of Russia:*[5]
"Brothers against brothers, sons against fathers, slaves against masters; each one trying to kill the other from motives of self-interest, lust, and power; each one trying to rob the other of dignity; each one incapable of leading, but trying to be the smartest; each one wanting what the other one had and crying over what they have not. . . ."

Now these idiots are convinced that Russian history has undergone a great "shift," and that this "shift" will lead to something completely new and unprecedented!

This "Russian history" has always been a tragedy (and a terrible one at that), but no one has the slightest understanding of it.

April 20 / May 3, 1919
I rushed to read the newspapers—but there is nothing noteworthy in them. "The enemy offensive is being met with equally strong resistance. . . ." But, in the end, who is this enemy?

The newspapers all have one and the same tone—a high-blown yet vulgar jargon—along with the same threats and the same frenzied boasting. But it is all so flat, so false, so transparent, and so obvious that one cannot believe a single word of it, the result

5. Bunin is quoting from Tatishchev's *Russian History from the Very Earliest Times (Istoriia rossiiskaia s samykh drevneishikh vremen)*, 5 vols. (Moscow, 1768–1848).

being that the individual lives fully cut off from the world, as one from some Devil's Island.

[Our maid] Anyuta says that already for two days now she cannot even get that terrible pealike bread which makes everyone around scream with colic.[6] And precisely who is not getting any bread? Why, that very same proletariat who was having such a good time the day before yesterday. But the walls are plastered with posters saying: "Citizens! Everyone take up a sport!" It's absolutely unbelievable, but completely true. Why sports? How did their cursed skulls come up with sports along with everything else?

Voloshin was here. Some people want to get him to the Crimea with the help of Nemits, the navy commissar and commander of the Black Sea Fleet. Incidentally, this Nemits is also a poet who, some say, "writes particularly good rondos and triolets." They're trying to come up with some secret "mission" to send Voloshin to Sevastopol'. The only problem, though, is that there's nothing to send him down there for: Nemits's entire navy consists of a single sailing ship, an old tub which can't be sent out in any kind of weather.[7]

A flurry of rumors: Petrograd has been taken by General Gurko, Kolchak is near Moscow, and the Germans are about to enter Odessa. . . .[8]

How fiercely everyone yearns for the Bolsheviks to perish! There's not the most terrible biblical punishment that we wouldn't wish on them. If the devil himself would burst into the

6. "The bread [in Odessa] has one remarkable quality," Konstantin Paustovsky wrote to a friend at this time, "the crust is quite separate from the inside . . . and the space between the two is filled with . . . a sour, slightly fermented liquid." See Lincoln, *Red Victory*, 371.

7. The rumor was only partly true. German troops captured the Russian naval base, and with it the Black Sea Fleet, on May 1, 1918. Some ships, including the dreadnought *Free Russia* (*Svobodnaia Rossiia*), found a temporary refuge off the Kuban but were scuttled in June.

8. None of the rumors had any basis in fact.

city and literally go about with Bolshevik blood up to his neck, half of Odessa would weep from joy.[9]

There is so much lying going around that I could scream. All my friends, all my acquaintances, people whom earlier I never would have thought of as liars, are now uttering falsehoods at every turn. They cannot help but lie; they cannot help but add to *their own lies, their own flourishes* to well-known falsehoods. And they all do so from an agonizing need that everything be just as they so fiercely desire. They rave on like they have a fever; and when I hear their rantings I take their words in greedily and become infected by them. Otherwise it seems that I won't survive the week.

And every day this self-deception gains such momentum that by evening I go to bed as if in a drunken stupor, almost completely certain that something will happen during the night. I cross myself firmly and furiously. I pray with such force that my body hurts. It seems that God, or a miracle, or the heavenly powers cannot but help us. I fall asleep, exhausted from the unbelievable fervor with which I have begged for an end to the Bolsheviks. I send my soul over thousands of miles, into the night, the darkness, and the unknown so that I will be with my family and loved ones, and so that I can express my fear for them, my love for them, my agony for them, and my hope that God will save and protect them. Then suddenly in the middle of the night I jump up with a wildly beating heart: somewhere I hear the rat-a-tat-tat of a machine gun. Sometimes it is very close by, like a hail of stones on the roof. Here it is, I think. Something has finally happened; someone, perhaps, has attacked the city and will finally put an end to this cursed life!

But the next morning I again sober up with a heavy hangover. I rush to the newspapers; no, nothing has happened. Again I read

9. Appeals to the devil for rescue from the Bolsheviks were common in this time. "If only the devil, if only Satan himself would come," Gippius wrote in Petrograd in 1919. See O. Mikhailov, *Ivan Alekseevich Bunin: Ocherk tvorchestva* (Moscow, 1967), 141.

all the same insolent and self-assured cries, all the same new "victories." The sun is shining, people are going about, the stores have lines in front of them . . . and again I fall into a torpor, overwhelmed by hopelessness and the feeling that I have to face another long, empty day; no, not just one day but many days, empty, long, and good for nothing! Why bother living? For what? Why bother to do anything? In this world, in their world, in the world where the lout and the beast hold sway, I need nothing. . . . [People say:] "Our country has an extremely special psyche, one which people will write about for the next hundred years." But what comfort do I take in that? After all, what do I care about a time when even the dust from my remains will be gone? These notes will not be worth anything. But who cares? The very same human being will be living through these hundred years—and I know very well how much he's worth!

It's night. I'm writing this in a slightly tipsy frame of mind. This evening A. V. Vas'kovsky stopped by. Like a conspirator, he opened the door and whispered all kinds of things, insisting that everything people had been saying during the day was the absolute truth. . . . Pyotr[1] got so upset that his ears turned red. He crawled under the stairs and pulled out two bottles of wine. My nerves are so shot that I got tipsy from only two glasses of wine. I know that all these rumors are nonsense—but I believe them nonetheless. And so I am writing with cold and shaking hands. . . .

"Oh, revenge, revenge!"—Batyushkov wrote [to Gnedich] after the fire of Moscow in 1812.[2]

Savina wrote to her husband when she was in the Caucasus in the summer of '15: "If God allows our dear little soldiers, our wondrous little knights to suffer such shame and grief—then we will be the ones who will be defeated!"

1. Pyotr Nilus, a writer and artist.
2. From a paraphrase of a letter from the writer, Konstantin Batyushkov, to another writer, Nikolai Gnedich, written in October 1812 and referring to the burning of Moscow during Napoleon's invasion of Russia.

But what happened? Did our stupidity and ignorance come from the fact that we didn't know the people, or because we didn't want to know them? Both. At that time, though, people usually had a lot to gain by telling falsehoods for which they were somehow rewarded. "I believe in the Russian people," someone would say, and applause would follow.

A well-known segment of society suffered particularly from such lying. People became so depraved in professing to be "friends of the people, of youth, and of all that is enlightened," that they seemed completely sincere. Almost from adolescence on, I lived with such types—and I was constantly, every minute, outraged by their behavior since I could sense their hypocrisy, especially when they often would scream at me about someone else altogether:

"This one is lying, one can see right through him—has he ever given his entire life to the people!?"

One whom everyone called "an honest man" was a handsome old gent with glasses, a huge, white beard, and a soft hat. . . . But his brand of lying was very special, as if he did it almost unconsciously. The fact that he could overlay everyday life with sham emotions had, it seemed, long become second nature to him; but they were false nonetheless.

I can remember so many of these "liars"!

Indeed, this type would be an unusual subject for a novel, and a terrible novel at that.

How we lied to each other when we said that our "wondrous knights" were the best patriots in the world, that they were so very brave in battle and so very merciful with the conquered enemy!

"Does that mean that there was no one like this at all?"

No, there were some people. But who? There are two types of people among the folk. Ancient Rus' resides in one; Chud and Merians in the other.[3] Both are terribly fickle in emotion and ap-

3. Chud was the name given in Old Russian chronicles to the Estonians and related Finno-Ugric tribes who lived in the area around Novgorod. The Merians were a now extinct group of closely related Finnic-speaking tribes that settled along the upper Volga.

pearance; they're "real shaky," as people used to say in the old days. The very folk have said about themselves: "We're like the tree; from it comes both the icon or the club"; the result depends on circumstances, on who tends to the tree: Sergei Radonezhsky or Emel'ka Pugachev.

If I did not love, if I had not seen this "icon," this Rus', then why have I gone nearly insane all these years, why have I suffered so incessantly, so cruelly for my homeland? People say I only hate. But who are these people? In reality they are those who would readily spit on the folk—if the folk were not an impetus for their splendid feelings about life. Not only did they not know or want to know anything about the folk, they didn't even take note of the faces of the cabbies who would carry them off to some Free Economic Society.[4] Skabichevsky once confessed to me:

"I never saw the rye grow. Perhaps I saw it, but I didn't pay any attention to it."

But did Skabichevsky ever see the peasant as a separate individual? No, he knew only the words "folk" and "humanity." Even the famous phrase "help for the hungry" came to us through literature and only from a desire to kick the government for the umpteenth time, to undermine it again.

It's a terrible thing to say, but it's the truth: if it were not for the misfortunes of the folk, thousands of our intellectuals would be profoundly unhappy people. How else could they have sat around and protested? What would they have cried and written about? Without the folk, life would not have been life for them.

The same thing happened during the war. In truth there was the same very cruel indifference to the people everywhere. The

4. The Free Economic Society (*Volno-Ekonomicheskoe Obshchestvo*) was founded in Saint Petersburg by large landowners who, with the growth of grain markets and trade, wanted to set agriculture on a rational course and raise the productivity of the serfs. In 1900 the tsarist government sought to reduce the scope of the Society's activities and to transform it into an institution of applied agronomy. As a first step it called a halt to the Society's programs on literacy and hunger. By 1915 the activities of the Free Economic Society had virtually ceased, and in 1919 the Society was formally abolished.

"little soldiers" were an object of ridicule. How everyone poked fun at their speech in the hospitals, how they indulged them with candy, rolls, and even ballet dances! And these same "little soldiers" went along with them and pretended to be terribly noble, meek, and painfully resigned. "What can you do, little sister, it is God's will!" they said, agreeing with everything the nurses, and the ladies with the candy, and the reporters said. They lied when they said how much they enjoyed Gel'tser and the dances. (When I once asked a soldier what he thought was going on as he watched the performance, he answered: "Why, it's the devil . . . they're playing the devil, dressing up as goats. . . .")

People were terribly indifferent to the folk during the war. They lied like criminals about the folk's patriotic spirit, even when a child could not help seeing that the war repelled them. Where did this indifference come from? Why, from our terribly innate carelessness and frivolity, and from the fact that we were unaccustomed and unwilling to be serious when the times called upon us to be so. Just think how carelessly, haphazardly, and even gaily all of Russia looked upon the beginning of the Revolution as one of the greatest events in all history, and one of the greatest wars in the world!

Yes, before the Revolution we all lived (the peasants included) extremely freely, with rustic carefreeness; we all supposedly lived on a very rich estate, where even someone who was down and out, or who had shoes that were beyond repair, or who lay down after having taken off these shoes, did so in a fully relaxed way, since his needs were so elementary and limited.

"We all studied a little somehow and somewhere." Yes, we did only those things that we had to, sometimes with great passion and talent, but for the most part any old way—only Petersburg wanted to do things right. We cared little for long daily routines; in truth, we shirked work terribly. And from this, incidentally, came our idealism—in essence, a very gentrylike idealism—our eternal opposition, our criticism of everyone and everything. After all, it was much easier to criticize than to set ourselves down to work. Take, for example, the following quotation:

"Oh, how I'm suffocating under Tsar Nicholas. I cannot be a bureaucrat and sit next to Akaky Akakievich[5]—a carriage, someone get me a carriage and get me out of here!"

Thus the Herzens, the Chatskys.[6] And also Nikolka Seryi from my work *The Village*, [a peasant] who sits on a bench in a cold dark hut waiting for some "genuine" work to show up—and who continues to sit, wait, and languish. What an old Russian disease is all this languishing, this boredom, this babbling—this eternal hope that a frog with a magic ring will come and do it all for us, that we only have to step out onto the porch and throw a ringlet from one hand to another!

All of this is rooted in a type of nervous illness, and not at all in the famous "questions" that supposedly arise from our "depths."

"I never did anything because I always wanted to do something special."

This is Herzen's confession.

I recall other remarkable lines of his:

"We are sobering up humanity. . . . We are its hangover. . . . We canonized humanity. . . . We canonized revolution. . . . We are sparing future generations sorrow by our disenchantment, our suffering. . . ."[7]

No, we're still a long way from sobering up humanity.

I close my eyes and I keep seeing the image of a person as if alive before me: [he is an individual] with ribbons coming from a sailor's cap, pants with huge bell-bottoms, and fancy slippers from

5. The reference is to Tsar Nicholas I. Akaky Akakievich is the hapless hero in Gogol's story "The Overcoat" ("*Shinel'* "), written in 1842.

6. Chatsky is a character in Griboyedov's play *Woe from Wit* (*Gore ot uma*), written in 1825. He is also an archetype for the so-called "superfluous man" in Russian literature, i.e., an individual who is long on anger or analysis but short on action.

7. Bunin is here paraphrasing excerpts from Herzen's famous memoir, *My Past and Thoughts* (*Byloe i dumy*), written between 1852 and 1868.

Weiss's[8] on his feet; his teeth are firmly clenched, the muscles of his jaw twitch. . . . I will never forget this, even if it means that I will turn over in my grave!

April 21 / May 4, 1919
"An Ultimatum from Rakovsky and Chicherin to Rumania!— Clear out of Bukovina and Bessarabia in 48 hours!"[9] This is so improbable, so stupid (even if someone is poking fun at the mob) that it has even occurred to me to think: "Maybe this is all being done on someone's order, the Germans, perhaps—and, with the intention to discredit the Communists, the revolutionaries, and in general, the Revolution on a daily basis?" Then I read—"From Victory to Victory—New Successes for the Valiant Red Army. Twenty-six Members of the Black Hundreds Have Been Shot in Odessa. . . ."

Izvestia—oh, the cursed orthography it uses![1]—follows its headline about the ultimatum first with a published list of the names of the twenty-six who were shot yesterday, then with a small article on how well "work is going on" with the Odessa secret police and that "in general, there's still a lot of work to do"; and, finally, with a proud declaration: "Yesterday Coal Obtained to Repair the Trains in Kiev." Oh, happy day! And this right after an ultimatum!

But what if the Rumanians do not obey Rakovsky, then what? And how devilishly monotonous are all these clownish stunts! But

8. Weiss's was a fashionable shoestore in Moscow.
9. Bessarabia was a so-called "Ukrainian ethnographic land" that lay between southwest Ukraine and northeast Rumania; it was seen by Western powers as a base of operations in their struggle against the Soviets. With their support, Rumania invaded Bessarabia in December 1917. On May 1 and 3, 1919, both the Russian and Ukrainian Soviet republics demanded that the Rumanians withdraw their troops from Bessarabia and the neighboring territory of Bukovina to the immediate west. Their demand was ignored.
1. The changes ordered by the Bolsheviks in Russian orthography deeply disturbed Bunin and others, even though these changes had been formulated and approved by the Russian Academy of Sciences immediately before the Revolution. As with the changes in the Russian calendar, the reform in orthography

perhaps it's all just some coarse dramatic production, or a reason for someone to raise objections? But precisely who?

The "bourgeoisie" are just on the verge of affirming their faith in Petrograd. After all, they keep saying they have actually seen a telegram [saying] that Petrograd has been taken (after the English supposedly brought bread to the city).[2] . . .

There is also a rumor that we will have the same type of savage plundering that is already going on in Kiev—that clothes and shoes will be "collected."[3]

I recently read about the shooting of twenty-six men, but it didn't seem to faze me.

I'm now in a stupor. Yes, twenty-six men, and not just any old time but yesterday, here, right next to me. How can I forget, how can I forgive the Russian people? But everything will be forgiven; everything will be forgotten. I only *try* to be horrified; for I'm not

---

would have been accepted without much resistance or further discussion had it been promulgated before February 1917. Because the world war postponed its implementation, and because it was the Bolshevik government that gave legal force to these changes, the reform was regarded as anathema by many in Bunin's group.

2. As the Allies could neither recognize nor destroy bolshevism, they believed they should send food to Russia so that its people could fight the Soviets from within. The relief planned for Saint Petersburg was considerable: 24,000 tons of grain for the two months between the liberation of the city and the resumption of normal trade. The food was never delivered, however, because of the objections of the Finnish government, which was seeking to capture the city. See M. Kettle, *Russia and the Allies, 1917–1920*, vol. 3 (Routledge, 1992), 247, 308, and 327.

3. The rumor was true. Bolsheviks in Odessa took hostages from among the bourgeoisie and threatened to execute them if their families did not raise funds for the indemnity charged to the city. The campaign soon broadened to include all of Odessa's citizens. Red Guards and the Cheka began searching block after block, apartment after apartment, confiscating clothes, food, and valuables. By mid-May the Odessa Bolsheviks decided to regularize this mass expropriation with this order: "In accordance with the decision of the workers' soviet, today on May 13 the registration of property will begin according to a special questionnaire with the aim of expropriating from the propertied classes foodstuffs, shoes, clothes, money, valuables, and other items which are needed by the entire working people. . . . Everyone is obligated to render assistance to this sacred task. . . . Those who will not abide by this directive will be arrested immediately; those who offer resistance will be shot." See Brovkin, *Behind the Front Lines*, 121.

shocked by anything anymore. This is the hellish secret of the Bolsheviks—to kill all sensitivity. People live as best they can; their sensitivity and their imagination have been taken away from them, for the people have crossed the fatal line. Take the price of bread or beef, for example. "What? Three rubles a pound!" Then it goes up to a thousand—but there comes an end to the shock and screaming; stupor and passivity take their place. "What? Seven were hanged?!" "No, my dear, not seven, but seven hundred!" Already you are stunned beyond measure—you can still imagine seven being hanged, but try to imagine seven hundred, even seventy! . . .

At three o'clock—it has been raining all day—we took a walk. We met Polevitskaya and her husband [Schmidt]. "I so very much want a role in a mystery play; I so would like to play the Mother of God!" Oh, good Lord, good Lord! And to do all this and also be on the closest terms with bolshevism! But it's been like that for a long time both in literature and in the theater.

I bought some matches at six rubles a box; a month ago they cost only fifty kopecks.[4]

When I go out, I feel as though I'm on the verge of getting seriously ill.

It's now 8 p.m., but by "Soviet" time it's already 10:30.[5] Having returned home from my walk, I started closing the shutters of my apartment when I caught sight of a large flat moon that was completely golden-colored, and that was shining brightly through the new green leaves of the tree under my window. The western sky had already cleared, exquisite and still bright.

I had gone out at seven o'clock. It was raining constantly, like an evening in the fall. I went along Khersonskaya Street, then

4. Odessa was particularly hit hard by inflation. If a dinner cost five rubles in Ekaterinodar in January 1919, the same meal cost thirty rubles in Odessa. See Kenez, 183.
5. The Soviet government introduced daylight savings time in the summer of 1918, and "time zones" on February 8, 1919.

turned to go to Cathedral Square. It was still light out, but everything was already closed, including all the stores. A burdensome,
anxious emptiness filled my soul. When I got to the square, the
rain had stopped. So I made my way to the cathedral along the
bright wet asphalt and under the cover of chestnut trees with their
new green leaves and bright flowers.

I recalled the gloomy evening on the First of May. People
were getting married in a cathedral; a women's choir was singing.
I entered; and, as always as of late, this churchly beauty, this island of the "old" world amidst a sea of the dirt, vileness, and baseness of the "new," touched me in a most unusual way.

How the evening sky shone through the windows! The altar,
the recesses of the church, the windows were all purplish blue—
my favorite color. The dear little faces of the choir singers, the
white veils on their heads, the little gold crosses on their foreheads,
the music in their hands, and the golden lights of their small wax
candles—this was all so charming that, looking and listening to
them, I cried quite a bit. I went home with such a feeling of light-
ness, of youth. And together with that—such sadness, such pain!

When I returned, I ran into some people who were playing a
piano and dancing both in the apartment of a policeman and also
in our courtyard. I also saw our cook Marusya. In the twilight she
seemed so very beautiful and alive. Her eyes were so bright that
my *heart* momentarily recalled the distant, irretrievable charm I
had once experienced sometime in my early youth, on a similar
April evening in the village garden.

Last summer Marusya was living as a cook at our dacha, and
for an entire month she kept hiding our bread in the kitchen and
feeding it to her lover, a Bolshevik. I knew what was going on
and did nothing. So much for any bloodthirstiness on my part; but
that's precisely the point: we cannot be like them, for once we are,
that's the end for us!

I am writing all this by the light of a lamp—the oil and the
wick are in a jar. Darkness and soot. I'm ruining my eyesight.

In truth, we should have hanged ourselves a long time ago. We have been so beaten, muzzled, deprived of all rights, and stripped of all laws. We live as such vile slaves amidst incessant insults and slaps in the face!

How self-possessed
Are work-a-day horses
For they pay no need
To life's dark forces!

These humorous lines were written by a young poet,[6] a student who became a policeman last winter for ideological reasons but was later murdered by the Bolsheviks. A dear boy, may the kingdom of heaven be his! Yes, we too are very much "workaday horses."

April 22 / May 5, 1919
I remember a loathsome day complete with rain, snow, and dirt. It was last year, the end of March in Moscow. A poor funeral procession was stretching its way across Kurdinskaya Square when suddenly this animal on a motorcycle came madly dashing out from Nikitskaya Street. Wearing a leather cap and jacket, he kept making threatening gestures, waving a huge revolver, and splashing mud on the coffin bearers:
"Get off the road!" he said.
The coffin bearers dashed to the side and, stumbling and jiggling the coffin, ran as fast as they could. An old lady was standing at the corner, and, having bent over, she was crying so bitterly that I automatically stopped and began to console her, to put her at ease. I muttered, "What will be, will be. God be with you!" Then I asked her, "Was the dead person a relative of yours?" The old lady paused for breath and dried her tears. Finally she said with difficulty:

6. Anatoly Fioletov, a favorite poet with Odessa's youth, published this piece in that city in 1916.

CURSED DAYS

"No . . . I don't know him . . . *But I envy him. . . .*"

I remember other things. It was again Moscow, the end of March, the year before last. Prince Trubetskoy, big and fat, was shouting and theatrically shaking his small fists:

"Remember this, ladies and gentlemen: The Rissin' boot will mercilessly crish these tender sp'rits of Rissin' freedom! Everyone to the rescue!"

What the prince said was repeated by hundreds of thousands at that time. But they were silent about precisely whom they had to find to defend this "Russian freedom" for!

In the winter of '18 these same hundreds of thousands hoped for salvation (but not for "Russian freedom") precisely from the Germans. All of Moscow raved on about their coming.

Today is Monday. There are no newspapers, so I can rest from the insanity that comes from my reading them, an insanity that has grown since the very beginning of the war. Why am I so brutal with myself? Why do I tear my heart to shreds by reading them?

All these Peshekhonovs are so certain, so unusually and firmly assured, that the fate of Russia belongs only to them. When did that happen? When should they be punished, if only for the shame they brought on themselves when they paraded before the entire world during their six-month reign in '17?[7]

I find this Bolshevik jargon intolerable. Generally speaking, what kind of jargon does our left speak? "Cynicism, bordering on gracefulness . . . Now a brunette, today a blonde . . . Reading with a passion . . . To conduct an interrogation with passion . . . Either-or: there is no in-between . . . To draw the proper conclusions . . . Whom it is necessary to inform . . . To stew in one's own juice . . . The dexterity of hands . . . New-era lads . . ."

They also attempt to use high style with some supposedly high bitter irony (though it is not clear who or what is the target). It all

7. Alexei Peshekhonov was minister of food supply for the Provisional Government. Unable to satisfy the peasant hunger for land and the urban hunger for food, he resigned his post in August 1917.

sounds like Korolenko (especially in his letters). It's not a "horse" but invariably a "Russian High-Stepper"; it's not "I sat down to write" but "I mounted my Pegasus"; they're not "policemen" but "uniforms of a sky-blue color." Speaking about Korolenko, what a thundering article he wrote in defense of Rakovsky in *Russian News* in the summer of '17![8]

It is terrifyingly mystical in the evenings. It is still light out, but the clocks show something absurd, that it is night. The fountains are not lit, but all the "government" buildings, all the offices of the Cheka, and the theaters and clubs bearing the names of Trotsky, Sverdlov, and Lenin blaze forth brightly, like medusas or rosy glass stars.

All kinds of people rush off to these theaters and clubs (to see their own serf actors perform). They travel down the strangely empty but lighted streets in cars and cabbies, very often accompanied by dolled-up girls. They are the red aristocracy: sailors with huge revolvers in their belts, pickpockets, criminal villains, and shaved dandies in service jackets, depraved-looking riding breeches, and dandylike shoes with the inevitable spurs. All have gold teeth and big, dark, cocainelike eyes. . . .

But the afternoon is also petrifying. This whole huge town does not live; it stays home and goes out but little. It feels it has been conquered by an allegedly special type of people who seem much more terrible than our ancestors, the Pechenegs.[9] But these conquerors only stagger, trade at hawkers' stands, spit out sunflower seeds, and "swear in the foulest language."

Deribasovskaya Street is host to two groups of people: one bunch amuses itself by accompanying the coffin of some hoodlum, who is invariably being called a "fallen warrior" (and who lies in a red coffin, preceded by an orchestra and hundreds of red and

8. Korolenko defended Rakovsky in a "letter to the editor" published in *Russian News* on June 30, 1917.

9. The Pechenegs were a confederation of predominantly Turkish nomads who dominated the southern Russian-Ukrainian state from roughly 900 to 1040. During this time they waged continual war with the Russians of Kievan Rus.

black banners); the other group appears to turn dark as they play on their accordions and dance and cry out:

"Hey, my little apple,
Where are you rolling along?"

Generally speaking, as soon as a city becomes "red," the crowd that fills the streets changes suddenly and sharply. There is a new assortment of faces; the street becomes transformed. How such faces affected me in Moscow! It was because of them that I left there.

It is now the same in Odessa—from that very holidaylike day when the "revolutionary people's army" marched into town, and when, even from the horses of cabbies, red bows and ribbons burned like fire.

There is nothing simple or ordinary about these faces. They are almost all so extremely and sharply repulsive, so frightening in their evil dullness, that they constitute a threatening, lackeylike challenge to everyone and everything.

This is already the third year this monstrous thing has been going on. A third year of only baseness, only dirt, only brutality. If only for a laugh, if only for fun, one wishes for something that is not even good but just simply ordinary, simply different!

"No wholesale making fun of the people!"

The "Whites," of course, are fair game; but the people, the Revolution, are always being forgiven. "It's all just excesses," people say.

Regarding the Whites, whom the people have profaned, assaulted, and murdered, and from whom they have taken everything away—their homeland, their native cradles and graves, their mothers, fathers, and sisters—none of these things, of course, can be seen as "excesses."

"Revolution is an elemental force...."

Earthquake, plague, cholera are also elemental forces. No one extols them, though; no one canonizes them; no one overcomes them. And the Revolution is always "deepening."

"The people who gave us Pushkin, Tolstoy."

But the Whites are not people, they say.

"The nobility took in Saltychikha, advocates of serfdom, and other diehards. . . ." What everlasting baseness—to pull the wool over people's eyes and to include Saltychikha, this most ordinary madwoman.

But what about the Decembrists, the famous Moscow University of the '30s and '40s, the conquerors and colonizers of the Caucasus, the Westerners and the Slavophiles, the agents of the "era of the Great Reforms," the "repentant noblemen," the first members of "The People's Will," the government Duma? What about the editors of the well-known journals?[1] And all the greats of Russian literature? And its heroes? No other country in the world can lay claim to such nobility.

1. Briefly, the Decembrists were a group of Russian noblemen who staged an unsuccessful revolt against autocracy in 1825.

Moscow University in the 1830s and 1840s was a center of Western idealist and rationalist thought in Russia.

Between 1796 and 1864 Russia had conquered all political entities north and south of the Caucasus Mountains, though they did not control the main range itself.

The Westerners and Slavophiles were two opposing groups in the mid-nineteenth century who argued over whether Russian society should follow European or indigenous patterns of thought, culture, and government.

The Great Reforms took place during the reign of Alexander II. They began with the emancipation of the serfs in 1861 and included changes in local government, the courts, and the military.

The so-called "repentant noblemen" (*"pokaiashchiesia dvoriane"*) included such writers as Nikolai Nekrasov, Alexander Pleshcheev, and the brothers Zhemchuzhnikov, and all who professed both outrage and guilt for the condition of the folk in Russia.

The members of the "The People's Will" (*"Narodnaia volia"*) were angered both by the highly centralized nature of the Russian state and by the failure of populism in Russia. Having exited the Land and People party in 1879, they quickly became a revolutionary terrorist organization, dedicated to liquidating the most harmful members of the tsarist government and responsible for the assassination of Tsar Alexander II in 1881.

The four dumas (1906–1907, 1907, 1907–1912, and 1912–1917) were nationally elected assemblies and attempted parliamentary government in Russia.

"The disintegration of the Whites . . ." they say.

What monstrous nerve to talk like this after the unprecedented world "disintegration" that marked the appearance of the Reds.

But, to tell the truth, many things arise from stupidity. Tolstoy used to say that nine-tenths of human folly can be explained exclusively by stupidity.

"When I was young," he would say, "we had a friend, a poor fellow, who once, with his last pennies, suddenly bought a windup metal canary. We cracked our heads trying to explain this stupid act, until we recalled that our friend was simply very stupid."

April 23 / May 6, 1919
Every morning I make an effort to dress quietly, to overcome my impatience to read the newspapers—but all in vain. And in vain I again try to do so today. It is cold and rainy, but I again run out into the slime and again waste five whole kopecks to get the news. What is going on in Petersburg? What about the ultimatum to the Rumanians? Of course, there is not a word about one or the other. But here is an important item: "Kolchak must not see the Volga!"[2] This is followed by stories that a "Provisional Worker-Peasant Government" has been formed in Bessarabia,[3] and that Nansen is begging "The Council of Four"[4] for bread for Russia where "hundreds

---

The so-called "thick" journals were monthly publications that included sections on science, politics, philosophy, fiction, literary criticism, and international affairs. The two most famous "thick" journals in the nineteenth century were *The Notes of the Fatherland* (*Otechestvennye zapiski*, 1818–1884) and *The Contemporary* (*Sovremennik*, 1847–1866).

2. On April 21, 1918, the First, Fourth, Fifth, and Turkestan Red Armies launched a counteroffensive against Kolchak's forces east of the Volga, defeating them on April 28, 1919. This marked the beginning of the end for Kolchak's armies.

3. In truth, a "Provisional Bessarabian Worker-Peasant Government" had been founded in Odessa in anticipation of Bessarabia's liberation by the Bolsheviks.

4. On April 3, 1919, Fridtjof Nansen proposed to the Allied Council of Four

of thousands are dying monthly from hunger and disease."
Abrashka the Accordion Player (Reginin from *Exchange News*)[5]
continues to amuse the members of the Red Army with such ditties as "Kolchak jumps as if hit/ And from fright, he takes a shit,"
along with pieces of news: "Blockades in Paris, the old henchman
Clemençeau in panic"; the Bulgarian Communist Kasabov has
"declared war on France";[6] and the last item—this is literally what
was said—a French dispatch boat arrived in the port of Odessa yesterday, but "the blockade continues, and the French have been
abandoning even their sailing vessels. . . ."[7]

Everyone in town is surprised by the behavior of the French;
they all run to Nikolaevsky Boulevard to look at the French torpedo boat, looking grey in the distance on a completely empty sea;
and they shake in fear as they think: God forbid that it leave! Everyone seems to think that the ship is some kind of a protector, and
that, should extreme savagery break out around us, the torpedo
boat will start shooting . . . but the people also think that, should
it leave, that means the end of everything, that there will be all
kinds of horror, and that the world will be completely destroyed. . . .

Voloshin was here all evening. He had high praise for the navy

---

(the United States, Britain, France, and Italy) that a neutral commission be organized to carry out relief work in Russia.

5. During the Civil War, Vasily Reginin wrote plays, poetry, and feuilletons
for the Red Army press. *Exchange News* (*Birzhevye vedomosti*) was a moderately
liberal newspaper published in Saint Petersburg from 1880 to 1917. It was closed
in October 1917 for publishing anti-Soviet propaganda.

6. Like all of Lenin's followers, the Communists in Bulgaria believed in an
imminent world revolution and their own accession to power. At their first party
congress in 1919 they unanimously voted to join the Comintern and called for
the formation of soviets for the masses. Enmity toward France was another part
of their program.

7. Beginning in March 1919 it was now the Bolsheviks' turn to blockade
Odessa.

commissar Nemits—"he sees and believes in the ongoing union and building of Russia." Voloshin also read from his translations of Verhaeren. Again I think—not for the first time—that Verhaeren is a great talent; but, having read ten or so of his poems, I begin to suffocate from his devilishly monotonous devices, his wild hyperboles, and the insane "Bolshevik" pressure that he exerts on the reader's imagination.

Russian literature has become extremely depraved over the past few decades. The street and the mob have begun to play a very great role in it. . . . Everything—and especially literature—has gone out into the street, has joined up with it, and has fallen under its influence. And the street corrupts and rankles, because it becomes so terribly unrestrained in its praises when it is catered to. Russian literature now has only "geniuses." An amazing harvest! The genius Bryusov, the genius Gorky, the genius Igor Severyanin, Blok, Bely. . . . How can one stay calm when someone can become a genius so quickly and easily? Anyone can fight his way through, dazzle the mob, and call attention to himself.

Take Voloshin, for instance. The day before yesterday he called Russia the "Angel of Revenge,"[8] who had "to stab a maiden's heart with the ecstasy of murder and to pierce a child's soul with bloody dreams." Yesterday he was a member of the White Guard, but today he is ready to sing the praises of the Bolsheviks. For the past few days he has tried to drum the following into my head: The worse it gets, the better it will be; for nine seraphims are descending to earth and are entering into us so as to reconcile us with crucifixion and burning, and to transform us into new, tempered, and enlightened beings. I advised Voloshin to choose someone a bit more stupid for such conversations.

A. K. [Alexei Konstantinovich] Tolstoy once wrote, "When I recall the beauty of our history before the cursed Mongols came,

8. "Angel of Revenge" ("*Angel mshcheniia*") was the introductory cycle for Voloshin's work *Deaf-mute Demons* (*Demony glukhonemye*), published in 1919.

I want to throw myself on the ground and roll about in despair."[9] Yesterday Russian literature had Pushkins and Tolstoys, but now it has almost only "cursed Mongols."

Nighttime, the same day
The last time I was in Petersburg was in early April '17.[1] Then something unimaginable had just happened in the world. One of the very greatest countries on earth was thrown to the full whim of fate—and not just at any time but during a very great world war. The trenches still stretched for three thousand miles in the west, but they had already become simple pits. The deed was done, and in a way that was simply unprecedented and absurd. A power that had extended over three million miles, and that had comprised an armed horde, an army of millions of men,[2] was transferred into the hands of "commissars," of journalists such as Sobol' and Yordansky. But more awesome was the fact that the magnificent, centuries-old life that had reigned throughout the entire great expanse of Russia was suddenly cut short and replaced by a bewildering existence, one that was rooted in a pointless, holidaylike atmosphere and in an unnatural abandonment of everything that human society had lived by.

Having arrived in Petersburg, I stepped out of the train car and began walking around the station. There, in Petersburg, things seemed even more terrible than in Moscow. It seemed as though

9. More accurately, Alexei Tolstoy wrote to a friend on April 26, 1869: "When I think about the beauty of our language, when I think about the beauty of our history before the cursed Mongols and before the rise of cursed Moscow which was still more infamous than the Mongols, I feel like throwing myself on the ground and rolling about in despair because of what we did with the *talents* that God gave us." See A. K. Tolstoy, *Sobranie sochinenii v chetyrekh tomakh*, vol. 4 (Moscow, 1964), 281.
1. Bunin had gone to Petersburg to meet with Gorky about the publication of Bunin's works. Though the encounter between the two men was friendly and warm, it would be their last meeting; Bunin declined to see Gorky after the October Revolution.
2. Almost sixteen million men—more than one-third of all those mobilized by the Entente and its allies—had been mobilized for the Russian armed forces.

even greater numbers of people had absolutely no idea of what to do and were roaming about the station in a completely senseless way. I walked out to the entranceway to hail a cabbie; but he also did not know what to do—whether he should take me or not—as well as what to charge me for the ride.

"To the Europe Hotel," I said.[3]

He thought a bit and answered randomly: "Twenty rubles."

The cost was completely out of line for the times, but I agreed, got in, and took off—but, as I traveled around, I did not recognize Petersburg.

Life had already stopped in Moscow. Its new rulers, though, had come up with an imitation of it, an existence that was insane, chaotic, and fevered, and that was rooted in some allegedly new structure, a new ritual, even a parade of life. The same thing was happening in Petersburg but even to a far greater degree. Meetings, assemblies, and mass gatherings were going on nonstop; appeals and decrees were being published one after another: a well-known "hot line" was operating at a frenzied pace—who wasn't shouting, who wasn't giving orders on this "line" in those days! Government cars sporting little red flags rushed along Nevsky Prospekt;[4] trucks overflowing with people rumbled and roared; detachments with red banners marched to music in an excessively lively and precise manner. . . .

Nevsky was being trampled underfoot by a grey mob, soldiers with overcoats thrown over their shoulders, unemployed workers, strolling servants, and drunkards of all kinds. Vendors were selling cigarettes, red ribbons, obscene postcards, sweets, and anything else one might want from their stands. The sidewalks were filled with litter and piles of sunflowers; in the streets were frozen manure, humps, and holes. Halfway to my destination, the cabby sud-

3. The Europe Hotel (*Gostinitsa Evropeiskaia*), one of the most famous hotels in Saint Petersburg, was built between 1873 and 1875.
4. The main thoroughfare in Saint Petersburg.

denly told me what many bearded peasants were saying at that time:

"The people are now like cattle without a herdsman; they keep shitting all over and destroying themselves."

I asked: "So what should be done?"

"What should be done?" he said. "There's nothing one can do now. All we got now is an orgy going on. There's no government at all."

I looked around, at this Petersburg. . . . "Truly, there's an orgy going on now." But in the depths of my soul I still hoped for something. I still could not believe that the government had vanished.

But I also could not help believe.

In Petersburg I felt the following in a particularly lively way: there had been a great death in our huge, thousand-year-old home. This home had now been thrown open wide and filled with a huge holiday mob, which no longer saw anything sacred or forbidden in its rooms. Amidst this crowd were the heirs of the deceased, individuals dazed by cares and a need to give orders—which no one, though, obeyed. The crowd wandered from chamber to chamber, room to room. They never stopped nibbling or chewing on sunflower seeds; they only looked around and held their tongues, waiting for a better time to talk. But the heirs played up to the crowd, talking incessantly and assuring both the people and themselves that it was precisely they, the sovereign crowd, who, in their "sacred anger," had broken the "chains" that had bound the deceased and the heirs. They kept instilling into the people as well as into themselves the idea that in no way did they consider themselves heirs—only temporary administrators who supposedly represented the crowd.

I went to the Field of Mars.[5] The people there had just finished celebrating something that looked like a traditional sacrifice

5. The Field of Mars (*Marsovo pole*) measures some thirty acres and is one of the most beautiful places in Saint Petersburg. In pre-Revolutionary times it was also a place for folk festivals and military parades.

to the Revolution, but which was really a comic funeral for heroes who had allegedly fallen for freedom. Why was this necessary? What was this really, other than a mockery of the dead? The deceased were being deprived of an honest Christian burial. For some reason they were boarded up in red coffins and buried in the very center of town, right among the living! The comedy was done with great levity. Though the deceased were known to no one, their humble remains were mocked by high-blown speeches. From one end to the other, the great square had been dug up and trampled underfoot. It was disfigured with mounds of dirt; pierced with tall, bare poles topped with very long, thin black rags; and closed off by fences which had been hastily joined together and which, in their savage primitiveness, looked no less loathsome than the poles.[6]

I attended a very large gathering, the opening of an exhibit of Finnish art. What pictures we had then! Or so it seemed. The powers-that-be tried to have as many people as possible at the event. "All Petersburg" showed up, headed by several new ministers and well-known deputies of the Duma. They all simply *begged* the Finns to send Russia to the devil and to do whatever they pleased. I do not know any other way to describe the delight with which the Finns were addressed as regards "the dawn of freedom that shines over Finland." And from the windows of that very grand building in which all of this took place, and which stood just across from the Field of Mars, I again looked out onto that terrible gravelike disgrace which it had become.

I was also present at a celebration honoring the very same Finland—a banquet given for their people after the opening of the exhibit. And, good Lord, the Homeric chaos that poured out of this banquet made everything else that I had seen in Petersburg seem harmonious and relevant! Everyone who attended the exhibit

6. Bunin was not alone in his sentiments. The young literary critic Viktor Shklovsky thought the atmosphere in Saint Petersburg seemed "like an explosion, when it's all over, when everything's blown up." Others felt that "the city of Peter the Great was dying." See Lincoln, *Red Victory*, 53.

seemed alike—all "the flower of the Russian intelligentsia," i.e., famous artists, actors, writers, social figures, new ministers, and one
tall foreign representative, the ambassador of France himself.[7] But
the poet Mayakovsky prevailed over them all. I was sitting with
Gorky and the Finnish artist Gallen. Mayakovsky immediately
began acting up, coming over to our table without any invitation.
He shoved a chair between us and began to eat from our plates
and to drink from our glasses. Gallen's eyes popped out of his head.
It was almost as if he were looking at a horse that had just been
led into the banquet hall. Gorky tittered. I moved aside.
Mayakovsky noticed this.

"Do you really hate me that much?" he asked me in a merry
way.

I said "no" quite freely; that would be too much of an honor
for him. He was about to open his trenchlike mouth and ask me
something else, but at that moment the minister of foreign affairs[8]
rose to give the official toast. Mayakovsky rushed over to him, to
the middle of the table. Once there, he jumped up on a chair and
began to yell something so obscene that the minister froze to the
spot. He immediately got hold of himself and again proclaimed,
"Ladies and gentlemen!" But Mayakovsky yelled something even
fouler than before. The minister made a final and fruitless attempt
to speak; then he shrugged his shoulders and sat down.

As soon as the minister had taken his seat, the French ambassador got up. Apparently he felt fully assured that the Russian
hooligan would back off in confusion. He couldn't have been more
wrong! Mayakovsky drowned him out in a still shriller voice. Moreover, and to the ambassador's extreme amazement, the entire hall
suddenly erupted into a savage and senseless frenzy. Infected by
Mayakovsky, everyone began to shout for no reason at all. They

7. Maurice Paleologue was the French ambassador to Russia from 1914 to
1917. Although Paleologue's knowledge of Russia and its people exceeded that of
any senior diplomat in Europe, he was recalled to Paris three months after the
February revolution.
8. The individual in question was Pavel Milyukov.

began to stamp their shoes on the floor and to beat their fists on the table. They laughed, howled, yelped, and grunted; they even turned off the electricity. Suddenly a Finnish artist, who looked like a shaved walrus, drowned out everyone else in a truly tragic wail. Drunk and dreadfully pale, he was apparently shaken to the depths of his soul by the *extreme* swinishness that was going on; and, wishing to protest, he began, with all his strength and literally with tears in his eyes, to scream out one of the few Russian words he knew:

"That's too much! That's too-o-o much! That's too-o-o much!"

I happened to be at still another celebration in Petersburg— when Lenin came to town.[9] "We bid you welcome!" Gorky wrote in a newspaper, acting as just one more claimant to the inheritance. But he was extremely serious and open in his claims. Lenin was met at the station by an honor guard and music; he was whisked off to one of the best Petersburg homes, which, of course, Gorky did not own.

"That's too much?" But how else could one say it? After all, there were banquets going on all over the place, and the only sober ones at these feasts were the Lenins and the Mayakovskys.

One-eyed Polyphemus wished to devour the wandering Odysseus. Lenin and Mayakovsky (whom high school students prophetically dubbed "Idiot Polyphemovich") were also both gluttonous and extremely powerful in their political one-eyedness. At one time everyone looked upon them as little more than street clowns. Not for nothing was Mayakovsky called a Futurist,[1] that is, a man of the future. Without a doubt the polyphemiclike future

9. With the help of the German foreign office, Lenin returned to Petrograd in a "sealed" railway car on April 3, 1917.
1. Briefly, the Russian Futurists were a group of anarchically inclined artists and poets who wanted nothing less than a radical reformation of the arts. In such manifestos as "A Slap in the Face of Public Taste" ("*Poshchechina obshchestvennomu vkusu*") (1912), they attacked all culture and demanded a language of "transsense" that violated the rules of syntax, semantics—and propriety. The Futurists did everything they could to attract attention, shock the bourgeois, and arouse indignation. As they saw it, they were people of the future, and their art was the

of Russia belonged to the Mayakovskys and the Lenins. Mayakovsky instinctively sensed what the entire Russian feasting of those days had turned into, and recognized how splendidly Lenin could shut the mouths of all other tribunes as he spoke from Kshensinskaya's balcony. Even more splendid was the fact that Mayakovsky himself could shut mouths, and at a banquet that was ready to sell us down the river to Finland!

The world was host to Easter, to spring, and to such splendid days, the likes of which ordinarily never occurred in Petersburg at that time of year. But an immense sadness held sway over anything else I felt then. Before I left Petersburg I visited the Peter and Paul Cathedral.[2] Everything was wide open—the fortress gates, the cathedral doors. Idle people were roaming about everywhere, looking around and spitting out sunflower seeds. I walked around the cathedral, looked at where the tsars were buried, and, with a bow to the ground, I begged their forgiveness. Coming out onto the church porch, I stood for a long time in a state of shock: the entire endless universe that was Russia at springtime was opening up before my very attentive eyes. Spring and the Easter chimes called forth feelings of joy and of resurrection, but an immense grave yawned in the world. Death was in this spring, the final kiss. . . .

"The world did not know disappointment," Herzen said, "until the great French Revolution; skepticism arrived together with the Republic of 1792."[3]

As far as Russia is concerned, we will carry to the grave the greatest disappointment in the world.

I have just reread what I have written. No, we probably could still have saved ourselves. For the most part at that time, the depravity had only taken hold in the cities. The villages still had some

---

seedbed for new life. For more on Mayakovsky and the Futurists, see Lincoln, *Red Victory*, 351–354.

2. The Peter and Paul Cathedral lies inside the Peter and Paul Fortress and was built between 1712 and 1733. It contains the tombs of all but two of the Russian emperors and empresses from Peter the Great to Alexander III.

3. Bunin is again paraphrasing from Herzen's *My Past and Thoughts*.

sense, even shame. I recall notes I had written earlier, ones that I now pulled out and opened: for example, an excerpt from May 5/18, 1917:

"I was at a mill. There were many peasants present, several of them women. The noise of the mill failed to drown out the loud conversation that was going on. A peasant was leaning up against the lintel of the door. He was tall, but with hunched shoulders; his face had a dark black beard and a soft reddish hue that went up to his hair. A hat was pushed way down over the bridge of his nose. Having cocked his ear, he listened attentively to what [Bunin's nephew] Kolya was saying; but he kept looking down at the ground.

"Kolya was saying that the soldiers were not obeying anyone and that they were leaving the front. A peasant suddenly roused himself and, fixing his shining black eyes at him, began speaking in an angry way:

" 'There you have it! There you have it! That's those sons of bitches for you! Who dismissed them? Who needs 'em here? Those sons of bitches, they all should be arrested!'

"At that very moment a young soldier came riding by on a grey horse, singing and whistling. He was wearing khakis and a pair of quilted pants. The peasant rushed toward him, saying:

" 'There's one! See how he goes? Who let him go? How did he get drafted? How did he get tricked into going?'

"The soldier was bowlegged, with a feigned carefree air. He got down, tied up the horse, and entered the mill.

" 'How come you won so few battles?' the peasant shouted after him. 'Tell me, your soldier's hat, your soldier's pants, did you put 'em on just to stay at home?' (The soldier turned around with an awkward smile.) 'You'd better not come around here at all, you son of a bitch, you bastard! I'll come and take them myself. I'll strip you of your pants and shoes, and then I'll smash your head against a wall! I'm glad you got no bosses now, you bum! Why did your father and mother even bother feeding you?'

"The peasants caught up with the soldier, raising a collectively indignant cry. The soldier with the awkward smile tried to be scornful, but he merely shrugged his shoulders."

April 24 / May 7, 1919
Yesterday evening I took it into my head to hide these notes so well that not even the devil himself could find them. Incidentally, the devil is now a little boy and his puppy. All the same, these notes can still be found, and they will be my ruin. *Izvestia* has already written about me: "It is long overdue to pay attention to this academician with the face of a Gogolian Christmas eve,[4] to remember how he extolled the arrival of the French in Odessa!"[5]

I looked through the newspapers. But the same puppet show is going on. "Yesterday the Bessarabian worker-peasant government published a manifesto, declaring war against Rumania. But this is not the predatory war of imperialists. . . ." and so forth.[6]

There was also an article by Trotsky "on the necessity of finishing off Kolchak." Of course, this is a primary agenda not only for Trotsky but for those who, wishing to destroy the "cursed past," are also ready to destroy *en masse*—even if it be half the Russian people.

In Odessa the people have been waiting for the arrival of the Bolsheviks. "Ours are coming," they say. Many everyday citizens are also waiting for them—they are tired of the change of governments; they want something stable and hope that life will be cheaper, too. But oh, how they keep rushing to get things! Well, that's nothing; they'll get used to it. It's like the story of the old peasant who so wanted a pair of glasses that when he got them he literally burst into tears.

---

4. Most likely *Izvestia* is referring to the character of the devil in Gogol's story "The Night Before Christmas" ("*Noch' pod rozhestvom*"), published in 1832.
5. This poem, entitled "December 22, 1918," appears in full on pages 218–219.
6. Such a manifesto was futile.

His neighbor said: "Makar, you've gone crazy! After all, you'll go blind if they're not the right ones for your eyes!"

"Who are you, a *barin* or something? You're concerned about my glasses? That's nothing, they'll *change with my eyes....*"

Voloshin told me that Severnyi, the son of Dr. Yuzefovich and head of the Odessa Cheka, told him: "I'll never forgive myself for letting Kolchak escape. I once had him in my hands!"

I've never heard anything more offensive in my entire life!

Of Dybenko or "Torture-rack"[7] ... Chekhov once told me: "Now here's a great name for a sailor: 'Cat-crusher.'"

Dybenko is better than "Cat-crusher."

Yesterday Shchepkina-Kupernik told me about Kollontai:

"I know her very well. She once resembled an angel. At the beginning of the day she would don the simplest little dress and gallop off to the workers' slums—'to go and work there,' she said. And when she returned home, she took a bath and put on a small bluish shirt and, rushing off to bed with a box of candy in her hands, she would say to her girlfriend: 'Well, dear, let's chatter on now to our heart's content!'"[8]

The judicial system and psychiatric medicine have long classed this (angelic-looking) type as belonging to inbred criminals and prostitutes.

From *Izvestia*:

"The peasants say: 'Give us the commune, only *deliver* us from the Cadets....'"[9]

A huge poster stands near the doors of the Political Adminis-

---

7. From the Russian word *dyba* or "torture-rack."

8. Kollontai did in fact work in the "slums" as a volunteer at the Mobile Museum of Teaching Aids, whose members hoped to spread political education among urban workers through Sunday schools and evening classes. Shchepkina-Kupernik's allegation as to what Kollontai did "after hours" is, to say the least, highly suspect. See Cathy Porter, *Alexandra Kollontai: The Lonely Struggle of the Woman Who Defied Lenin* (New York, 1980), 37–38, and Lincoln, *Red Victory*, 330–336.

9. The Cadets, or the Constitutional Democratic party, were organized in 1905 and embraced liberal monarchist constitutionalists as well as republicans.

tration Office. A red-skinned peasant woman, with an insanely savage snout and savagely bared teeth, is running full speed and sticking a pitchfork into the backside of a fleeing general. Blood pours
forth from his rear. The inscription says:
"Don't hanker, Denikin, for land that is not yours!"
"Don't hanker" must mean "don't think to bury yourself."[1]

I swear by Michael the Archangel himself that I will never accept the Bolshevik orthography. If only because the human hand
has never written anything like what is being written now in this
script.

Just think, I *still* have to explain first to one, then to another,
why I will not go and work for the Proletkult.[2] I still must *prove*
that I cannot sit down right next to the office of the Cheka, where,
almost every hour, someone's head is being broken, and enlighten
some idiot with sweaty hands about "the latest achievements in the

---

They advocated proper legal procedure, civil liberty, and political democracy.
Having been condemned by the Soviet government as "enemies of the people"
on December 11, 1917, the Cadets went underground and collaborated with White
generals and such anti-Bolshevik movements as the National Center and the
League of Restoration.

    1. In Russian, "don't hanker" is "*ne zaris'*," and "don't think to bury your-
self" is "*ne zar'sia.*" Mayakovsky, together with the graphic artist Mikhail Cherem-
nykh, had conceived the idea of spreading political commentary and educational
propaganda among the masses by placing large posters of captioned cartoons in
shop windows. These "Windows of Satire" rendered political messages into two-
liners that could be easily remembered, and were illustrated by cartoon figures
that dramatized the main points of the message for men and women who still
found it difficult to comprehend the letters.

    The "Windows of Satire" thus allowed the Bolsheviks to send powerful po-
litical messages quickly to semiliterate men and women and, at the same time,
to conserve paper, which by 1919 had become one of the scarcest resources in
Soviet Russia. See Lincoln, *Red Victory*, 352–353.

    2. The Proletkult, or "Proletarian Cultural and Educational Organizations"
(*Proletarskie kul'turno-prosvetitel'skie organizatsii*) (1917–1932), was an early Soviet
project to develop a distinctly proletarian literature and art. Ironically the Proletkult later recommended Bunin's *The Village*, even though the work was not
reprinted in the first years of Soviet rule.

instrumentation of verse"! One should curse these lepers to the nth generation, even if they claim to be "intristed" in verse!

Generally speaking, what is most horrible, terrible, and repulsive now is not even the horrors and disgraces that the students of the Prolekult write, but the fact that I must first read through them and then argue with people as to whether they are good or bad. The absolute worst thing, though, is that I must *prove* to others that, for example, it is a thousand times better to die from hunger than to teach iambic verse and trochees to some idiot so that he can sing the praises of the Revolution, in which his colleagues rob, beat, rape, ruin churches, whip with belts taken from the backs of officers, and marry priests to horses!

Speaking about the Odessa Cheka, there is now a new way of shooting people—over the latrine hole.

Voloshin says that Severnyi, the head of the secret police here, has a "pure, crystallike soul"; but he also says that he just met the man several days ago—"in the living room of an attractive woman."

Anyuta said:

"The Red Army have been chased from Russia."[3]

I know, for I have already seen some of them. Today I came across yet another one—a thick-mugged, short-legged individual who, when he spoke, raised the left corner of his lip. I was at the end of Torgovaya Street, overlooking the port. He was lying with another soldier on a stone fence, cracking sunflower seeds with monkeylike quickness, and looking at me distrustfully from under his brows. Why was I, unhappy man that I am, there in the first place? I wanted to look at the empty berths, at the sea, but all the time feeling that hopes for rescue from that quarter were melting away!

I finished reading Bulgakov's memoirs.[4] Tolstoy once said to him:

3. Nothing could have been further from the truth.
4. Valentin Bulgakov was Leo Tolstoy's secretary in 1910. The work in question is *At L. N. Tolstoy's Home in the Last Year of His Life* (*U L. N. Tolstogo v poslednii god ego zhizni*), published in 1911, 1918, and 1920.

"Schoolgirls who read Gorky and Andreev sincerely believe they cannot penetrate the depths of their writing. . . . I have just finished reading the prologue to *Anathema*—and it is complete nonsense. . . . What is going on in their heads, all these Bryusovs and Belys?"[5]

Chekhov also did not understand these writers. In public he would say they were "marvelous" writers, but at home he would laugh loudly: "What characters! They should be arrested!" And about Andreev: "First I'll read two pages—and then I'll need two hours of fresh air to clear my head!"

Tolstoy also said: "Today one is a literary success only by being stupid and insolent."

He forgot to say that the critics were helping.

Who are they, these critics?

People turn to doctors for medical advice, lawyers for legal affairs, engineers to construct a bridge, and architects to build a home. But when it comes to art, anyone who wants to can be a critic, often people who, by nature, are completely alien to art. But these are the only ones that readers listen to. . . . Tolstoy's opinion does not count for a thing—because it is the opinion of one who, first of all, possessed a profound critical sense. For example, the writing of each word in *War and Peace* was weighed most carefully; it underwent the most precise evaluation.

Even when I completely give up hope, I harbor a secret dream that there will come a day of revenge, a time for a universal damnation of these days. One cannot live without this hope. But how can one believe now, when such an unbelievably horrible truth has been revealed about humankind?

Everything will be forgotten and even extolled! And *literature*

5. Andreev's *Anathema* (*Anafema*) was written in 1910. More accurately, Tolstoy said about the work: "I have just read the prologue to Leonid Andreev's *Anathema*. It is complete jibberish . . . madness, absolute madness! . . . It is surprising that the public likes such an incomprehensible thing as this. Indeed, it is precisely from a work such as this that readers demand and seek some kind of special meaning." See V. Bulgakov, *L. N. Tolstoy* (Moscow, 1960), 194, 229.

will be the first to help. It will soundly distort everything, just as it did with the French Revolution, when poets, the most noxious tribe on earth, outnumbered each conscientious writer with thousands of verse-idlers, degenerates, and charlatans.

> Blessed are those who will visit this world
> In its fatal moments![6]

We complicate, we philosophize over everything, even over the unspeakable things that are now going on about us. With us it's not a "rope" but a "thing to tie things up with," just like Krylov's wise man who jumped into a pit but continued to expound upon things once he was there.[7] For example, we are still arguing about Blok: are his drunkards who killed a street girl really apostles or something less?[8] Mikhryutka,[9] who shattered a Venetian mirror with a club, is invariably our version of a Scythian, a Hun, and we take great comfort in affixing this label to him.

Generally speaking, we have been poisoned by the literary approach to life. For example, look at what we've done to the very great and colorful life that Russia lived in the last century. We have smashed it and broken it up into decades—the twenties, the thirties, the forties, the sixties—each decade defined by its *literary hero*: Chatsky, Onegin, Pechorin, Bazarov.[1] . . . It would make a cat laugh, especially when one recalls that these heroes were eighteen, nineteen, or, at the most, twenty years old! . . .

---

6. Bunin is quoting from Tyutchev's poem "Cicero" (*"Tsitseron"*), published in 1832.

7. Bunin is mistaken here. The story in question is Khemnitser's *"The Metaphysician"* (*"Metafizik"*), published in 1799.

8. Bunin is here referring to Blok's famous poem "The Twelve" (*"Dvenadtstat'"*), published in 1918.

9. Mikhryutka is a generic name for a feeble or unprepossessing person; he appears as a character not in Blok but in such writers as Grigorovich and Pisemsky.

1. Onegin is the hero of Pushkin's *Eugene Onegin*; Pechorin, of Lermontov's *A Hero of Our Time* (1837–1840); and Bazarov, of Turgenev's *Fathers and Sons*.

ODESSA 1919

The newspapers are calling for a crusade to Europe. I remember the fall of '14, a meeting of Moscow intellectuals at the
Juridical Society.[2] Gorky, green from excitement, said in a speech:
"I fear a Russian victory because our savage country will have
its hundred-million-man belly fall on Europe!"

Now the belly is a Bolshevik one, but Gorky is no longer
afraid.

The newspapers have also issued a "warning": "Due to a complete lack of fuel, there will soon be no electricity." Thus in one
month they have brought chaos to everything: no factories, no railroads, no trams, no water, no bread, no clothes—no nothing!

Yes, yes—"Seven thin cows will devour seven fat ones, but
they themselves will not become fat."[3]

Now (it's 11 p.m.) I open the window and look out onto the
street. The moon hangs low behind the houses, there is not a soul
in sight. It's so quiet that one can hear, somewhere on the street,
a dog gnawing on a bone. But where did it get a bone? Look at
what we've come to—we're even surprised to find a bone!

I'm reading *The Precipice*.[4] It is long but very intelligent and
forceful; but I have to force myself to read it—since I find these
Mark Volokhovs[5] so repulsive. How many hooligans have de-
scended from this Mark! "Why are you creeping into someone
else's garden and eating their apples?" "But what does this mean:
'someone else's garden or apples'? Why can't I eat when I feel like
it?" Mark is a brilliant creation, one that is the remarkable business of artists. An individual captures, distills, and embodies a type,
one that was supposed to dissolve into thin air. But sometimes his
presence and influence increase a hundredfold—in complete dis-

2. The Juridical Society (*Iuridicheskoe obshchestvo*) was founded in Moscow
in 1863 and brought together legal scholars and practitioners.
3. Bunin is here paraphrasing Joseph's interpretation of Pharaoh's dream in
Genesis 4:4.
4. Goncharov's *Precipice* (*Obryv*) was written between 1849 and 1868.
5. Mark Volokhov is a "nihilist" and a fictional brother of the better-known
Bazarov in *Fathers and Sons*.

regard of what his portrait was supposed to represent. Goncharov wanted to poke fun at the remnants of knighthood. He created a figure who never existed in life but who was the catalyst for hundreds of Don Quixotes to spring into existence. Goncharov wanted to castigate all the things that were associated with Mark, but he wound up giving birth to thousands of Marks who took their beginnings not from life but from books.

Generally speaking, how does one distinguish between that which is real and that which books, the theater, and films give us? Most likely, the people who have taken part in my life and who have had an impact upon me are fewer in number than the heroes of Shakespeare and Tolstoy. Others have allowed Sherlock Holmes to enter their lives, while some maid has been captivated by some woman whom she saw in an automobile on film.

April 25 / May 8, 1919
Late yesterday evening some people, together with the "commissar" of our home, came to measure the width, length, and height of all our rooms in order "to consolidate the proletariat." These damn monkeys are measuring all the rooms in the city and are creating havoc wherever they go! I didn't say a word. I silently lay on the couch while they measured all around me, but I got so upset from this new insult that my heart started to flutter and my veins pulsated in a sickly way on my forehead. This will not be good for my heart. I used to have a good heart, but I wonder about it now!

The "commissar" of our home became a commissar only because he was the youngest person among all the occupants in our building and because he came from a completely humble calling. He accepted the office out of fear. He's a modest, shy individual, and he now shakes at the mere mention of the "revolutionary tribunal." He runs through the entire building, begging us to fulfill the decrees. How these villains are able to instill fear and terror into people! How they take every opportunity to emphasize and parade their savagery! I get a sharp pain next to my left nipple whenever I hear words like "revolutionary tribunal." Why "commissar," why "tribunal," why not simply "court"? All because when the Bolsheviks take cover under such sacred revolutionary words, they can bravely wade in blood up to their knees. Thanks to such words, even the most intelligent and decent revolutionaries can become indignant over everyday pillaging, robbery, and murder. They know perfectly well that they should tie up and drag a bum into the police station because he has seized a pedestrian by the throat *in ordinary daylight*. By the same token, though, they choke from ecstasy before this tramp if he does the same thing in so-called "revolutionary" times, because he has the fullest right to do so.

As I was finishing writing the above words—I heard a knock at the front door which immediately turned into frantic rapping. I opened the door—and again it was the commissar with a mob of his friends and members of the Red Army. With hurried vulgarity they demanded that I hand over to them any extra mattresses. I said I didn't have any extra ones. They came in, looked around, and left. Again my head became stiff, my heart started fluttering, and my arms and legs shook from outrage, from insult.

I suddenly heard music coming from the courtyard. A roving Jew wearing a hat, a woman, and a German-type accordion. They were playing a polka—how strange all this is now, how inopportune!

The day is sunny but almost as cold as yesterday. There are clouds, but the sky is blue and the tree in the courtyard is already thick, dark green, and resplendent.

In the courtyard where the mattresses are being collected, cooks scream (about us): "That's fine, that's quite all right. Let them sleep on shingles and boards for a while!"

Kataev was here (he is a young writer). The cynicism of today's young people is unbelievable. He told me, "For a hundred thousand rubles, I'll kill anyone you want. I want to eat well, I want to have a nice hat, an excellent pair of shoes. . . ."

I went out to take a walk with him. Suddenly my entire being was momentarily taken up with the enchantment of spring, whose coming, for the first time in my life, I had not yet completely felt. I also felt that my vision had suddenly widened physically and spiritually, and that it was unusually powerful and clear. Deribasovskaya Street seemed unusually short, and the buildings bordering it unusually close. The statue of Catherine, all wrapped up in rags, Levashov's house where the Cheka were, and the sea—all were small, flat, like the palms of my hands. Suddenly I realized clearly, vigorously, dispassionately—without any sorrow or fear but only with a vibrant despair—that everything going on in Odessa and in all of Russia was heading for an abyss.

When I left my home, I heard the janitor saying to someone:

"Oh, these Communists, they'll steal beds to the last bastard. They'd rob their own father—swindle him with moonshine and pay him off with cigarettes!"

Everything is this way, and the lunacy is genuine, though it is surprising that everyone I meet affirms this—especially when one considers what happened to me (as if on purpose) on Pushkinskaya Street: an automobile rushed madly toward me from the station. In it, amidst a pile of friends, was an absolutely rabid-looking student with a rifle in his hands. Everything about him was harried-looking. His dilated eyes were fixed savagely forward; he was extremely thin; the features of his face were incredibly thin and sharp; the ends of a red hood fluttered in the wind behind him.

Generally speaking, one rarely sees students these days, but this one was rushing off somewhere, all in tatters. He was wearing a dirty nightshirt under an old overcoat that was flung open wide. The cap on his disheveled head was faded; the shoes on his feet were worn through; and a rifle, its barrel downward, hung from his shoulder. Incidentally, the devil knows if he really was a student.

Everything else is just as unreal. For example, it just so happened that a detachment of soldiers was coming out of the gates of what used to be the Crimea Hotel (located across from where the Cheka is) at the same time a group of women was crossing the

bridge there. The soldiers stopped suddenly, turned in their direc-
tion, and took a piss, laughing as they did so. And what about the
huge poster that hangs on the wall outside the police station?
Someone has drawn a series of steps, and on the highest one is the
picture of a throne from which blood flows in rivers. At the bottom is the inscription:

Thrones covered with the people's blood
But we'll stain our enemies scarlet!

And on the square next to the Duma[6] the rostrums for the
First of May still assault the eye with their red color. Farther on,
something incomprehensibly foul, enigmatic, and complex rises
high in the distance. This something, held together by boards and
apparently conforming to some Futurist design, is daubed with
paint in every way possible. It is an entire edifice, narrowing at the
top and graced with gates all around. Posters again hang all along
Deribasovskaya Street: two workers are turning a press, under
which lies a flattened bourgeois. Golden coins pour forth in ribbons from his mouth and ass. And the mob walking about? First
of all, how filthy they are! How many old, unbelievably soiled soldiers' overcoats, how many reddish brown leg-wrappings on their
feet, how many greasy caps on their lice-ridden heads—all looking
as though they had been used to sweep up the street! And I'm
seized with horror when I think about how many people are going
about in clothes, stripped from the corpses, of those who have already been murdered!

The members of the Red Army display a key trait—their dis-
soluteness, their lack of discipline. Their teeth have a cigarette between them, their eyes are cloudy but insolent, their caps are
perched way back on their heads, and a clump of hair falls on their
foreheads. They are dressed in some kind of collective rags. Some
wear a full-dress uniform from the '70s; some, for no reason at all,

---

6. Bunin is referring to the government offices in Odessa.

have red riding breeches along with an infantryman's overcoat and a huge overfashioned saber.

Sentinels sit on chairs next to the entrances of confiscated homes, and in the most tortuous poses. Sometimes a plain tramp sits there with a revolver in his belt; a German cutlass hangs from one side, a dagger from the other.

In order to have hot water in the city, these "builders of the new life" have ordered that Odessa's famous elevated railway be torn down,[7] i.e., the many-miled wooden track that runs to the port and is used to deliver bread. People are complaining in *Izvestia*: "Everybody is taking apart the railway!" Branches and trees are also being lopped off and chopped down—already two rows of bare trunks stick out on many streets. Members of the Red Guard also heat samovars by breaking the butts of their guns into chips.

When I got home I looked through a book of pulp fiction that had been lying round here for a long time: *The Library of the Working Masses. Songs of Folk Anger.* Odessa, 1917. Yes, the inscription that was on the poster is also here:

Thrones covered with the people's blood
But it will stain our enemies scarlet,
Heartless revenge on all our foes
And death to capitalist leeches and harlots!

There is the "Worker's Marseillaise," the "Warsaw Anthem," the "Internationale," the "Hymn of the Volunteers," "The Red Ban-

---

7. Odessa was long proud of its two-mile *estakada* or "elevated railway," which allowed trains to carry grain directly to ships in port. The *estakada*, though, was more show than substance. Most of the grain in the area had to be delivered to the docks by carts and loaded onto the ships by hand. The result was chronic delays and skyrocketing costs which, coupled with civic unrest, widespread thievery, numerous strikes, the absence of huge elevators and specialized equipment, and the need for extensive improvements around the harbor left Odessa at the mercy of rival cities on and around the Black Sea. The city's share in total national trade fell from 45 percent in 1897–1901 to 28.7 percent in 1908. See Herlihy, *Odessa*, 224–227.

ner"[8] ... and it is all so malicious, so unbelievably bloody, so sick-eningly false, so flat and unbelievably wretched:

Vicious whirlwinds give us pause
But all our warriors we will call
The banner for the worker's cause
We'll raise both proud and tall. . . .

And we'll begin a new life
And make plowshares from swords
By sending our enemies to the knife
And killing the enemy hordes. . . .

Good God, what has happened! What a terribly abnormal thing has happened, the result of entire generations of boys and girls who memorized Ivanyukov and Marx by heart; who published their writings in secret; who disseminated them in gatherings of the Red Cross[9] and under the guise of "literature"; who shamefully pre-tended they were dying of love for all the Pakhoms and Sidors;[1] and who constantly inflamed themselves with hatred for the no-

8. Briefly, the words for the "Internationale" were written by the French revolutionary poet Eugene Pottier during the period of the Paris Commune in 1871; the music for the piece was composed by a French wood carver, Pierre Degeyter, in 1888. Although the piece was banned in tsarist Russia, it was trans-lated into Russian in 1902 and circulated among Russian revolutionaries both at home and abroad. The "Internationale" was the official anthem of Soviet Russia until 1943.

The "Warsaw Anthem" ("*Varshavianka*") was a popular Polish and Russian revolutionary song that was written in Polish in 1883 and translated into Russian in 1897. Its subject was the Polish uprising against the Russians in 1863.

The "Hymn of the Volunteers" ("*Dobrovol'cheskii gimn*") was taken from a song written by Mikhail Mikhailov. It was one of the most popular songs among members of the Russian underground before 1917.

The "Red Banner" ("*Krasnoe znamia*") is a translation of the French hymn *Le Drapeau Rouge*. It was written in 1877 by a member of the French Commune and sung by Russian revolutionaries from 1900 on.

9. The Red Cross (*Krasnyi krest*) was the generalized name for a number of revolutionary organizations in Russia throughout the 1880s, their purpose being to help political prisoners and exiles.

1. Bunin is using the names of "Pakhom" and "Sidor" as generalized epi-thets for Russian peasants.

bleman, the factory owner, the philistine, and all "bloodsuckers, spiders, obscurants, and knights of darkness and violence!"

Yes, it's universal insanity. What is in people's heads? The other day I went walking along Elizavetinskaya Street. Some guards were sitting next to the doorway of a confiscated home and playing with the bolts of their guns. One said to another:

"And all of Petersburg will be under a glass ceiling . . . so there'll be no snow, no rain, no nothin'. . . ."

Not long ago, out on the street, I met Professor Shchepkin, the commissar for education. He was moving slowly, his eyes fixed forward and with a dull, idiotic look on his face. He was wearing a dust-ridden cape about his shoulders with a huge greasy stain on the back. His hat was also so filthy that it made one sick to look at it. His paper collar was also very dirty; it was propped up by a huge pus-filled boil on the back of his neck that looked like a volcano about to erupt. His tie was old, thick, and died a *red oily color.*

People have been talking about how Fel'dman delivered a speech before some peasant "deputies":

"Comrades, soon the power of the soviets will take over the entire world!"

Suddenly a voice rang out from the crowd: "Not a chance!"

Fel'dman asked angrily:

"And why not?"

"Because you haven't got all the Jews yet!"

That's nothing to worry about; [the Bolsheviks] have got all the Shchepkins they need.

April 26 / May 9, 1919
I woke up at six because my heart was beating so strongly.

Going to get the newspapers, I heard an old lady cursing. The small fish in her basket had cost her eighty rubles!

The newspapers from Moscow report: Shipments of firewood on all railways have fallen by 50 percent. . . . The People's Commissars have decided to restore works of art. . . . India has been seized by bolshevism.[2]

Izvestia has been answering letters from its readers:

"Dear Citizen Guberman, So you think that the war with those bastards Kolchak and Denikin is fratricide?"

"Dear Comrade A., Praises to Russia, even if they be to a Soviet Russia, transcend a Marxist approach to the question."

"Dear Citizeness Glikman, Have you still not understood that the way of life in which, with money, one can have everything, but without it one can die from hunger—that way of life is gone forever?"

We took a walk to Nikolaevsky Boulevard. Along the way we saw white springlike clouds and a huge and clear vista—the empty berths in port, the charming colors of distant shores, and the bright blue ripples of the sea. . . . We ran into Osipovich and [Semyon] Yushkevich.[3] Again it's one and the same thing. With a look of indifference, they said quickly, in a whisper: "Tiraspole has been taken by the Germans and the Rumanians—this is already a fact. Petersburg too has fallen. . . ."[4]

At three this afternoon our maid Anyuta came in with a frightened look on her face: "Is it true that the Germans are entering the city?[5] Everybody is saying they have supposedly surrounded the city. They themselves got the Bolsheviks started; now they've been ordered to destroy them, but it will take them fifteen years before they surrender all of them to us. Ain't that great!"

What's all this? Most likely savage nonsense, but just the same I got so upset that my hands grew cold and shook. To calm

---

2. At this time Ghandi had begun India's struggle for independence from England.

3. There are two Yushkevichs in the narrative. The Social Democrat and philosopher Pavel Solomonovich Yushkevich, and his brother, the writer Semyon Solomonovich Yushkevich.

4. The rumors were still false.

5. The rumor was not true.

myself down I began reading a manuscript by Ovsyaniko-Kulikovsky, his memoirs of Dragomanov, Ziber, and P. Lavrov.[6] They're all marvelous people, like everyone who appears in Kulikovsky's works. He writes: "The Creator made these living souls from the best ethers. . . ." Good Lord! What a thing to read in my old age!

I then read Renan. *"L'homme fut des milliers d'anneés un fou, après avoir été des milliers d'anneés un animal."*[7]

April 27 / May 10, 1919
From *Izvestia*: "The counterrevolutionaries are sitting and are thinking up great thoughts about how to confuse proletarians and Communists. . . . Their narrow foreheads are covered with wrinkles, their mouths are open, and yellowing teeth peek out from under the thick, baggy lips of these Fedula Fedulyches. . . . Good God, they are either comedians or simple tavern rogues and swindlers. . . ."

From *The Voice of the Red Army*, a lushly written piece:
"Comrade Podvoisky has ordered that Rumania be invaded. . . . The Rumanian scallywags, along with their bloody king,[8] have seized the young Soviet Hungarian republic by the throat in order to snuff out the revolution that has seized all of Europe."

A resolution from Voznesensk:[9]

"We, the members of the Red Army and citizens of Voznesensk who are fighting for the liberation of the world, protest against boorish anti-Semitism!"

6. Ovsyaniko-Kulikovsky wrote these memoirs in 1919 and 1920 in Kharkov and Odessa. They were published in Petrograd in 1923.

7. "For thousands of years man was a fool, after having been for thousands of years an animal." Ernest Renan's book *Life of Christ* (*Vie de Jesus*), first published in 1863, attracted the attention of both Tolstoy and Dostoevsky.

8. The king in question is Ferdinand I, who ascended the Rumanian throne in 1914. Nothing came of Podvoisky's directive. After being checked by the Allies on May 9, 1919, the Rumanians regrouped their forces and captured Budapest six months later.

9. Voznesensk is a small city about one hundred miles northeast of Odessa.

ODESSA 1919

From Kiev there is news that "the statue of Alexander the II[1] is slated to be destroyed." A typical thing to do these days. As early as March '17 people were beginning to tear down eagles[2] and coats of arms. . . .

Again there is a rumor that Petersburg has fallen, Budapest too. Such rumors, though, always start off in the same hackneyed way: "A friend of a friend visited me and said . . ."

Great news, Radetsky and Koiransky came by, all excited. "Grigoriev is coming to Odessa!" they said.

"What Grigoriev?"

"The very same one who chased the allies out of Odessa.[3] Now he has joined up with Makhno and is beating the Bolsheviks. And Zelyonyi is heading for Kiev.[4] 'Beat the Jews and the Communists for the faith and fatherland!' that's what they say. I myself am a Jew, so to speak, but let the devil himself come at this point. Yesterday Shpital'nikov told me that he was a democrat who was against all intervention and interference. I replied: 'And what would you say against such intervention and interference if there were an all-Russian pogrom against the Jews?' "

April 28 / May 11, 1919
It is so!

1. The statue of Alexander II in Kiev was erected in 1911.
2. Bunin, of course, is referring to the famous double-headed eagle, which, initially of Byzantine origin, was one of the imperial accoutrements that accompanied the reign of Ivan III after his marriage to the Byzantine princess Sofia Paleologus in 1472. Although various representations of the double-headed eagle were dismantled by the Bolsheviks during the Revolution, they are being restored to prominence throughout Russia today.
3. The rumor was true. Grigoriev fought first for the Bolsheviks, then for the counterrevolution. On May 7–9, 1919, he refused to carry out the order of the Soviet command to move his division to the Rumanian front, and instead undertook an anti-Soviet rebellion in the rear of the Red Army which was fighting the troops of Denikin in the region of the Donbas.
4. Danylo Zelyonyi, a Ukrainian peasant warlord who fought both Reds and Whites, was unsuccessful in his quest. Kiev was taken by the counterrevolutionaries at the end of August 1919.

"In order to offset rumors circulating about the city, the head-quarters of the third Ukrainian Soviet army hereby announces that the Cossack chieftan Grigoriev, having gathered a mob of follow-ers, has proclaimed himself as hetman and has declared war on the Soviet government. . . ."

Next an order from Antonov-Ovseenko:[5]

"The White Guard bastard is seeking to thwart Red power and to exterminate it in a peaceful settlement. . . . This base traitor of the homeland, this wretched servant of our Cains, must be de-stroyed like a mad dog. . . . He must be crushed and ground into the dirt, like worms into the earth which he has defiled. . . ."

Then an appeal to the members of the military-revolutionary soviet:

"To one and all! To the children of the working classes of the socialist Ukraine! Grigoriev—an adventurer and a drunkard, the servant of the gang of the old regime, the lackey of priests, landowners, and mama's boys—has taken off his mask and has sur-rounded himself with a flock of black ravens with greasy mugs. . . . He preaches that Bolsheviks want to lock everyone up in a commune . . . even though the Communists are not forcing any-one to join. We are only making clear what everyone already knows, that is, that it is not the business of the Bolsheviks to cru-cify Christ because, after all, He, as the Savior, taught the same thing as we do. He too rebelled against the rich. . . . Such an ab-surd provocation was written in a drunken stupor; and, of course, it can have no effect. . . . Hurrah! Down with the adventurist who has taken it into his head to bathe in the blood of starving work-ers. . . . We must catch these traitors and pimps and hand them over to the workers and peasants. . . ." It was signed: "Comrades Dyatko, Golubenko, and Shchadenko." No one signs letters with

---

5. Vladimir Antonov-Ovseenko was a revolutionary street tactician who com-manded the Bolsheviks' attack against the Winter Palace in October 1917. For more on Antonov-Ovseenko, see Lincoln, *Red Victory*, 84–87.

the word "comrade." It would be like me finishing a letter with "Mr. Bunin."

Everyone's been upset the entire morning. [Semyon] Yushke-vich was here. He very much fears a pogrom against the Jews. The anti-Semitism in town is fierce.

Still more—an excerpt from "local life": Yesterday, by order of the military-revolutionary tribunal, eighteen counterrevolution-aries were shot.

The savagery and panic brings one to despair. "All bourgeois must be registered." How is one to understand this?

Yesterday I went out at sunset and ran into Rozenthal, who told me that someone had thrown a bomb on Cathedral Square. I took a walk with him to visit Lazrusky. There, from the windows of his apartment, I saw a rose-colored west amidst pale blue clouds. It was already twilight when I headed back on Deribasovskaya Street. On one side there were a great many people, but it was empty on the other. Angry soldiers kept crying out: "Comrades, to the other side of the street!" Several automobiles rushed by madly; they were followed by an ambulance with an anxious siren, two riders on horseback, and a dog who barked after them. . . . No one was allowed to go farther.

Thomas, our doorman, informed me that the day after to-morrow will "truly be the end of the world": it will be the "Day of Peaceful Insurrection," when every last bourgeois will be stripped of his things.

April 30 / May 13, 1919
It has been a terrible morning! I went to visit D. [Shpital'nikov]. He was wearing two shirts and two pairs of pants. He said that the Day of Peaceful Insurrection has already begun, that the pillaging was in full swing, and that he was afraid that someone would take his second pair of pants.

We went out together. A detachment of horsemen were going along Deribasovskaya Street. In their midst was an automobile with a horn that wailed the highest notes. We ran into Ovsyaniko-Kulikovsky, who said: "Rumors lacerate my soul; there's been shooting all night long; now people are being robbed."

It is three o'clock. I again take a walk into town: the Day of Peaceful Insurrection has suddenly been called off. It seems that the workers themselves have revolted. They were about to be robbed too, because they had helped themselves to piles of stuff earlier. The insurrectionists were met with firing, boiling water, and rocks.

Today we had a terrible storm with a downpour and hail. I took cover under the gates. Trucks, filled with comrades armed with rifles, were going by with a roar. Two soldiers walked under the gates. One was a big, hunched-over man with a cap on the back of his head. He was gobbling up a sausage, tearing pieces with his teeth while, with his left hand, he was slapping himself below the stomach.

"Here it is, here's my commune!" he said. "This is what I said to him right off, 'Don't scream, your Jerusalem excellency. It's hanging right below my belly.' . . ."

May 1 / 14, 1919
Everyone is in an anxious frame of mind, not only here in Odessa but in Kiev and in Moscow itself. Things have gotten so bad that Kamenev, as the plenipotentiary representative of the Soviet Ministry for Defense, has issued an appeal: "To one and all! One more push and worker-peasant power will conquer the world. At this very moment the traitor Grigoriev wants to stick a knife into the back of worker-peasant power."[6]

The commissar of our building came by to verify how old I am. The powers-that-be want to recruit all bourgeois into a "rear-guard militia."

---

6. This assertion was true. In his revolt against Soviet power, Grigoriev had the support of Ukrainian kulaks and of middle-class peasants who were dissatisfied with food requisitioning.

It has been cold all day long. This evening I went to visit [Semyon] Yushkevich. He's been trying to establish a theater for his friends in some "military hotel"; but, as he's afraid to go alone to the soviet to ask for this theater, he wants to involve me in all of this. He's out of his mind! I returned home through the rain, through a dark and gloomy city. Here and there, girls and lads of the Red Army were laughing and cracking nuts.

May 2 / 15, 1919
Members of the Red Army in Odessa led a pogrom against the Jews in [the town] of Big Fountain.

Ovsyaniko-Kulikovsky and the writer Kipen happened to be here and told me the details. Fourteen commissars and thirty Jews from among the common people were killed. Many stores were destroyed. The soldiers tore through at night, dragged the victims from their beds, and killed whomever they met. People ran into the steppe or rushed into the sea. They were chased after and fired upon—a genuine hunt, as it were.[7] Kipen saved himself by accident—fortunately he had spent the night not in his home but at the White Flower sanitorium. At dawn a detachment of Red Army soldiers suddenly appeared. "Are there any Jews here?" they asked the watchman. "No, no Jews here." "Swear what you're saying is true!" The watchman swore, and they went on farther. Moisei Gutman, a cabby, was killed. He was a very dear man who moved us from our dacha last fall.

I went by the Duma today. It was very cold and grey. The sea was deserted, the port was dead. The French torpedo boat was far off in its berth, looking very small and somehow lonely, pitiful, and absurd—God knows why the French are staying around here.

What are they expecting, what are they going to do? A crowd of people was standing next to a cannon. Some were upset about

---

7. Kipen's story is most likely true. Anti-Bolshevik Ukrainians took particular pleasure in throwing Jews overboard into rivers and seas. See Lincoln, *Red Victory*, 320.

the Day of Peaceful Insurrection; others were preaching boldly, passionately, and giving it good and hot to those who stood around.

I went along and thought. More accurately, I felt: "If only I could manage to get out of here and go somewhere, perhaps to Italy or to France. But it would be repulsive everywhere—for humankind itself has become repugnant! Life has forced us to feel so sharply, and to look at it, its soul, its loathsome body. What good were our former eyes—how little they saw, even mine!"

Now I'm out in the courtyard. There is night and darkness; rain is pouring down; there's not a person in sight. All of the Kherson Province is in a state of siege. We dare not go out when it gets dark. I'm writing, sitting as though I'm in a fairy-tale dungeon: the entire room flickers with dusk and the fetid soot of the night light. On the table is a new appeal: "Comrades, take heed! We are bringing you the true light of socialism! Quit your drunken gangs, vanquish the parasites once and for all! Cast aside the strangler of the folk masses, the former excise officer, Grigoriev! For he has a weakness for the bottle and owns a home in Elizavetgrad!"[8]

May 3 / 16, 1919
I fight the tension, I try to get out from under it, this intolerable waiting for something to happen—and all in vain. It is especially horrible when I yearn for time to fly by as quickly as possible.

A resolution of the regiment bearing the name of one Starostin:

"We declare that we will collectively enter the struggle against the new uncrowned hangman, Grigoriev, who, like a spider, again wishes to suck all our energy in drunkenness and debauchery!"

The Odessa committee of the Russian People's Government Alliance[9] was arrested (sixteen people in all, including a professor);

---

8. Elizavetgrad (now Kirovgrad) is an important agricultural and industrial center in the Ukraine.

9. The Russian People's Government Alliance (*Russkii narodno-gosu-darstvennyi soiuz*) was one of many political groups liquidated by the Bolsheviks

and they were all shot yesterday evening "because of their overt attempts to disturb the peaceful tranquility of the population."

Imagine! They're worried about the tranquility of the population!

We visited the Varshavskys. We returned home through the dark city; the streets were full of twilight but not as they are during afternoon or sunrise, though now one could hear the sounds of steps in a much sharper way.

May 4 / 17, 1919

The weather is clearing. The courtyard is under a blue sky, and the trees are showing a spring, festivelike splendor; behind it the wall of the house is dazzling white but spotted with dark shadows. A Red Army soldier rode into the yard and tied his stallion to the tree. The animal was black, with a wavy tail that fell to the ground, brilliant markings on his croup, and even grander ones on its back. In the living room, Evgeny [Bukovetsky] was playing the piano. Good God, how painful all this is!

We visited V. A. Rozenberg. He is working in a cooperative; he is living together with his wife in one room. We drank some weak tea and had some dried-up old raisins alongside a lamp that gave off little light. . . . Here's an editor for you, the boss of *Russian News*! He spoke passionately about the "horrors of tsarist censorship!"[1]

May 5 / 18, 1919

In a dream I saw myself on a sea that was milky white in the light blue night. I also saw the pale rose lights of a ship; and I said to myself that I had to remember that the lights were pale rose. What does this all mean?

---

in Odessa. See Iu. Fel'shtinskii, *Krasnyi terror v gody grazhdanskoi voiny* (London, 1992), 244–245.

1. "Tsarist censorship" paled in comparison with the restrictions that the Bolsheviks placed on publications immediately after the Revolution.

A notice from the *Voice of the Red Army*:

"Death to counterrevolutionaries who take part in pogroms! The enemies of the people wish to drown the revolution in Jewish blood. They want the masters to live in storybook mansions and the peasants to go back to the fields, to tending sores on their cows, and to bending their backs for parasites and lazybones. . . ."

A millionaire is getting married in our courtyard. He came in a carriage. They had forty bottles of wine for the feast. Just two months ago a bottle cost twenty-five rubles. What must it cost now, especially when it is forbidden and one can get it only on the sly!

An article by Podvoisky appeared in *Kievan Izvestia*:

"If the black jackals who are *congregating* in Rumania can fulfill their plans, then the fate of the world revolution will be decided. . . . The black band of scoundrels . . . The predatory talons of the Rumanian king and the landowners. . . ." Next an appeal by Rakovsky, which, incidentally, included this item: "Unfortunately the Ukrainian village is just the same as it was in Gogol's time: ignorant, anti-Semitic, illiterate. . . . Commissars bribe, extort, get drunk, and violate the law at every turn. . . . Soviet workers win and lose thousands at cards, and distilleries support the drunkenness."

And then there's a new piece by Gorky, a speech that he gave the other day at an assembly of the Third International[2] in Moscow. Its title was "The Day of the Great Lie."[3] Its contents:

"Yesterday was the day of the great lie. The final day of its power.

"From time immemorial, people, like spiders, have carefully spun a strong web of discreet bourgeois life, which, more and more, sustains itself by lies and greediness. The most cynical falsehood is considered to be an unshakable truth: the individual must live off the flesh and blood of the person next to him.

2. The Third International was established in March 1918 in Moscow and disbanded in May 1943.
3. Gorky's speech, "The Day of the Great Lie" (*"Den' velikoi lzhi"*) was published in the January issue of the journal *Communist International* (*Kommunisticheskii internatsional*) in 1919.

"Only yesterday this kind of thinking led to the insanity of the all-European war, to its nightmarish glow which immediately illuminated all the shocking nakedness of this ancient lie.

"The patience of the peoples of the world was exhausted; the rottenness of existence was destroyed by an explosive force; and life cannot be restored to its old forms.

"This present day burns so brightly; that is why the shadows are so thick!

"Today the great work of liberation has begun. People are being freed from the powerful iron web of the past. The work is like childbirth: terrifying and difficult. . . .

"It just so happens that the Russian people are leading all other nations in this decisive battle. Only yesterday the entire world looked upon them as half-savages, but today these half-savages are like old, experienced warriors. With passion and courage they are going either to victory or death.

"What is now going on in Russia must be understood as a gigantic attempt to realize, in life, in action, the great ideas and words that the teachers of humankind, the sages of Europe have uttered.

"And if upright Russian revolutionaries, individuals who are surrounded by enemies and tormented by hunger, if they are vanquished, then the consequences for this terrible catastrophe will rest heavily on the shoulders of all the revolutionaries of Europe, on the entire working class.

"But the honest heart will not waver, the honest thought will be alien to tempting compromise, the honest hand will not tire of working—the Russian worker believes that his brothers in Europe will not allow Russia to be strangled, that it will not permit the resurrection of everything that is breathing its last, that is disappearing and will disappear!"

And here's a clipping from [the newspaper] *New Life*, dated February 12/25, 1918:

"We have before us a company of adventurists who—because of their own personal interests and because the agony of their dying autocracy has been extended for several weeks—are ready to betray, in a most shameful way, the interests of socialism and the interests of the Russian proletariat, the very same one in whose name they commit outrages on the vacant throne of the Romanovs!"

The only thing we live for is to gather in secret and to exchange news with each other. For us the main source for such counterintelligence is on Khersonskaya Street, at the home of Shchepkina-Kupernik. News from the Bureau of the Ukrainian Press finds its way there. Yesterday it supposedly received a decoded telegram: Petersburg has been taken by the English.[4] Grigoriev is surrounding Odessa and has issued a universal decree in which he acknowledges the soviets but only those that "have fewer than 4 percent of those people who crucified Christ." News from Kiev has supposedly stopped coming completely, since the peasants are being swayed by Grigoriev's slogans[5] and are destroying railways for thousands of miles.

I am not a strong believer in their "ideology." Most likely this will later be seen as a "battle of the people with the Bolsheviks" and be placed on the same level as that of the Volunteer Movement. This is terrible. Of course, communism and socialism are for peasants what the saddle is for the cow; both will drive the people to frenzy. But, most of all, what is going on now is akin to the "thief-like wandering" that Rus' has so loved since the beginning of time, i.e., the wish for the free, pirate's way of life, a wish that has now seized hold of hundreds of thousands of people who are corrupt in every way possible, who have broken away from or have grown unaccustomed to home and work. Less than a decade ago I wrote an epitaph to my stories about the people and their souls, using the words of Iv. Aksakov: "Ancient Rus' has not yet passed us by!"

4. The telegram was not true.
5. In his so-called universal decree or "manifesto," Grigoriev vaunted such slogans as "Ukraine for Ukrainians," "Free Grain Trade," and "Power to the Soviets of the Ukrainian People Without the Communists."

I was correct to have done so. Klyuchevsky notes the extreme "repetitiveness" of Russian history. But to our supreme misfortune, no one has paid any attention to this repetitiveness. The "liberation movement" came into being with lighthearted amazement, with indispensable, obligatory optimism, and with all kinds of meanings and interpretations: "warriors" and writers of realistic populist literature thought one thing; others saw events with a certain kind of mysticism. Everyone "put laurel wreaths on lice-covered heads," to use Dostoevsky's words.[6] Herzen was a thousand times right when he said:

"We have divorced ourselves profoundly from existence. . . . We have become capricious, we do not want to know reality, we continually excite ourselves with our dreams. . . . We endure the punishment of people who come forth from our country's present. . . . Our misfortune has been that we have abrogated the theoretical and practical aspects of life. . . ."[7]

Incidentally, many have found it—and continue to find it—simply disadvantageous *not* to divorce themselves from reality. They needed "young people" and "lice-covered heads" as cannon fodder. They burned incense before youth because youth were passionate; they did likewise to the peasant because he was dark and "unstable." Did many people not know that revolution is only a bloody game in which people merely trade places and which, in the final analysis, only ends up with their going from the frying pan into the fire—even if they manage temporarily to sit, feast, and raise hell where their masters used to be?

Extremely clever and cunning ringleaders knew full well what they were doing when they prepared this insulting sign: "Freedom, brotherhood, equality, socialism, and communism!" And this sign will hang for a long time—as long as these ringleaders do not weigh too heavily on the necks of the people. Of course, thousands

6. Bunin is quoting from the character Stepan Verkhovensky, from an early chapter in Dostoevsky's *The Possessed* (*Besy*), published in 1872.
7. Bunin is quoting from a diary excerpt by Herzen on September 17, 1844.

of boys and girls have cried out this ditty in a rather simplehearted
way:

The folk, the people, the nation
Will lead us to salvation!

And, of course, most of them have sung this rather silly thing
with their deep bass voices:

The cliff and the colossus
All that Stepan[8] thought for us
He'll retell to the brave ones
Who'll glow like phosphorus. . . .

"But what was all this after all?" Dostoevsky asked. "It was the
most innocent, sweet, and liberal chatter. . . . We were captivated
not by socialism but by the emotional side of socialism. . . ." But
this too is the underground after all; and in this underground the
right person knows exactly where he must direct his steps and
which qualities of the Russian people are extremely useful to him.
And this Stepan knew very well.

"A people—young, unbalanced, perpetually dissatisfied, and
spiritually dark—readily ceded to disturbances, waverings, and in-
stability. . . . And they did it again in an extremely grand
way. . . . The spirit of materialism, of unrestrained will, of coarse
self-interest wafted destructively over Rus'. . . . The hands of the
righteous were paralyzed, and those of evil men were untied to
commit all kinds of atrocities. . . . Crowds of outcasts, the scum of
society, devastated their own homes under the banners of the leaders, impostors, hypocrites: under the guise of leading degenerates,
criminals, and ambitious people. . . ."

This is from Solovyov, about the Time of Troubles.[9] Here is
an excerpt from Kostomarov, about Sten'ka Razin:

8. The reference is to Sten'ka Razin.
9. Bunin is quoting from Solovyov's multivolumed *History of Russia from
the Most Ancient Times* (*Istoriia Rossii s drevneishikh vremen*), published between
1851 and 1879. The Time of Troubles (*Smutnoe vremia*) (1598–1613) refers to the

"The people followed Sten'ka. They were deceived and in-flamed by him, for they did not understand much of what he had in mind. . . . There were promises, bribes, lures, but always with traps all along the way. . . . All types of Asians and pagans rose up— Zyrians, Mordavians, Chuvash, Cheremis, and Bashkirs[1]—people who rose up and slashed, not even knowing why they did so. . . . There were Sten'ka's 'flattering letters'[2]—'I will go to the bo-yars, the officials, and other powers-to-be, and I will bring about equality among them. . . .'[3]

"But full-scaled pillaging was the result. . . . Sten'ka, his asso-ciates, and his armies were drunk from wine and blood. . . . They hated laws, society, religion, everything that checked personal in-centive. . . . They breathed vengeance and envy. . . . They were fugitives, idlers, and thieves. . . . All these bastards and scum Sten'ka promised freedom in everything; but in reality he made them debtors, complete slaves. He tortured and executed them for the slightest disobedience; he honored everyone with the term 'brother,' and so they all fell prostrate before him. . . ."

Don't think the Lenins of this world didn't know and count on all this![4]

From *Red Army Star*:[5] "Wilson, one of the greatest scoundrels

---

interregnum between the Ryurokivichan and the Romanov dynasties. In his stud-ies of this period, Solovyov focused on the moral decline of the nation. It should also be noted that Bunin was not alone in comparing the current Russian crisis to the Time of Troubles. See Lincoln, *Red Victory*, 81.

1. The Zyrians are a tribe well known as traders in northern Siberia. The Mordavians and the Cheremis belong to one of the Finnic peoples of the Mid-dle Volga region. The Bashkirs are primarily a Turkish group who live in south-western Siberia and Central Asia.

2. Razin's letters were so-called because they "flattered" the people to re-volt. See I. Stepanov, *Krest'ianskaia voina v Rossii v 1610–1611 gg.* (Leningrad, 1966), 8–9.

3. Bunin is citing Kostomarov's *The Rebellion of Sten'ka Razin* (*Bunt Sten'ki Razina*), published in 1858.

4. Lenin took great care to stress his kinship with Sten'ka Razin in the strug-gle against oppression in Russia. See Lincoln, *Red Victory*, 76.

5. *Red Army Star* (*Krasnoarmeiskaia zvezda*) was a newspaper published by

and spongers among the bourgeois, is demanding an invasion of the north of Russia.[6] Our answer: Get your paws off! We will go as one to prove to the dumbfounded world. . . . Any lackeys will know in their souls that they *have fallen overboard and that they are far beyond our anchor of salvation.*"

Joyous rumors—Nikolaev[7] has been taken; Grigoriev is close at hand. . . .

May 8 / 21, 1919
The *Odessa Communist*[8] has published an entire poem about Grigoriev:

At night the tired Hetman sleeps
But he has a "terrible" dream
He sees a rifle, the proletariat.
And he's ready to scream.
The folk have a burning glance,
And for the while they keep mum.
But then they horrify "pan" by saying:
"Know that you are traitor, scum.
You think you've figured out
How to feather your bed,
But the golden Hetman crown
Will not rest on your head!"

---

the political division of the Revolutionary Military Council for the Red Army on the eastern front in 1919.

6. This was not true. In fact, President Woodrow Wilson, facing the failure of the limited American engagement at Archangel in the Russian north, as well as severe domestic criticism for the Allied intervention, had decided to withdraw American forces from Russia as soon as possible. See D. Foglesong, *America's Secret War Against Bolshevism: U.S. Intervention in the Russian Civil War, 1917–1920* (Chapel Hill, 1995), 188–230.

7. Grigoriev's rebels occupied many cities in the Ukraine, including Nikolaev and Kherson.

8. *Odessa Communist* (*Odesskii kommunist*) was a newspaper published from 1918 to 1920.

I went out to get a shave and had to take cover from the rain under an awning on Ekaterinskaya Street. Next to me stood an individual eating a radish. He was one of those who "firmly holds the red banner of world revolution in his calloused hands," i.e., a peasant from around Odessa. He kept complaining that the harvest was good but that he and others had planted too little. He very much feared the Bolsheviks: "Let the bastard Grigoriev come and lock 'em up!" He said this about twenty times. At the end of Elizavetskaya Street I saw about a hundred soldiers who had assembled on the sidewalk and with rifles and machine guns in their hands. I turned off on Khersonskaya Street, and there on the corner of Preobrazhenskaya, I saw the same thing. . . . There are rumors all over town that the "revolution has begun!" One could simply get sick from all these endless lies.

We took a walk after dinner. I cannot express how tired I am of Odessa; I'm simply devoured by angst. And there's absolutely no way for me to get out of here! Gloomy blue clouds stand on the horizon. The sounds of wild music and dancing blast from the windows of a splendid home next to the police station, across from Catherine's statue. I also hear the despairing cry of one of the dancers, as if he had been stabbed with a knife: a-ah!—the cry of a drunken savage. All the surrounding homes have their lights on; everyone is busy doing something.

It's evening. But I don't dare turn on any lights or go outside! Oh, how terrible these nights are!

From the *Odessa Communist*:

"The Ochakovsky Garrison[9] realizes that, as evidenced by the assault of the arrogant drunkard Grigoriev, the counterrevolution never rests, and also that it has raised its head with complete impudence by pouring poison into the heart of the worker and the peasant, and by setting one nation against another. Also, the drunkard Grigoriev's slogan: 'Beat the Jews and save the Ukraine!' has brought terrible harm to the Red Army and hastened the demise

9. Ochakov is a small city in the Ukraine about thirty miles northeast of Odessa.

of the socialist Revolution! And so we affirm: to send our curses to the drunkard Grigoriev and to his nationalist friends!"

The *Odessa Communist* also writes: "Having discussed the question of the members of the White Guard whom we have taken captive, we demand that they be shot forthwith, for otherwise they will continue to carry on their dark work and to spill blood in vain. Already way too much blood has been shed, thanks to the capitalists and their stooges!"

Alongside was this doggerel:

The Communist worker
Knows where power is:
For if he loves labor
A living spring is his . . .
He sees bastards rot,
He doesn't accept nations.
He'll give all he's got
To Soviet organizations!

May 6 / 19, 1919
Ioann, i.e., Ivan the peasant from Tambov, the saint and miracle worker who lived not so very long ago—in the last century—once prayed before the icon of Prelate Dmitry Rostovsky, the great and well-known bishop, and said to him: "Mityushka,[1] dear one, hear me!"

This very same Ioann was tall but somewhat hunched. His face was swarthy, his beard was thin, and his hair long and sparse. He would compose simplehearted verse like this:

Doors won't open
And windows are far
For those who don't pray
To God their tsar.
So return to him
Wherever you are,

1. Mityushka is the diminutive form of Dmitry.

ODESSA 1919

Quietly, simply,
Like a shining star. . . .

Where has all this gone, what has happened to it all?[2]
"The holiest of callings," the calling of the "human individual," has been discredited as never before. The Russian person has
also been discredited—no matter what, no matter where our eyes
fall, it's as if Nevsky's "ice crusades"[3] had never happened! How
terrible are the old Russian chronicles: records of endless sedition,
insatiable self-interest, ferocious struggles for power, deceptive kissings of the cross, flights to Lithuania and to the Crimea "for the
rising up of non-Christians for their own native ancestral homes,"
the obsequious missives to one another ("I bow to the earth, as
your faithful slave") only to fool someone, to hurl evil and shameless reproaches from one brother to another. . . . You have abandoned words that belong to another time:
"Shame and disgrace to you: You wish to abandon your father's blessings, your native graves, your sacred fatherland, and your
Orthodox faith in our Lord, Jesus Christ!"[4]

May 9 / 22, 1919
At night I am plagued by anxious dreams about trains and seas and
very pretty landscapes, but they leave me morbid and sad—and
tensely expecting something. . . . I also see a huge talking horse. It
was saying something related to my poem on Svyatogor and Il'ya,[5]

2. Bunin's description of Ioann is accurate. See, for instance, *Istoriko-
statisticheskoe opisanie tambovskoi eparkhii* (Tambov, 1861), 293–294.
3. A reference to the famed "battle on ice" in which Alexander Nevsky and
his troops defeated the Livonian army on Lake Peipus (Lake Chud to the Russians) on April 5, 1242, and as immortalized by Sergei Eisenstein in his 1939 film
Alexander Nevsky.
4. Bunin is paraphrasing the famous correspondence between Ivan IV and
Prince Andrei Kurbsky, which was written at various intervals between 1564 and
1579, and which illustrated the momentous conflict between Muscovite rulers
and Russian princes over the nature of national government at this time.
In this excerpt, Ivan castigates Kurbsky for defecting to Lithuania on April
30, 1564.
5. Svyatogor and Il'ya (Muromets) are well-known heroes of the so-called
Kievan cycle of Russian *byliny* or "epic folktales."

but in an ancient language; and it was all so terrible that I woke
up and mentally repeated these verses for a long time:

On long-maned, shaggy steeds
With stirrups, gold and wide,
Two brothers rode—one younger, one older,
One, two, three days in stride.
They see a trough in the field,
A coffin and a big one at that;
Deep, with hollowed-out oak,
And a roof, black, heavy, and flat.
Svyatogor opens it, lies down
And jokes: "It fits me just fine!
But help me out, Il'ya,
For today's not my time!"
Il'ya, laughing, grabs the top
And pulls up with all his might,
But he soon finds he has to stop;
For the black lid's way too tight.
A voice from the coffin—"Get a sword!"
Il'ya goes for it—but seized by spite
That fills his mind and heart
He hacks the coffin to pieces
But cannot break it apart.
For wherever he strikes
There appears an iron brace;
Svyatogor in his gravelike crypt
Will never lift his face!

I wrote this in '16.

We too are crawling into a gravelike trough, but we do so mer-
rily, in a joking frame of mind. . . .

Again the newspapers say: "Death to the drunkard Grigoriev!"
Further on, though, they adopt a more serious tone: "*This is not
the time for words!* The issue at hand is neither the dictatorship of

the proletariat nor the building of socialism, but the most elementary achievements of October. . . . On one hand, the peasants affirm that they will struggle for world revolution with every drop of their blood; but, on the other, everyone knows that they have attacked Soviet trains and have killed our best comrades with axes and pitchforks. . . ."

A new list of people who have been shot has been published—"by way of conducting affairs in the life of the red terror." Then a small article:

"It was a happy and joyous time at Club Trotsky. The main hall of what used to be the Garrison Assembly, where whole groups of generals formerly huddled together, was now filled to overflowing with members of the Red Army. The closing music portion of the evening was especially successful. People first sang the 'International.' Then Comrade Kronkardi stirred and delighted the audience by imitating a barking dog, a chirping chick, a singing nightingale, right up to a bad-tempered pig. . . ."

The "chirping" of a chick and the "song of a nightingale" and other animals—which, it turns out, everyone there also did "right up to" the pig—this is something I think even the devil himself could not write up. Why was the pig the only "bad-tempered" creature there, and why was the "International" performed right before Kronkardi began imitating such an animal?

Of course, all this is "pornographic literature." But isn't this "porn"—its swinelike and international aspects—the essence of almost all Russia, of almost all Russian life, of almost all Russian writing? And will it ever be possible for us to break from this "porn"? But then, isn't all this pornographic writing tied by blood to almost all of the "new" Russian literature? After all, people have long published—not just anywhere but in "leading" journals— things like the following:

The garden flowers have already bloomed . . .
The flax has been turned into rope . . .
I go to sort our kernels of wheat . . .

But for that woman you must not mope . . .
For now isn't it good all around?
One should not set the queen to rest . . .
I'd describe it all, but can words be found?

The decline and destruction of the word, with its hidden sense and its sound and weight, have been going on in literature for a long time.

"Are you going home?" I once asked the writer Osipovich as I was saying farewell to him on the street.

He answered: "Ain't goin' nowhere!"

But what happened when I told him that one can't say that in Russian? He didn't understand, for he had no feeling for the language.

"And how am I supposed to say it? You'd probably say: 'No, I'm not going anywhere?' What's the difference?"

He did not understand the difference. Of course, he's got an excuse; he's from Odessa. He can also be excused if only because, in the end, he had an inkling that he had done something wrong and promised to remember that one must say, "No, I'm not going anywhere."

Now, though, our literature has such an incredible number of self-assured, impudent fellows who pass themselves off as all-knowing connoisseurs of the word! How many champions do we have of an ancient ("fresh and juicy") folk tongue? How many in-dividuals are there now who never say a simple word but who ex-haust themselves with their arch-Russianness!

The latter is now becoming quite fashionable (the result of all these international "searchings," that is, of all these Young Turk imitations of every kind of Western model). How many writers of poetry and prose are creating a nauseating Russian language! How many of them are taking the most precious folk legends, fairy tales, and "golden words" and shamelessly passing them off as their own! How many of them are defiling these legends, tales, and words with their own retellings and additions, rooting about in regional dictionaries and coming up with the most obscene arch-Russianness, a language that no one speaks now or ever spoke in old Russia, and that is even impossible to read! How our Moscow and Petersburg salons are host to all the Klyuevs and Esenins who even dress like pilgrims and nice Russian lads, but who sing through their nose about "dear little candles," and "sweet little rivers," or who pretend to be someone or something with their "sweet bold little heads"?

The Russian language is becoming fractured; the people have made it sick. I once asked a peasant what he fed his dog. He answered:

"What d'ya mean 'what'? Nothin'. He eats whatever. I got an eatable dog."

This happens to the language whenever the folk get the upper hand. But what if it gets the upper hand now?

May 10 / 23, 1919
From the newspapers: "Kolchak has lost Belebey[6] and is flogging peasants to death. . . . Mikhail Romanov is riding with him.[7] . . . They are traveling on an old troika: autocracy, orthodoxy, nationality.[8] . . . They are conducting pogroms against the Jews and carrying vodka in their hands. . . . Kolchak has entered into the service of international predators . . . so that the cold-blooded, *fattened* hand of Lloyd George[9] can cause an exhausted country to shudder. . . . Kolchak looks forward to the day that *he'll be able* to drink the blood of the workers. . . ."

---

6. Belebey is a small town in the eastern part of European Russia.

7. Mikhail Romanov, the brother of Nicholas II, renounced the throne on March 15, 1917. He was arrested in February 1918 and shot by the Bolsheviks on July 13, 1918.

8. "Autocracy, orthodoxy, and nationality" was the national policy pursued by the reactionary Nicholas I in the second quarter of the nineteenth century.

9. At this time Lloyd George was prime minister of England. (He resigned in 1922.) Toward Russia he pursued a somewhat contradictory policy in which he sought to assist anti-Bolshevik forces, engage in commerce with the Soviets, and

Next to this is an article scolding and threatening the Left SRS:[1]

"These hacks are becoming such fussy little prisses. For a while they've taken up dancing and are . . . even smearing their mugs with cold cream. But no matter how they clean themselves up, their faces still show the same kulaklike freckles. . . ."

The people who write these things are worried not only about the peasants who have been "beaten to death" by Kolchak but also about the Germans: "The vile comedy in Versailles is over, but even Scheidemann's[2] followers insist that the conditions set by the Allied fleecers and the bourgeois sharks are completely unacceptable. . . ."

We took a walk along Gimnazicheskaya Street. A charming springlike rain greeted us almost the entire way; and there was also a marvelous springlike sky among the storm clouds. But I almost fainted twice. I have to stop writing these notes; jotting them down, I irritate my heart even more.

Again there are rumors—now ten transports of what the people around here are calling the "c'lored'" troops (i.e., "colored" in Russian)[3] are supposedly coming to rescue us.

A person who is rather close to Podvoisky says that "he's a dim-

---

uphold the independence of the newly formed states that had recently sprung up on the periphery of the former Russian empire. He also openly advocated the dismemberment of Russia, thereby following in the footsteps of Disraeli, who had seen a great and powerful Russia as a menace to Great Britain's interests in India, Persia, and Afghanistan.

1. The Left Social Revolutionaries became a separate political party in November 1917. Throughout the civil war they advocated terrorism and uprisings against the Bolsheviks, having condemned both the Treaty of Brest-Litovsk and the Bolsheviks' readiness to incite internecine war among Russia's peasants. In July 1918 the Left Social Revolutionaries staged an unsuccessful revolt against the Bolsheviks.

2. At this time Philip Scheidemann was the first chancellor of the Weimar Republic, but he chose to resign in June 1919 rather than approve the Versailles Treaty.

3. Bunin is most likely referring to the so-called "Greens," i.e., anarchist peasants and deserters who stood apart from both the Red and White armies, and

witted seminarian with piglike eyes and a long nose, and that he is also a maniac when it comes to discipline.

May 11 / 24, 1919
Slogans in the classic Russian style:
"Forward, native sons, do not count *the corpses* around you!" One can conclude only one thing from the news of Grigoriev's "pogrom"—that almost all of the Ukraine has been seized by *Grigorievshchina.*[4]

Yesterday people were saying that Trotsky himself had come to Odessa. But it turns out that he was in Kiev. "The arrival of the leader was an inspiration to all workers and peasants of the Ukraine. . . . The leader delivered a speech in the name of all the folk millions, at a time when the backbone of bourgeois confidence has been broken, and we hear the cracking in its voice. . . . The leader spoke to the people from the balcony. . . ."

I am now reading Le Notre.[5] Saint-Just, Robespierre, Couthon[6] . . . Lenin, Trotsky, Derzhinsky . . . Who are the most base, bloodthirsty, and vile? Our Muscovites, of course; nonetheless, those from Paris are right up there too.

Le Notre says that Couthon was a dictator, a very close asso-

---

who opposed the former while hoping for a truce with the latter. They took cover in the "greenery" of forests (hence their name) and sprang up in the mountains of the North Caucasus and along the Black Sea coasts. See Kenez, *Civil War,* 239–245, and Brinkley, *Volunteer Army,* 225.

4. This was true. In fact, Grigoriev's rebellion was so extensive that it helped Denikin's troops begin an offensive in the southern Ukraine and prevented the prompt transfer of Red Army troops to the Rumanian front to support the Hungarian Soviet Republic in 1919.

5. The book in question is Le Notre's *Paris Revolutionnaire: Vieilles maisons, vieux papiers,* which was repeatedly published between the years 1901 and 1909, and which was dedicated to the leading figures of the French Revolution.

6. Saint-Just was a Jacobin and a member of the Committee of Public Safety. He was famous for his energy, oratorical ability, military leadership, and political role in the French Reign of Terror. Couthon was also a Jacobin and a member of the Committee of Public Safety. He was executed together with Robespierre.

ciate of Robespierre, the Attila of Lyons, a legislator and a sadist, who sent thousands of absolutely innocent souls to the guillotine, "a passionate friend of the People and of Virtue"; and, as is also well known, a cripple who had lost the use of his legs. But how and under what circumstances did he lose his legs? It so happened that it was a rather shameless affair. He was spending the night with his mistress, a woman whose husband was out of town. Everything was going along splendidly until suddenly they heard a knock at the door and the steps of the returning husband. Couthon leapt out of bed, jumped out the window to the courtyard below—and landed in a cesspool. He stayed there till dawn, but he lost the use of his legs forever—and he was paralyzed for the rest of his life.[7]

People are saying that a pogrom against the Jews is going on in Nikolaev. Apparently it is far from fact that all the peasants of the Ukraine "are welcoming the arrival of the leader."

The tone of the newspapers, though, is getting more strident and insolent. Was it all that long ago that their people were writing that "it is not the business of Bolsheviks to crucify Christ who, being the Savior, also rose up against the rich"? Now they are singing other songs. Here are several lines from the *Odessa Communist*:

"The spit of such a famous wizard as Jesus Christ must also have an appropriate magic force. Many people, who do not even recognize Christ's miracles, continue to sentimentalize over the morality of his teaching, trying to show that the 'truth' of Christ is head and shoulders over their own moral worth. But in reality such a view is completely false and can be explained only by an ignorance of history and a lack of intellectual development."

May 12 / 25, 1919
Again there are flags, processions. Again, there is a holiday—"a day

7. The more accepted version is that a disease (probably meningitis) had paralyzed Couthon's legs.

of solidarity of the proletariat with the members of the Red army."
The place is rife with drunken soldiers, sailors, and tramps. . . .

Today they carried a corpse past us (the deceased was not a
Bolshevik). "Blessed are those, O Lord, whom you have chosen
and taken onto Yourself. . . ." Truly, the dead are the blessed ones.

The rumor is that Trotsky has arrived and that he "was greeted
like a tsar."[8]

May 14 / 27, 1919
"Kolchak and Mikhail Romanov are bringing vodka and pogroms
to the people. . . ." Kolchak is in neither Nikolaev nor Elizavetgrad,
but one reads this nonetheless:
"There is a savage pogrom against the Jews going on in Nikolaev. . . . Elizavetgrad has also suffered terribly at the hands of the
dark masses. People are reckoning the material losses in the millions. Stores, private apartments, small shops, and even refresh-
ment counters have been leveled. Soviet depots have also been
destroyed. It will take Elizavetgrad many years to recover from this
disaster!"
There's more:
"The head of the soldiers who rose up in Odessa and then
left it is threatening Ananiev—more than a thousand people have
been killed and stores have been looted. . . ."
"A pogrom that is going against the Jews in Zhmerinka is *just
like the one that took place* in Znamenka.[9] . . ."
The Bloks of the world look upon all this and say, "The people have fallen under the sway of the music of the Revolution—
listen, listen to the music of the Revolution!"

---

8. At the time Trotsky was not far from Odessa, though he never entered
the city.
9. Ananiev is a small city one hundred miles north of Odessa. Zhmerinka
is situated one hundred miles further northwest. Znamenka is approximately two
hundred miles northeast.

Nighttime, the same day
I was looking through my briefcase, and I tore up several poems and stories that I never finished. I already regret what I did. All this from grief, a sense of hopelessness (though this is not the first time I have felt like this). I also hid the various notes I made about the years '17 and '18.

Oh, these nightly furtive hidings and rehidings of papers and money! Over the years millions of Russians have endured this corruption, this degradation. And how many treasures will people find someday! This entire era will become a fairy tale, a legend. . . .

The summer of '17. It is twilight. A group of peasants are standing on the street next to a hut. They are talking about "the grandmother of the Russian Revolution."[1] The owner of the hut says in a measured way: "I've heard about this old lady for quite some time. She's a soothsayer, that's for sure. The word on her is that she's been predicting all these goings-on for the past fifty years. But God help us, she's really beastly looking: fat, angry, with very small, penetrating eyes—I once saw her portrait in a feuilleton. She was chained up in a stockade for forty-two years, but they couldn't break her. She was never left alone day or night, but they couldn't hold her back: even in the stockade she managed to get hold of a million rubles![2]

"Now she's buying people for support, promising to give them land and not to draft them for war. But what's in it for me? I don't need to own the land. I'm better off leasing it because I don't have the capital for manure and other things. And they won't take me into the army 'cause I'm too old. . . ."

As it turned out, someone in a shirt that made him look all white in the twilight—"the pride and joy of the Revolution"—dared to interrupt, saying:

1. The person in question is Ekaterina Dmitrievna Breshko-Breshkovskaya.
2. Throughout her life in Russia, Breshko-Breshkovskaya endured repeated arrest and imprisonment. Although she did indeed spend some forty years in tsarist prisons, the stories here are untrue—the stuff of tabloid accounts of her life and work.

"Such a provocateur in our country, we should arrest and shoot him right off!"

But the peasant objected quietly but firmly:

"You may be a sailor, but you're also a fool. I'm old enough to be your father. I remember when you used to run past my hut without your pants. What kind of a commissar are you when you're always around the girls and look up their dresses right in broad daylight? Just wait, just you wait, pal—someday there'll be holes in your official-looking pants; the money you've stolen you'll waste on drink; and you'll be asking shepherds for work! As I said, pal, you'll be arresting my pig. It won't be like laughing at the masters! I'm not afraid of you and all your Zhukovs!"

(By Zhukov, he meant Guchkov.)

For no reason at all, Sergei Klimov added:

"Yeah, Petrograd, we should have given it up a long time ago. There's only chaos going on there. . . ."

Girls scream in the park:

Love the Whites, with curly strands
With silver watches in their hands. . . .

From under a hill comes a crowd of boys carrying accordions and a balalaika:

We are comrade hedgehogs,
Our boots show we're no punks,
But we love to drink and have a bite
And go about drunk as skunks. . . .

I think: "No, these Bolsheviks will be a bit smarter than the heads of the Provisional Government were! Not for nothing do they keep up their insolence; they know their public well."

Alongside a village hut, a deserter-soldier sits smoking and singing:

"The night is dark, like two minutes. . . ."

I asked him: What kind of nonsense is this? What does this "like two minutes" mean?

"What can I say? I give it a sincere try and sing: 'like two minutes.' It all depends on the stress."

A neighbor chimes in: "Oy, pal, when the Germans get here, are we gonna get it!"

Another replies: "There's only one thing I fear—to be under the Germans, to be really at their mercy!"

A huge gathering in a garden alongside a hunter's cabin. A watchguard, a worldly-wise peasant with a very fine sense of speech, is passing along a rumor that a mare twenty miles long has fallen from the sky somewhere near the Volga.

Turning to me, he says: "Ginuin' nonsense, huh, *barin?*"

His friend ecstatically recounts his "revolutionary" past. In 1906 he was sitting in a stockade for breaking into houses—and the best memory of his time there, the one thing he talked about constantly, was that: "Any wedding there was a very merry affair, and the lamb stews were excellent!"

He went on to say: "When I was in jail, it was cust'mary that the political prisoners were on the topmost floor and their assistants were on the second. They were afraid of no one, these political ones; they would swear the foulest things at the warden himself, but in the evenings they would sing. We were at their mercy. . . .

"One of these officials the tsar himself had once ordered to be hanged; and he had even gotten the most terrible hangman from the Synod[3] to do the job. But then this official got pardoned. Another time this new head warden came to visit the officials. He was a third-rate figure at the tsar's court who had just passed his preparatory exams. He came and right away went out carousing with the staff: he first had a huge dinner, then sent the village constable for a gramophone—and then they all poured out into the

3. The Synod, or more accurately the "Holy Synod," was the central administrative organ of the Russian Orthodox Church from 1721 to 1917.

street. The warden had eaten and drunk so much that he could not put one foot in front of the other; the constables had to carry him along in a sleigh. . . . He pr'mised to give each of us twenty kopecks, a half a pound of Turkish tobacco, and two pounds of bread made from sifted flour; but, of course, he was lyin' up his sleeve. . . ."

May 15 / 28, 1919
I go for walks and listen carefully to what people are saying on the streets, around the gates, in the market. The air is filled with pervasive spite toward the "communes" and the Jews. The most vicious anti-Semites are the workers in Ropit (Russian Steamship Society).[4] But what scoundrels they are! Every minute they're being bought off with a sop here and a present there. Three-quarters of the people are like that: for crumbs or the right to pillage and rob, they'll give up their conscience, soul, and God. . . .

I walked through the market—and encountered dirt, smells, poverty. I saw Ukies (males and females) at least a hundred years old, thin oxen, and antediluvian carts—and amidst all this, posters and calls for people to join the struggle for the Third International. Of course, even the most mangy, stupid Bolshevik could not help understand all this nonsense. Even they, I imagine, must often be rolling with laughter.

From the *Odessa Communist*:

> With bayonets we'll kill the hellish hydra,
> And then we'll be happy and gay!
> For if we don't, they'll surface quickly
> And come back to life right away.
> Like parasites they'll come and live,
> And suck our blood night and day.

---

4. Ropit (*Russkoe Obshchestvo Parakhodstva i Torgovli*) or the Russian Society for Steamship Navigation and Trade was founded in 1856 and was the largest monopoly of its type in Russia before 1917. It was nationalized in 1918.

The pharmacies are being pillaged: everything is closed, "nationalized and to take inventory." God forbid we get sick!

As if I were in an asylum, I'm lying down and rereading Plato's "Symposium," sometimes looking about with perplexed and, of course, crazed eyes. . . .

For some reason I recall Prince Kropotkin (a famous anarchist). I once visited him in Moscow. He was an absolutely enchanting old man, a real society type; but he was also a complete child, and a cruel one at that.

Kosciusko is being called "the defender of *all kinds* of freedom." This is remarkable. He was a specialist, a professional person. And a terrible individual.[5]

May 16 / 29, 1919
As far as I can make out, the Bolsheviks are doing poorly both around the Don region and beyond the Volga. May God help us!

I've just finished reading a biography of the poet Polezhaev, and I've been greatly moved—it was painful and sad and sweet (not because of Polezhaev, of course). Yes, I am the last who feels this past, the time of our fathers and forefathers. . . .

It's been drizzling on and off. There's a cloud high in the sky, the sun is peeping out, and birds chirp sweetly in bright yellow-green acacia trees in the courtyard. I keep having snatches of thoughts and memories, of things that are truly gone forever. . . . I remember a small place called Toadstool Forest—a backwoods, a small birch tree, and grass and flowers that were as high as your belt—and how I once ran through them in the same drizzle that we're having now, and also how I breathed in the sweetness of the birches and the wheat and the fields; I think of all, all the charm of Russia. . . .

5. Within the context of *Cursed Days,* Bunin may be objecting to the fact that French revolutionaries had named Kosciusko an honorary citizen of their country in 1792; or that Kosciusko had appealed to both the Girondists and the Jacobins for help in the struggle of Poland against Russia the following year.

Nikolai Filippovich[6] was run off his estate (near Odessa). Not long ago he was also run out of his apartment in the city. He went to church and prayed up a storm—it was the feast day of his guardian angel. Then he went to talk to the Bolsheviks about his apartment—and died right there on the spot. It was decided to bury him at his estate. So now he lies in eternal rest in his native haunts, amidst all his loved ones. A hundred years will pass—and will there be anyone then who, when by Nikolai's grave, will feel his time? No, never, no one. The same goes for my time as well. But what if I will not be laid to rest with my loved ones. . . ?

"Popov has been searching through the university archives to find information on the Polezhaev affair. . . ."[7] Why was Popov so interested in Polezhaev? All from a yearning to impugn the reputation of Nicholas I.

The Murids[8] were suppressed along with their leader, Kazi-Mullah. Kazi's grandfather had been a fugitive Russian soldier. Kazi himself was an individual of average height, with pockmarks on his face, a thin beard, and eyes that were bright and penetrating. He killed his own father by pouring boiling oil down his throat. Then he sold vodka, proclaimed himself a prophet, and undertook a holy war. . . . How many rebels and leaders have been like this one!

May 17 / 30, 1919
The Whites have apparently taken Pskov, Polotsk, Dvinsk, and

---

6. It was at Nikolai Filippovich Shishkov's dacha that the Bunins lived when they first arrived in Odessa.

7. Polezhaev's 1825 poem "Sashka" was considered so seditious by tsarist censors that it led to the poet's impressment into the Russian armed forces the following year. The article in question is entitled "New Information on Polezhaev" ("*Novye svedeniia o Polezhaeve*"), published in 1881.

8. In Muslim countries, Murids are individuals who dedicate themselves to Islam and who seek to master the fundamentals of mystical Sufism.

Vitebsk. . . . Denikin has also supposedly taken Izyum and is mercilessly pursuing the Bolsheviks. . . . But what if it's not true?[9]

Desertion from the Bolsheviks has been going on at a terrible rate. In Moscow they have even had to come up with a "central office for deserters."[1]

May 21 / June 3, 1919
Ioffe was in Odessa—"in order to inform the Entente[2] that we will be appealing to the proletariat of all countries . . . in order to nail the Entente to the pillar. . . ."

What are they going to appeal about?

I heard this about Ioffe:

"He's a prominent *barin*, a great lover of comfort, wine, cigars, and women. He's also a wealthy individual—with a steam mill in Simferopol and with Ioffe-Rabinovich automobiles. He's very ambitious. Every five minutes he says: 'When I was ambassador in Berlin. . . .' He's a handsome man, your typical well-known woman's type of doctor. . . ."

The person who told me this was secretly in love with him.

May 23 / June 5, 1919
The *Odessa Alarm*[3] is requesting information about the fate of these missing people: Valya Zloy, Misha Mrachny, Furmanchika,

---

9. Pskov is an old historic city in northwestern Russia. Dvinsk (renamed Daugavpils in 1920) is a city in Latvia. Polotsk and Vitebsk are cities in Belarus. The rumors of their capture are true. Izyum is a small city in the eastern Ukraine. The rumor of its capture is in fact false. Denikin was then in the Caucasus.

1. According to the first edition of *The Great Soviet Encyclopedia*, there were more than 2.8 million deserters from the Russian army between 1919 and 1920. Of these, approximately 1.5 million "voluntarily returned to the front." A central committee "to halt desertion" was founded late in 1918.

2. The Entente is the name frequently applied to the collaboration of Britain, France, and Russia in the years 1907–1917.

3. The *Odessa Alarm* (*Odesskii narbat*) was a newspaper run by the Odessa Federation of Anarchistic Groups in 1919.

and Muravchika.[4] . . . It also has this obituary about some Yashen'ka:

"You, too, have perished, splendid Yashen'ka . . . like a luxu-
rious flower which has just opened its petals . . . like the ray of a
winter sun . . . indignant at the slightest injustice, rising up against
oppression and force, you became a sacrifice of that wild horde
that is destroying everything valuable in humankind. . . . Sleep quietly, Yashen'ka, we will seek your revenge!"

What wild horde? And what and whom are they seeking revenge for? The obituary also goes on to say that Yashen'ka was a
sacrifice of "that universal scourge, venereal disease."

The walls on Deribasovskaya Street have new pictures on
them. In one, a sailor and a soldier of the Red Army, together with
a Cossack and a peasant, are twirling a repulsive green toad with
goggling eyes at the end of a rope—a symbol for the bourgeois.
Underneath is this inscription: "You've been crushing us with your
fat belly." In another a huge peasant waves a club while, over him,
a hydra raises its toothy, bloodstained heads. The heads all have
crowns on them. The largest of these is that of the terrible, deathly,
mournful, resigned Nicholas II. He has a bluish face with a crown
off to the side of his head. From under it blood flows in streams
down the cheeks of his face.[5] . . . But the editorial staff of "Agit-
Enlightenment,"[6] which includes many acquaintances of mine,
tell me they have been called upon to ennoble art. They sit and

4. Most likely these are assumed names, i.e., *"zloi"* ("evil"), *"mrachnyi"*
("gloomy"), *"furman"* ("driver"), and *"muravei"* ("ant").
5. Of such "hydras," Muromtseva-Bunina wrote on March 25, 1919: "All the
posters are now being drawn in absolutely realistic tones—just like pictures from
tobacco or cigarette boxes. This is what the public wants. The citizens still have
not taken to Cubist art. The inscriptions under these pictures are milder in
tone. . . . The posters keep showing the Red soldiers beating up fat generals. . . .
"A huge poster in the middle of the square: A five-headed snake, two heads
have been chopped off . . . and a knife hangs over a third.
" 'Take a look at that,' a woman in a kerchief says to her husband, nudg-
ing him with her elbow. 'I have never seen a snake with five heads. . . .'
"The hydra of the counterrevolution!" See Grin, *Ustami*, 255–256.
6. So-called "agitation-enlightenment centers" (*"agitatsionno-prosvetitel'nye*

meet, think up things to do, and coopt new members like Osipovich and Professor Varneke—and then they eat their rations of moldy bread, spoiled herring, and rotten potatoes. . . .

May 24 / June 6, 1919
I went for a walk. It had stopped raining and was warm out. The sun was nowhere to be seen, but the verdure of the trees was soft and lush, festive and joyous. The pillars of the buildings had these huge posters on them:

"The hall of the Proletkult has a huge exhibit going on. There will be prizes after the show: one for the most delicate leg, another for the prettiest eyes. Modern-style kiosks will benefit unemployed speculators. There will also be a closed kissing booth (lips and legs) a 'red' tavern, games with electricity, a cotillion, paper streamers, two orchestras playing military music, and an armed guard. Lighting has been secured; closing will be 6 a.m. old style. The hostess for the evening will be the spouse of the commander of the Third Soviet Army, Klavdia Yakovlevna Khudyakova."

I've copied all this down word for word. I can just imagine these "little legs" and what these "comrades" will do when they'll play "tricks," i.e., turn off the electricity.

I'm going through and tearing up some papers, cuttings from old newspapers. Here's some very sweet poetry that the *Southern Worker*[7] (a Menshevik newspaper that was published before the Bolsheviks came) addressed to me:

> Frightened, you suddenly bent
> Slavishly, with hurried praise,
> Before the Viking, spent. . . .

---

punkty") first appeared in 1918. Centralized by the government on May 13, 1919, they published leaflets, fliers, posters, and other "educational" materials.

7. *Southern Worker* (*Iuzhnyi rabochii*) was published in 1918 and 1919.

This had to do with some verse I published in the *Odessa Leaflet*[8] the day the French landed in Odessa.[9]

How these internationalists can turn into nationalists and patriots when it suits them! How arrogantly they make fun of "frightened intellectuals," as if there were absolutely no reason for these intellectuals to be frightened. How they poke fun at "frightened philistines," as if the Bolsheviks have some great superiority over them. And just who, precisely, are these philistines, these "well-off petty bourgeois"? And, generally speaking, who and what are these revolutionaries worried about, especially since they so despise the average individual and his well-being?

Imagine that one suddenly attacks any old house where a large family has lived for decades; the masters, stewards, and servants are killed or taken captive; the family archives are seized and ransacked so as to learn about the life of this family, this house. The perpetrator thinks how many dark, sinful, and unjust things will be discovered, and what a terrible picture will take shape, especially when he burns with that well-known desire, that passion to find something shameful no matter what, without any allowances whatsoever!

This was the case with one old Russian home that was seized so suddenly, so very, very suddenly. And precisely what was discovered? Truly, one had to marvel at the trifles that were found! After all, the house was seized by the very same regime that has brought fire and brimstone to the world. What was found? It's amazing: absolutely nothing!

May 25 / June 7, 1919
"Comrade Balabanova, secretary of the Third International, is visiting Odessa."

Today I came unexpectedly upon a funeral with music and

---

8. *Odessa Leaflet* (*Odesskii listok*) was a newspaper published from 1872 to 1918.

9. French troops landed in Odessa on December 18, 1918.

banners saying: "For the death of one revolutionary, a thousand bourgeois must die!"

May 26 / June 8, 1919
"The Union of Bakers announces the tragic death of the baker, Mat'yash, a noble warrior for the kingdom of socialism."

Other obituaries and articles:

"Still another one of ours has departed this world. . . . Mat'yash is no more. . . . He was strong, steadfast, and bright. . . . The banners of all the various unions of bakers were at his grave-side. . . . Day and night an honor guard stood by the place where he was buried. . . ."

Dostoevsky once said: "Give to all teachers ample opportunity to destroy the old society and to build a new one, and the result will be such darkness, such chaos, such unheard-of coarseness, blindness, and inhumanity, that the entire structure will collapse under the curses of humankind even before it is completed . . ." [1]

Such lines, now, seem vague and inadequate.

May 27 / June 9, 1919
Today is the Day of the Holy Spirit. [2] The way to the School of Saint Sergius was difficult, since we had to walk almost the entire way in a rainy gloom and in shoes that were worn out and soaked through. Weak from malnutrition, we went slowly; it took us almost two hours to get there. And, of course, as I also had expected, the person whom we had to see, and who had just arrived from Moscow, was not at home. So we had to make the same difficult trek back home. On the way we passed the now defunct railway station, with its broken windows and its rails red from rust. Next to it was a huge, dirty wasteland where people were on swings and carousels, screaming and laughing. . . . We were constantly afraid

1. Bunin is quoting from Dostoevsky's *Diary of a Writer* (*Dnevnik pisatelia*), written in 1877.
2. The Day of the Holy Spirit (*Dukhov den'*) is celebrated on the Monday after Trinity Sunday.

that someone would stop us, stick his mug in our faces, and grab hold of Vera. So I went along, having clenched my teeth and fully determined that if such a thing were to happen, I would grab hold of a rock, the biggest one I could find, and bring it down on his comradely skull. Let them haul me wherever they wanted to!

We returned home at three to hear this news: "The Bolsheviks are leaving. The English have issued an ultimatum—clear out of the city!"[3]

N. P. Kondakov was here.[4] He talked about the anger and spite that the people bear so devastatingly these days, and that "we ourselves had instilled in them for the past hundred years." Then Ovsyaniko-Kulikovsky came by; and after him A. B. Azart with more rumors: "Trunks, suitcases, baskets are being requisitioned. . . . The Bolsheviks are fleeing. . . . Communication with Kiev has been cut off. . . . Proskurov, Zhmerinka, and Slavyansk[5] have all been taken. . . ." But by whom? This nobody knows.

I've smoked almost a hundred cigarettes. My head burns, my hands are like ice.

Nighttime, the same day
Yes, very long ago, people established some "World Bureau for the Organization of Happiness for Humankind," for a "new and splendid life." It worked its way through everything, it accepted orders for everything, literally for the sordid and most inhumane types of baseness: "Do you need spies, traitors, and people to seduce the enemy army? You've found the right place—we've aptly shown our talents in this area. Do you want to 'provoke' something? We have just the thing for you. Nowhere else will you find more experienced scoundrels in provoking people. . . ." And so forth and so forth.

3. The ultimatum was ignored by the Soviet forces that had captured Odessa on April 6, 1919.
4. Kondakov would later escape with the Bunins from Russia. See V. Muromtseva-Bunina, "N. P. Kondakov," *Poslednie novosti* (February 21, 1930), 2.
5. Proskurov (renamed Khmelnytskyi in 1954) is a small city approximately two hundred miles southwest of Kiev. Slavyansk is a town in the far eastern Ukraine on the Donets River.

What nonsense! There was once a people that numbered 160 million and that possessed one-sixth of the earth's surface, but precisely which sixth did they possess? A truly legendary and rich land that blossomed with equally legendary quickness! Over the past hundred years, though, this same people was so beaten down that their only salvation was to take away from thousands of landowners those acres of land that wasted away in their hands not by days but by hours!

May 28 / June 10, 1919
I often do not get enough sleep. Today, too, I woke up early. From morning on, I am tortured by rumors. There are so many of them going around that they all come crashing down inside my head. Many of the rumormongers give the impression that liberation is at hand. Just before twilight an issue of *Izvestia* reported: "We have surrendered Proskurov, Kamenets, and Slavyansk.[6] The Finns have crossed the border and are shooting at Kronstadt[7] for no reason at all. . . . Chicherin is protesting their action. . . ." Dombrovsky has been arrested, his domains have been destroyed, and there's been shelling all around.

Dombrovsky was the mayor of Odessa. A former actor, he owned the Theater of Miniatures in Moscow. He just had a nameday, and the feast was a lavish, riotous affair. There were many guests from the Cheka. Everyone got drunk and caused a scandal with shooting and fistfights.

May 29 / June 11, 1919
The student Mizikevich has been named the mayor of Odessa to replace Dombrovsky. A news item from the papers: "Rumania is

6. Kamenets is a small city in Belarus, approximately a hundred miles northeast of Smolensk.
7. Kronstadt was a naval base located on Kotlin Island, about fifteen miles west of Saint Petersburg. The story was untrue. Finland took no part against the Soviets, preserving an armed neutrality to the very end.

in revolt. . . . All of Turkey has been seized by revolution. . . . The revolution in India is widening. . . ."[8]

At noon I went out to get a haircut. Two gloomy-looking comrades were "inviting" the owner of the barbershop to purchase tickets (at seventy-five rubles apiece) for some concert; but they were doing so with such swinish crudeness, and in such a shrill and imperious way, that even I, who seemingly has gotten used to everything, was taken aback. I met Louis Ivanovich (a famous sailor), who told me: "The deadline for the ultimatum expires at twelve. Odessa will be seized by the French."[9] I walked home in a dumbfounded state, as if I had had one drink too many.

May 31 / June 13, 1919
"Our valiant Soviet forces have taken Ufa,[1] along with several thousand captives and twelve machine guns. . . . The enemy is being energetically pursued and is fleeing in panic. . . . We have abandoned Berdyansk and Chyortkovo, and we are breaking to the south of Tsaritsyn."[2] Rosa [Luxemburg][3] is being buried today in Berlin. That's why Odessa has declared a day of mourning; all fun and games are forbidden; the workers are at their jobs only for the

---

8. To say that these countries were in the throes of "revolution" was an exaggeration. Although Rumanians were restive with their leaders, they expressed their discontent in parliamentary elections in November 1919. In Turkey the revolutionary Mustafa Kemal was organizing resistance against the legal Ottoman government. In India millions of citizens, including the young Mahatma Ghandi, were protesting their loss of civil rights in the wake of the so-called "black acts": measures passed by the British to extend wartime emergency measures that had been in effect since 1915.

9. The rumor was not true. Odessa remained in Soviet hands until August.

1. Ufa is a city in eastern European Russia. In the summer of 1919 troops on the Soviet eastern front defeated Kolchak's White forces, thereby breaking his drive westward and contributing to the collapse of his armies shortly thereafter.

2. Berdyansk is a city on the Sea of Azov in southeastern Ukraine. Chyortkovo is a small urban center about three hundred miles west of Volgograd.

3. After the suppression of the uprising of Berlin workers in January 1919, the German socialist leader Rosa Luxemburg was murdered by counterrevolutionary forces on January 15, 1919. Her body was found, though, only on May 29, and was buried two weeks later.

morning; and the *Odessa Communist* has an article entitled "Off with Your Hats!"

Ten eggs already cost thirty-five rubles and butter forty, because "bandits" rob the peasants who bring their wares to the city. The powers-that-be are also taking control of the cemeteries. "From now on all citizens will be buried for free," they say. Time here has been moved forth yet another hour—on my watch it's 10 a.m., but "according to the Soviets," it's 1:30 p.m.

Ioffe is living in a train car at the station and is working as a government inspector. He is surprised and disturbed by many people here in Odessa. "Odessa does things in an overzealous way," he says; but he shrugs his shoulders, spreads out his hands in despair, and "sets a thing or two to rights. . . ."

From an article entitled "Crown of Thorns": "The workers are spreading a persistent and cruel rumor that 'Mat'yash was murdered.' They are clenching their calloused hands and are already crying out hoarsely, 'An eye for an eye. Revenge!'"

It turned out, though, that Mat'yash had shot himself: "He could not endure the nightmarish reality about him . . . bandits, thieves, plunderers, dirt, and violence surrounded him on all sides. . . . The investigative commission has established that he recognized the difficulty of working among bandits, thieves, and swindlers. . . ." One more thing: it also turned out that Mat'yash was "slightly intoxicated."

June 2 / 15, 1919
The news is all confused. One thing, though, is clear—Denikin's successes continue.

After breakfast we took a walk. It began to rain, so we took cover under the gates of a home; and while there we ran into Shmidt, Polevitskaya, and the Varshavskys. Polevitskaya keeps asking me to write a mystery play in which she could play the role of the Mother of God or "something generally sacred, something that would call people to Christianity." "What people?" I asked, "Surely not these pigs." "Yes, who else if not they? After all, I recently saw a sailor who weighed about four hundred pounds and was sitting in the first row [of a theater] and crying. . . ." "Crocodiles also cry," I replied. . . .

We again went out after dinner. As always, the stone about my heart was terrible. Again those glassy rose stars in the evening twilight looked like something from the bottom of the sea. They were shining on Red Street, across from the Sverdlov Theater and over the entrance to the building. And again, a terrible poster— the head of Our Savior, dead, mournful, and blue. His crown knocked to one side by a peasant's club.

June 3 / 16, 1919
It was a year ago that we arrived in Odessa. How terrible to think that a year has already gone by! And how many changes of power have there been, and all for the worse. I now recall my trip from Moscow here as a splendid time.

June 4 / 17, 1919
The Entente has named Kolchak the Supreme Ruler of Russia.[4] *Izvestia* wrote an obscene article saying: "Tell us, you reptile, how much did they pay you for that?"

The devil with them. I crossed myself with tears of joy.

June 7 / 20, 1919
I stopped in at Ivansenko's bookstore. His library has been "nationalized"; he can sell only those books whose authors have "mandates." Cabbies and members of the Red Army appeared and bought up anything they could: Shakespeare, a book about concrete pipes, works on Russian civil law. . . . They grabbed them because they were cheap and with the hope that they could sell them for a higher price elsewhere.

---

4. This was old news. The British, anxious to have someone in their camp head an anti-Bolshevik government in Siberia, joined forces with Cossack units there to name Kolchak as Supreme Ruler on November 18, 1919.

No one wants to go to the front. Roundups of "draft dodgers" are proceeding apace.

For days on end, carts loaded with goods confiscated both from stores and the homes of the bourgeois make their way along the streets.

People say that Petersburg sailors, the most merciless beasts, have been dispatched to Odessa.[5] It's true, the number of sailors here in town is increasing, and they are not like the ones already here. Their bell-bottoms are monstrous-looking. Generally speaking, I find it terrible to walk the streets. The sentries keep playing with their rifles; they'll shoot at whomever comes in sight. Every minute one sees two hooligans standing on the pavement and stripping down a revolver.

After dinner we took a look at a cannon that had been mounted on the boulevard. Small groups of people in conversation, and political agitators—their sole topic is the atrocities of the White Guard. A soldier also talks about his previous job. But it's all one and the same thing: how the bosses "kept putting everything into their pockets." These pigs can't dream up anything else besides these "pockets."

"The generals have sold Peremyshl'[6] for ten thousand rubles," another said. "I know what I'm talking about. I myself was there."

There are all kinds of crazy rumors about Denikin and his military successes. Russia's fate is being decided.

June 9 / 22, 1919
The newspapers keep saying the same thing—"Denikin wants to take our family hearths into his paws"—along with the same terrible anxiety about the Germans, i.e., that Russia will have to sign the "shameful peace." It would be natural for one to cry out:

---

5. This was true. During the civil war a regular navy practically ceased to exist, since the Bolsheviks had dismantled ships to furnish badly needed artillery and sent Russian sailors to fight on smaller craft on rivers within the country.

6. Peremyshl' is a small city about one hundred miles southwest of Moscow. The rumor has no basis in fact.

"Scoundrels, what about the obscene treaty that Karakhan signed for Russia in Brest?" But this is precisely the nature of their satanic power, the fact that they managed to cross all limits, all permitted boundaries, so as to make any amazement, any outraged cry seem foolish and naive.

And once again the same frenzied reality, the same inexhaustible energy—one that, over the past two years, has not quieted down even for a minute. Yes, of course it is a phenomenon that is truly inhuman. Not for nothing have people believed in the devil for thousands of years. The devil—something devilish—is at work here.

"Extreme measures have been taken" in Kharkov.[7] But against what? All these measures come down to one and the same thing— to shoot people "on the spot." Fifteen more people were shot in Odessa (a list of victims was published). Also, "two trains filled with gifts for the defenders of Petersburg"[8] were sent from Odessa, that is, with foodstuffs (while Odessa itself is dying from hunger). This evening many Poles were arrested as hostages and out of fear that "Poles and Germans will move on Odessa after peace is concluded in Versailles."[9]

The newspapers are publishing excerpts from Denikin's declaration (his promise to pardon soldiers of the Red Army),[1] but also mocking it at the same time: "In this document one finds every-

---

7. Before the Whites took Kharkov from the Bolsheviks on June 24, 1919, the city was the scene of mass starvation and murders. The Soviets executed more than one thousand people there in the last days of their rule.

8. This may have been true. The Bolsheviks had taken command of the vast military stores left behind by the French.

9. Such fear was valid. By 1919 Poland had a fairly well-organized military force composed of trained soldiers and experienced officers who had previously served in the German, Austrian, and Russian armies. It also had at its disposal the ample military supplies of these three armies, together with new armaments being supplied by France. The Poles had been attacking Russia's western front since February 1919, and on April 21, 1919, had actually taken Wilno, the only major city on the Russo-Polish border. See Lincoln, *Red Victory*, 401–402, and Lehovich, *White Against Red*, 320.

1. Denikin's declaration of amnesty was in fact written by French and English officers, under pressure from the Allies. Denikin, though, did approve the

thing: the insolence of a tsarist upstart, the gallows humor of a man about to be hanged, and the sadism of an executioner."

For the first time in my life I saw a man with a pasted-on moustache and beard—not on stage but in broad daylight on the street. He was such a sight that I stopped as if thunderstruck.

Many wild peoples have had this ancient belief:
"The brilliance of the star to which our soul passes after death depends on the brilliance of the eyes of the people we have eaten in life. . . ."
Today that no longer sounds archaic.
"You will live by your sword, Esau!"[2]
So have we also lived up to this time. The only difference is that the contemporary Esau is a complete scoundrel when compared to the earlier one.

Another biblical citation:
"Honor will decline, and baseness will grow apace. . . . Social assemblies will turn into houses of ill repute. . . . And the face of a generation will become like that of a dog. . . ."

Still one more, which everyone knows:
"Taste—and you will become like the gods. . . ."[3]
People have often tasted—but always in vain.

"The French effort to restore the sacred rights of people and to win freedom for all has only revealed the full depths of human impotence. . . . What have we seen? Coarse anarchistic instincts, which, having been liberated, are destroying all social bonds with animal self-satisfaction. . . . But a powerful individual is coming to the fore, one who will check anarchy and whose fists will firmly grab the reigns of government!"

---

text, which was first sent to Clemençeau and Lloyd George before it was published in local newspapers. See M. Marguiles, *God interventsii* (Berlin, 1923), 91–92.

2. Bunin is quoting from Genesis 27:40.

3. Bunin is paraphrasing from the story of Adam and Eve (Genesis 3:5).

These words, most surprisingly, since they are so vindicating of Napoleon, belong to the singer of *The Bell*.[4]

But Napoleon himself once said:

"What makes a revolution? Ambition. And what puts an end to it? Also ambition. And freedom for all was such a splendid pretext for all of us to fool the mob!"

Le Notre once said about Couthon:

How did Couthon wind up in the National Convention?[5] As everyone knows, Couthon was a cripple, but he was one of the most active and tireless members of that political body. When he was not seeking a cure at the waters, he did not miss a single meeting. How then, by what means did he appear at the National Convention?

At first Couthon lived on Rue Saint-Honoré.[6] "I found this apartment to be very convenient," he wrote in 1791, "since it was two steps away from the very center of the National Convention, and since I could get there on crutches." But soon thereafter Couthon's legs refused to serve him, and he had also changed his place of residence: he lived first in Passy,[7] then next to the Pont-Neuf.[8] In 1794 he again established himself on Rue Saint-Honoré, in building No. 336 (now 338), where Robespierre also lived.

People have long thought that Couthon got to the National Convention from all these places by allowing himself to be *carried* there. But how, on what? In a basket made of branches? On the back of a soldier? Le Notre says these questions remained unan-

4. The newspaper *The Bell* (*Kolokol*) was the first Russian revolutionary newspaper. It was printed in London and Geneva by Alexander Herzen and Nikolai Ogaryov from 1857 to 1867.

5. The National Convention was the highest legislative and executive organ of the First Republic of France. It lasted from September 21, 1792, to October 26, 1795.

6. Rue Saint-Honoré is a main thoroughfare in Paris, extending to the northwest of the city.

7. Passy is an administrative district located on the Seine.

8. The Pont-Neuf was completed in the early seventeenth century and crosses the Ile de la Cité.

swered for hundreds of years; but he also digresses from the issue
at hand to portray this repulsive vermin in his domestic situation,
citing from a written story that was found among some revolutionary documents approximately twenty years after Couthon's death.

The story goes like this: There was once a certain individual
who came to Paris from the provinces in order to appear before
the National Convention and to vindicate his countrymen, i.e.,
revolutionary judges who, the people claimed, had been suspected
of "being condescending" to the people they served. This individual was advised to appeal to Couthon himself; and, a woman, an
acquaintance of Madame Couthon, arranged the meeting—"just
the mere recollection of which would later make him quiver for
the rest of his life."

"When we appeared before Couthon," the man from the
provinces said, "I was surprised to see a gentleman with a kind
face, who greeted me rather courteously. He occupied a splendid
apartment, with furnishings in excellent taste. He was wearing a
white robe and sitting in a chair, feeding a greenish-looking rabbit
perched on his arms. Alongside him was his three-year-old boy, a
handsome-looking child, who looked like a cupid and who was
tenderly petting this rabbit. 'How can I be of service to you?'
Couthon asked me. 'Any person whom my spouse recommends to
me has the right to my attention.' At this point I, won over by this
idyllic scene, gave full vent to describing the difficult situation of
my countrymen. Then, feeling even more emboldened by his kind
attention, I said with complete openheartedness: 'Monsieur
Couthon, you as an all-powerful member of the Committee for
Public Safety,[9] are you aware of the fact that the revolutionary tribunal is daily issuing death verdicts on people who are absolutely
innocent of everything? For example, today, sixty-three people will
be executed: and for what?

"Well, good Lord, how things immediately changed after I

9. The Committee of Public Safety was the provisional committee of the
French Revolutionary Government from 1793 to 1795.

said this! Couthon's face became savagely distorted, the rabbit flew out of his hand in a somersault, the child ran screaming to his mother, and Couthon himself pulled the rope for the bell that hung over his chair. Had I stayed there another minute, I would have been apprehended by the six 'police agents' who were constantly in Couthon's apartment. But, lucky for me, the person who had ushered me in managed to restrain Couthon's hand and kicked me out the door. That very day I fled Paris. . . ."

So, Le Notre tells us, this is what Couthon was like in his good moments. But it has been just recently discovered that Couthon went back and forth to the National Convention on a bicycle. In June 1889 a young woman turned up at Carnavalet.[1] She told the director of the museum there that she was Couthon's great granddaughter and that she was making a personal sacrifice by giving to the museum the very chair on which Couthon sat when he rode to the National Convention. And the week after this, the chair was sent to Carnavalet. It was unpacked—and "saw anew the Parisian sun, the very same Thermidor[2] sun which had not warmed his old trunk for 105 years." It was covered in a lemon-colored velvet and moved by means of a handle and chains that were joined to the wheels.

Couthon was almost like a corpse. "He had been weakened by the baths, he lived only on bouillon made from veal stock, he was emaciated by bone cancer, he was exhausted by constant nausea and hiccups." But his persistence and his energy were endless. The revolutionary drama was proceeding at a frenzied pace. "All its actors were so restless that they could imagine themselves only in motion, jumping up on stages, hurling thunderbolts of anger, and running around France from one end to another—all in a yearning to fan the fires that had to destroy the old world." And Couthon was right with them. Every day he ordered that he be

1. The Museé Carnavalet is situated in the Marais district of Paris. It was built in 1880 and traces the history of Paris in paintings, documents, and the like.
2. Thermidor was the month of July in the calendar of the French Republic (1792–1805).

lifted and seated in his chair. "By tremendous force of will he would force his bent arms to rest on a motor that recalled the handle of a coffee grinder, and fly off into the obstructions and crowds of Saint Honoré to the National Convention in order to send people to the scaffold. It must have been a horrible sight: the shell of a man who moved along the crowd in his rattling machine, his torso bent forward, his dead legs wrapped in a blanket, his face covered with sweat, and he always screaming: 'Out of my way!' The crowd would dash to the side in fear and amazement at the discrepancy between the pitiful sight of this cripple and the horror which his name would call forth!"

Speaking about the "elemental quality" of revolution:

In the Menshevik newspaper *Southern Worker*, published in Odessa last winter, the well-known Menshevik Bogdanov told this story about the famous Soviet of Workers' and Soldiers' Deputies there:

"Gimmer-Sukhanov and Steklov walked in. No one had elected them; no one had empowered them, but they announced that they would head a soviet that still did not exist!"

During the war Grzhebin organized the patriotic journal *Fatherland*.[3] He invited me for a talk. Incidentally, F. F. Kokoshkin was also there.[4] After we had talked, we went for a carriage ride and began talking about the people. I didn't say anything terrible — only that the people had grown tired of the war, and that all the cries in the newspapers saying that the folk were rushing off to battle were criminal nonsense. Suddenly Grzhebin interrupted me with his usual propriety, but this time he was also unusually sharp: "Let's drop this conversation. Your views of the folk have al-

---

3. *Fatherland* (*Otechestvo*) was an illustrated journal published in Saint Petersburg in 1914 and 1915. It owed much of its popularity to the fictional contributions of Leonid Andreev. Zinovy Grzhebin had published Bunin's writings in 1907 in a series of almanacs, entitled *Dogrose* (*Shipovnik*).

4. Fyodor Kokoshkin, a member of the Provisional Government and also a leader of the Cadet party, was brutally murdered in a hospital by anarchist soldiers in January 1918.

ways seemed to me—you will excuse me—extremely exclusive, they are . . ."

I looked at him in amazement and almost in horror. No, I thought, not for nothing will our nobility pass into oblivion! This nobility was a reward for service to the state,[5] but people play-acted at it, gave up applauding it, and even traded it in the market.

Then a company of little boys made up of all kinds of gross scum, but who did want to go off to the front, appeared at the Duma. They said they were "empowered by the confidence and the majestic will of the people." And they cried out to the world that the great Russian Revolution had been accomplished, that the people were now laying down their lives for them and for all kinds of freedom, and that the first order of affairs was to smash the Germans and bring the war to a victorious end. And if that weren't enough, in the course of several days they ended any and all sense of authority in Russia. . . .

Spring of '17. The Prague restaurant is filled with people, music, and waiters. Wine is forbidden,[6] but almost everyone is drunk. The music brings sweet anguish to one's soul. A well-known liberal lawyer wears a military uniform. He is huge, with a broad chest and shoulders, but also with a haircut that makes him look like a hedgehog. He is so drunk that he keeps crying out throughout the entire restaurant, demanding that the orchestra play "Oira."[7]

5. Bunin is here referring to the so-called Table of Ranks, established by Peter the Great in 1722, which defined the bureaucratic hierarchy of ranks in the army, navy, and civil service. Even the very lowest rank conferred the right of personal nobility as reward for service to the state. (Entrance into the higher ranks make such nobility hereditary.) Bunin is, of course, also using the word "nobility" in a more literal sense, i.e., "dignity," "honor," "integrity," and/or "virtue."

6. Prohibition on the manufacture and sale of alcoholic beverages in Russia was introduced with the outbreak of the world war in 1914, and continued until 1925. Russians evaded the law, though, with "home brew" and other concoctions.

7. "Oira-Oira" was a "polka française," written for the piano by A. Alexandrov and published in Leipzig in 1919. It soon became very popular in the repertoire of "restaurant music."

His drinking buddy, a Hussar, is even more drunk. He embraces and avidly kisses the lawyer, madly biting him on the lips.

At first the music was doleful and repulsively languid, and then lively:

Oh, you have run off.
You, my grey steed, are gone!

And the lawyer, having raised his thick shoulders and elbows, begins to jump and hop about on the sofa, all the while keeping time to the music.

June 10 / 23, 1919
Journalists from the newspaper *Russian Word* are fleeing on a small sailboat to the Crimea. They are going because bread is supposedly selling for eighty kopecks a pound there, the Mensheviks are in power, and there are other blessings as well.

I met S. I. Varshavsky on the street. He says that the post office is displaying an exultant telegram saying, "The Germans will not sign the shameful peace." [8]

More than a thousand Poles have been arrested in Odessa. The rumor is that as soon as they were taken into custody, they were savagely beaten. That's nothing; that's the way everyone is treated now.

In Kiev the "conducting of the red terror into life" goes on apace. Incidentally, several more professors have been murdered, including the famous clinical therapist Yanovsky. [9]

Yesterday there was something "urgent"—there's always something "urgent"!—a meeting of the Ispolkom. [1] Fel'dman said the usual stuff: "Comrades, the world revolution is approaching!" Someone answered him by shouting: "Enough already! We're sick

8. This was not true.
9. Actually, Yanovsky did not die until 1928.
1. The Ispolkom (*Ispolnitel'nyi komitet*) was the executive committee of the urban council or soviet. It oversaw the everyday administration of the city.

of hearing such things! Bread is what we need!" "Aha! So that's what things have come to!" Fel'dman yelled back. "Who said that?" The individual who had opened his mouth, jumped up bravely and said, "I said it!"—and was arrested right away. Then Fel'dman put forth a proposal that "the bourgeois should be used instead of horses to pull heavy things." This announcement brought stormy applause.

The rumor is that we have taken Belgorod.[2]

What vileness! The entire city is filled with the sounds of sandalwood trees knocking up against one another; and all the streets are covered with water—but from morning to night, "citizens" carry water from the port because the plumbing has not been working for quite some time. Also from morning to night, people seemingly talk only about getting food. Science, art, technology, all kinds of human endeavor or creative life—all this has perished. Thin cows have devoured Pharaoh's fat ones, but they have not only not grown fat, they themselves are dying!

Village mothers are now scaring their children:

"Quiet down! Or I'll send you off to the Odessa commune!"

People are passing on the brazen, impudently modest words that Trotsky used the other day:

"I would be sad if I were told that I'm a poor journalist. But when I'm told that I'm a poor military leader, I answer: 'I'm studying and will be a good one.' "

Trotsky was a shrewd journalist. A. A. Yablonsky told me that once when Trotsky was carried away, he stole someone's fur coat from the editorial offices of *Kievan Thought*.[3] Now, though, he's "learning" to wage war and conquer by questioning the tsarist gen-

2. Belgorod is a city in the Ukraine about fifty miles northeast of Kharkov. The rumor was true.

3. *Kievan Thought* (*Kievskaia mysl'*) was a liberal daily published from 1907 to 1918. Trotsky accepted an offer from *Kievan Thought* to serve as its military correspondent in the Balkans in September 1912, and two years later in France. He did an outstanding job in both places. See R. Segal, *Leon Trotsky* (New York, 1972), 100, 110.

erals whom he has captured. What the hell, he'll pass for a military leader.

Here is a portrait of the Red officer: a boy about twenty years old. His face is all bare and shaven, his cheeks are hollow, his pupils are dark and wide. He does not have lips but a loathsome sphinxlike slit. His teeth are almost all gold. A high school girl hangs onto his chickenlike body. She has military field belts about her shoulders. Her legs are thin, like skeletons, and they are covered with the most repulsive, bubblelike riding breeches. She wears superexpensive dandyish shoes. An absurdly huge pistol hangs from her thigh.

Everything in the university is in the hands of seven freshmen and sophomores. The main commissar is a student named Malich from the Kiev Veterinary School. When he talks with the professors he bangs his fist on the table and puts his feet up on it. The commissar for advanced women's courses is a freshman by the name of Kin. She does not tolerate objections but immediately yells: "No sounding like crows!" The commissar of the polytechnic institute always carries a loaded revolver in his hand.

Just before evening I met a Jewish acquaintance on the street: Zeeler, a Petersburg lawyer. He quickly told me:

"Greetings. Give me your ear. I have to whisper something to you."

I did as I was asked.

"It's going to happen on the twentieth! I'm warning *you* in advance!"

He shook my hand and quickly left.

He told me this in such a surefire way that he left me momentarily confused. But how could I not but be confused? Everyone keeps telling me that yesterday there was a secret meeting in which it was decided that the situation was desperate, that one had to retreat into the underground, from thence to destroy Denikin's men in any way possible—by penetrating their ranks, demoralizing them, bribing them, stirring up all kinds of chaos, putting on the uniform of a Volunteer and crying out "God save the tsar" and "Beat the Jews."

But it is entirely possible that, as has often been the case, the Bolsheviks themselves are the ones who are spreading all the rumors about a desperate situation. They very well know how devoted we are to optimism.

Yes, yes, this very optimism has also destroyed us. *This* we must firmly keep in mind.

But perhaps it is true that everyone is preparing to flee. The pillaging is terrible. The most faithful "Communists" are being given all kinds of things for free, anything that turns up: tea, coffee, tobacco, wine. Rumors have it that there's still a little wine left but that the sailors have drunk up most of it. (Rumor also has it that they are especially fond of Martell cognac.) So till now we've had no proof that these jailbird gorillas have been dying for the revolution, but rather for Martell.

I remember a day in September of '17. It was a gloomy evening. Dark clouds with yellowish fissures hung in the west. What few leaves remained on the trees by the church gate had a reddish glow, though it was already dark under our feet. I entered the watchman's room in the church. It was almost completely dark inside. The watchman was also a shoemaker, a small, snub-nosed individual with a broad, thick, red beard. A sweet-looking type, he was sitting on a bench, wearing a nondescript shirt and a jacket with a pouch of snuff sticking out of its pocket. When he saw me, he got up, bowed low, and threw back his hair which had fallen on his forehead. Then he offered me his hand.

"How's it going, Alexei?" I asked.

He sighed and said:

"Real borin'."

"What's the matter?"

"That's just the way it is. It's not good. Oh, dear *barin*, boy, is it not good! It's borin'."

"But why?"

"That's just the way it is. Yesterday I was in town. Before you could go about freely, but now you have to take some bread with you, 'cause the town is starving. Everywhere there's hunger, hunger! There are no goods to be had. There's absolutely nothing around. The salesman says: 'Give me some bread, and then we'll give you some goods.' But I say to him: 'No way, you can go eat your hides, but we'll hold onto our bread.' You can only talk about how bad things have gotten! Soles for shoes cost fourteen rubles! So long as the bourgeois are not all murdered, everyone else will be hungry and cold. Oh, dear *barin*, I'm telling you this with a clear conscience: The bourgeois will be slaughtered, yes, they will be slaughtered!"

When I left the room, the watchman also went out and lit the lamp next to the church gates. A peasant was coming from behind a hill. He kept falling and jerking forward—he was very drunk. He was screaming at the entire village and cursing out the deacon with the choicest swearwords. When he saw me, he leaned back as far as he could and stopped, saying:

"But *you* can't swear at him like that! For if you did, if you profaned a holy person, your tongue would be put out on a stretcher!"

"But allow me this: first of all, I haven't said a word, and second, why can you curse him out, but I can't?"

"And who is going to bury you when you croak? Surely won't it be the deacon?"

"But what about you?"

Having dropped his head and thought a bit, he said gloomily:

"That dog wouldn't give me any kerosene from the co'operative store. 'You,' he says to me, 'have already got your share.' But I says to him, 'But what if I want some more?' 'No,' he tells me, 'that's the law.' Not bad, huh? He should be arrested for saying that, the dog! There's no such law now. . . ."

"Just you wait, just you wait," the peasant said to the watchman, "you're gonna get yours! I'll remember you and your soles. I'll cut you up like a chicken—just give me a date!"

ODESSA 1919

I remember October of the same year. People were carrying posters; there were meetings and appeals, for instance:

"Citizens! Comrades! Realize your great duty before the Constituent Assembly. Fulfill your great dream before the majestic host of the Russia land! Everyone vote for list number three!"

The peasants, having heard these appeals in the city, told me when they got back home:

"What the hell? They keep screaming at us that our duties are great! Everyone get out there and vote, they say, but doesn't that mean I'll have to list what I own before the Constituent Assembly? And who must I do this for? Someone who should drop dead in the first place? No, this new leadership is no good, nohow. They pretend to be your friends, they promise pie in the sky; but they themselves yell, threaten, and try to tear the cross from your neck. Well, they'll just have to wait: so long as we don't have to whine about what we want!"

We sat and talked about this with a former elder, a peasant of average means but doing comparatively well. He said:

"Yes, everyone knows how they keep screaming about our duty and scare us about being in arrears.[4] Now they tell us that we're going to have a Constituent Assembly and that we have to choose a candidate. There's also a rumor that we'll have to draw up this here *understandin'* between him and us, that we'll have *this here discussin'* about it, and that he'll have to put his name to it. When and what road to take, when to declare war—he's now gotta ask us what we want. But do we really know which road we need? After all, I may be a rich man, but I have lived in Elets since I was born and have never been anywhere else. For twenty years now we haven't been able to fill up the hole in the road near the hill, 'cause whenever we get together—we fight for three days. Then

4. After the Emancipation, Russian peasants had to redeem the land allotted to them by their landlords or the government with the understanding that they would fully possess their holdings after a period of forty-nine years. Periodic crop failure, together with the fact that the peasants did not always pay their debts and that the price of redemptions was often set higher than the value of the land, meant that many former serfs fell into severe debt.

we gulp down three pails of vodka and take off. But the hole's still there. The same goes for declaring war against another country. I couldn't do it; I wouldn't know how or when. And what if the candidate is a good man? The powers-that-be say they can't do it without us. But why should I go and stick a dagger in someone's side? God be with this candidate in the Duma; that's what he's getting paid for!"

"That's just the point," I said, "the pay isn't half-bad."

"What's that? You say the pay's good?"

"Of course it's good. You should go there right away."

The elder thought a moment, but then said with a sigh:

"No, they won't let me in. I'm a Bolshevik: I've just bought over eight acres of land and two good horses."

"But," I replied, "who else is there except you? You're a landowner, after all."

Having thought a bit more, he became more lively:

"Yes! That's exactly what I've been trying to tell you! I'd be representing people who are in good shape. I'd be supporting nobility types. I'd be keeping your descendants in mind. And I wouldn't let them take any land away from my masters. But this one, this deputy we've just elected, he couldn't get anything on his own; but the devil helps him pull the wool over people's eyes with his smooth talking. So we elected him here in the region, but what kind of deputy is he? He talks in obscenities, he's got absolutely nothing going for him, his eyes have a drunken look, and he smells of something raunchy and burnt. He screams that he's got only one chicken on his farm, and that if they'd give him a hundred acres he'd be 'in the driver's seat' in two days' time. How could I replace him? He keeps rummaging through papers, but he can't find nothing. That foul shit can't read, he doesn't know how to read—but what kind of readers are we, after all? Any sheep can bleat better than what I read!"

I had another conversation about the Constituent Assembly with [the peasant] Pantysuhka, the most fervid revolutionary in all our village. He said some very passionate things:

"I myself, pal, am a Social Democrat.[5] For three years I sold newspapers and journals on Rostov-on-the-Don.[6] I dare say that a thousand issues of *Satirikon*[7] alone went through my hands; but I can also tell you directly: Who's this devil of a minister, this so-called Gvozdev? I got grey hair; is he that much whiter than me? He's no worse than me, though. He'll return to the village, for we're of the same cloth. I may crawl up to you in an insolent way, and say 'comrade, comrade'; but, to tell the truth, I really should get a clobbering. Your name is in the calendar,[8] you're a well-known writer, the most important prince can sit at your table because you're a nobleman, but what am I? I also tell the peasants: 'Hey, boys, let's not make a mistake here! After all, I'll tell you who you ought to choose for the Constituent Assembly; after all, it's already an understood thing. Vote for Comrade Bunin. He'll find good friends there and can worm himself in among anyone he wants to. . . .' "

Yesterday I visited V. A. Rozenberg. I again told him about the successes of the Volunteers, to which he replied they are "constraining freedom of speech" in the cities under their control. One could rush out and bite him.

5. The Social Democrats came into being in 1898, and, like other political parties of the time, endorsed freedom of the press, equality before the law, and other civil liberties. The group, though, had little use for the idealism of the Populists, especially their faith in the peasantry. Instead the Social Democrats focused on the proletariat, organizing unions and strikes, and endorsing practical economic goals, e.g., higher wages, shorter hours, and the like.

6. Rostov-on-the-Don is a city in Russia about seventy miles from the Sea of Azov.

7. *Satirikon* was an illustrated journal of satire and humor published in Saint Petersburg from 1908 to 1914. Its contributors included Nadezhda Teffi, Leonid Andreev, Alexander Kuprin, Alexei Tolstoy, and Osip Mandelstam.

8. The Russian publisher I. D. Sytin began publishing cheap, colorful, almanac-type calendars for the mass market at the beginning of this century. (Printings exceeded six million copies.) At the same time other publishing houses printed specialized calendars for both men and women as well as for people from various walks of life, e.g., jurists, children, military men, even beekeepers.

Nighttime, the same day
I remember when news came from the Austrian front[9] that Volod'ka had been killed. His mother, an old woman in a sheepskin coat, lay face downward on her plank bed for two days, but she didn't even cry. His father pretended to be happy. He kept walking by her and saying in a shy sort of voice:

"You're something else, old lady! You're really something else! Did you really think that the enemy would just look at our boys? After all, he also had to defend himself! How else could he have survived! Can your stupid head imagine anything else?"

Volod'ka's wife, a young peasant woman, kept running out into the vestibule, dropping her head on anything around, crying in various ways, and even howling like a dog. Volod'ka's father said to her:

"Here we go again! You too! You too! That means that the enemy shouldn't have had to defend himself, or that Volod'ka should have gone down on his hands and knees and begged the enemy for his life?"

Then there was this other person named Yakov. When he received a letter informing him that his son had been killed, he said, breaking out into laughter and strangely screwing up his eyes:

"It's nothing. It's nothing, after all. May the Heavenly Kingdom be his! I'm not gonna grieve, I'm not gonna regret what's happened! It's my candle to God, I tell myself! It's my candle to God, it's incense before Him!"

But, truly, both God and the devil are laughing at Russia every minute. Sitting in the garden alongside a hut lit by a warm, lone moon at the opposite end, and listening to the cries and wailing of Volod'ka's wife issuing forth from the village, a merchant said:

"Shit, listen to how she's carrying on! She ain't missin' her husband, she's missin' his dick. . . ."

I could hardly restrain myself. I so wanted to give him a good

9. Bunin is referring to the area of Galicia, situated between the Russian and Austro-Hungarian empires, and the site of furious battles between Austrians and Russians in early July 1919.

stiff caning. But in the hut a rooster cried tenderly and sweetly, re-joicing over the moon. The merchant continued on, saying:

"Good Lord, how great and sweet he sounds. That's why I keep him. I wouldn't take a hundred rubles for him! All night long he keeps my spirits high, he touches me deeply. . . ."

Pal'chikov's daughter (a quiet, pretty-looking thing) keeps ask-ing me:

"Is it true, *barin*, that forty thousand Austrian captives are being brought here?"

"I wouldn't say 'forty,' but yes, it's true. They're being brought here."

"And are we going to feed them?"

"How can we not feed them? What else are we going to do with them?"

She thought a bit.

"What do you mean? Why can't you just kill and bury them all? . . ."[1]

In the fall of '17, near Elets, there were some peasants who, after having destroyed a landowner's estate, got hold of some live peacocks and tore out and plucked their feathers just for fun. Then they let them go, all bloody, to fly and rush about, crying out shrilly wherever they went.

But what was the harm in this! After all, Pavel Yushkevich keeps asserting "one could not approach revolution with wrongful bias," and that to shudder over what had happened to the peacocks was "philistinism." He even recalled Hegel, saying, "Not for noth-ing did Hegel speak about the rationality of all existence: so if rea-son exists, then the Russian Revolution must make sense."[2]

Yes, yes, "Those who do the beating have ordered others not

1. In the battles between Russians and Austrians in Galicia in early July 1917, the Russians took at least seven thousand Austrian prisoners. (They were released after the October Revolution.) See R. Gray, *Chronicle of the First World War*, vol. 2 (New York, 1992), 64.
2. Yushkevich is quoting from the "Logic" section of Hegel's *Encyclopedia of the Philosophical Sciences*, written in 1871.

to cry." But what about the poor peacocks that did not suspect Hegel's existence? And with what kind of bias, other than a wrongful one, can priests, landowners, officers, children, old people "approach a revolution," especially when their skulls have been smashed by the triumphant people? But why should Pavel Yushkevich concern himself with such "philistine" questions?

People are saying that the sailors who were sent to us from Petersburg have become totally Satan-like from drunkenness, cocaine, and perversity. When they got drunk, they burst in on the prisoners being held at the offices of the Cheka, and, without any orders from their bosses, killed anyone they found there. Not long ago they tore off to some place to kill some woman with her child. She begged them to spare her for the sake of her young one, but the sailors answered back: "Don't worry, he's also gonna get it!"—and they shot him too. For sport the sailors chase prisoners out into the courtyard and force them to run around as they shoot at them—missing them on purpose.

June 11 / 24, 1919
Having awakened, I understand with horror, so especially clearly and soberly, that I am simply dying from this way of life, both physically and spiritually. Truth be told, the devil knows why I'm writing all this down, anything that comes to mind, like a madman. . . . After all, isn't it all the same, no matter what I do!

I can hardly wait for the papers. But the news is all very good:

"We've abandoned Boguchar.[3] . . . We've been pushed back 120 miles farther west of Tsaritsyn. . . . The hangman Kolchak is joining forces with Denikin's men. . . ."

Suddenly I read:

"That oppressor of the workers, Grishin-Almazov, has shot himself. . . . Trotsky writes in a newspaper from his train that one of our battleships has seized a ship on the Sea of Azov; that

---

3. Boguchar is a small city roughly two hundred miles northwest of Volgograd.

this vessel was carrying the well-known murderer and Black Hundred leader Grishin-Almazov, who was taking a letter from Denikin to Kolchak; and finally that Grishin-Almazov shot himself."[4]

What terrible news. In general the entire day has been very disturbing. The rumor is that Denikin has supposedly taken Feodosiya, Alushta, Simferopol', and Alexandrovsk. . . .[5]

4 p.m., the same day
Peace has been signed with the Germans.[6] Denikin has taken Kharkov.

I shared my joy with Foma, the janitor. But he's pessimistic:

"No, *barin*, the matter is hardly over. Now it'll be even more difficult to put an end to things."

"How do you think things are going to end? And when?"

"When! When hell freezes over! Now the villains will get stronger. Already the soldiers from the Red Army are saying: 'It's all on account of the Jews. They're all Communists, but all Bolsheviks are Russians.' But I think these very Red Army soldiers are the root of all evil. They're all drunkards, they're all scoundrels. Just count how many of them have crept out of their lairs. And how they scoff at all the citizens of the world! This type will go along the street and ask suddenly: 'Comrade citizen, what time is it?' And the person will take out his watch and blurt out: 'Two-thirty.' 'May your mother damn your soul! How can you think it's two-thirty when it's really five o'clock Soviet time? Does that mean you're for the old regime?' And then he'll rip the watch out of your hands and smash it on the sidewalk! No, this type will only get

---

4. This was true. To avoid capture by the Soviets, Grishin-Almazov committed suicide on May 5, 1919.

5. Feodosiya and Alushta are small cities in the Crimea; Alexandrovsk is in southeastern Ukraine. The rumor was true.

6. The Treaty of Versailles was actually signed on June 28, 1919. On this occasion Winston Churchill remarked prophetically to Lloyd George, "The war of the giants has ended, but the quarrels of the pygmies have begun." See Lincoln, *Red Victory*, 397.

stronger. But everyone else has gotten weak. Just look at how a former gentleman or a lady goes about on the streets these days; the man wears any old thing, his collar is crumpled, and his cheeks are unshaven. The woman is barefoot, without stockings; she drags a bucket of water all over town—she's ready to spit at everything. And I'll say this about myself: I keep waiting for something to happen, but I myself don't feel like doing anything. Even summer doesn't seem like it's here yet."

God marks the scoundrel. Even in ancient times there was a universal hatred for people with red hair and high cheekbones. Socrates could not bear palefaced individuals. Now there is a modern-day anthropology for the criminal type: a great number of so-called "born criminals" have pale faces, large cheekbones, a coarse lower jaw, and deeply shining eyes.[7]

How can one not recall this when one thinks of Lenin and thousands like him? (Incidentally, criminal anthropology makes note of a particularly contradictory type among innate criminals and especially women convicts: the doll-like, "angelic" face—like Kollontai once had, for example.)

How many pale faces, high cheekbones, and strikingly asymmetric features mark the soldiers of the Red Army and, generally speaking, also of the common Russian people—how many of them, these savage types, have Mongolian atavism directly in their blood! They are all from Murom,[8] the white-eyed Chud. . . . And it is precisely these individuals, these very Russichi,[9] who from time immemorial were known for their *antisocialness* and who gave us so many "daring pirates," so many vagabonds, escapees, scoundrels, and tramps—it is precisely these people whom we have recruited

---

7. Bunin is referring to the theory of *l'uomo delinquente* by Cesare Lombroso, who believed that one could determine "born criminals" by their anatomy, particularly their apish atavism. Bunin insisted that Trotsky was "a genuine murderer à la Lombroso."

8. Murom is an old Russian city two hundred miles directly east of Moscow.

9. Russichi was the name of one tribe of ancient Slavs.

for the glory, pride, and hope of the Russian *social* revolution. So why should we feign surprise at the results?

Turgenev once reproached Herzen: "You bow before the sheepskin coat;[1] you see in it such great grace, novelty, and originality of future forms." Novelty of form! The fact of the matter is that any Russian revolt (and especially the current one) primarily shows to what extent everything is *old* in Russia, and how radically Russia yearns for *formlessness*. From time immemorial there have been "pirates," brigands from Murom, Bryansk, and Saratov.[2] There have been runners, loafers, rebels against everyone and everything, drunkards, tavern riffraff, hypocrites, sowers of all types of lies, feuds, and unrealized dreams. Classical Rus is a rowdy country. It has the saint and also the builder, tall but cruel and firm. But what a long and incessant struggle these two have waged with the brawler, the destroyer, those who use all kinds of sedition, dissension, and bloody "disorder and absurdities"!

Criminal anthropology makes note of occasional criminals: people "who are not instinctively antisocial" and who commit crime by accident. But it also tells us of another group; "instinctive criminals." These always act like children, like animals, and their most distinguishing feature, their innate symptom, is their thirst for destruction, for *antisociality*.

Take a woman criminal, a girl. As a child she is stubborn, fickle. From adolescence on, she begins to show highly destructive behavior: she rips up books, breaks dishes, and burns her clothes. She reads avidly, and her favorite reading is passionate, involved novels, dangerous adventure stories, heartless and daring feats. She falls in love with the first fellow she meets, for she is ruled by her base sexual drives. She is always extremely logical in her discourse; she deftly blames others for her actions; and she lies so much, and

1. In other words, the Russian peasant. Bunin is citing a letter by Turgenev to Herzen, written on November 8, 1862. See I. Turgenev, *Pis'ma v trinadtsati tomakh*, vol. 5 (Moscow, 1963), 67.
2. Bryansk is a city roughly 150 miles southwest of Moscow. Saratov is a city on the Volga River, 200 miles northeast of Volgograd.

so brazenly or assuredly, that she paralyzes anyone who listens to her.

Take a male criminal, a youth. He is a guest at his family's dacha. He chops down trees, tears off wallpaper, breaks glass, pokes fun at religious symbols, and draws all kinds of vulgar things everywhere. He is said to be "typically antisocial. . . ." There are thousands of such examples.

In peaceful times we forget that the world teems with these degenerates because they reside in prisons and asylums. But then there comes a time when "the supreme people" triumph. The doors of the prisons and the asylums are flung open, the archives of criminal investigative units are burned—and the orgy begins. But the present orgy has exceeded everything that has gone before it. It has very much astounded and aggrieved those who, for many years, have called to Stepan's Cliff[3]—to hear "what Stepan thought." How amazing and strange! Stepan could not think about anything social; he was a "born" criminal—exactly from the same villainous tribe that perhaps foretold this new *many-yeared* struggle.

I recall the summer of '17 as the beginning of some terrible illness. I already felt sick. My head burned, my thoughts were confused, my surroundings took on a terrifying air. I still managed, though, to stay on my legs and to wait for something with the feverish tension of the very last of all my physical and spiritual powers.

But at the end of this summer, when I opened the morning newspaper with my perpetually shaking hands, I suddenly felt that I was getting pale, that the top of my head was being drained, like just before one faints. A cry written in big letters hit me in the eye "To one and all!"—a cry that Kornilov was a "rebel, a traitor of the Revolution and of the homeland. . . ."[4]

3. From a popular song, performed by Fyodor Chaliapin, about how Razin stood "on a cliff" to think deep thoughts.

4. Bunin is referring to the so-called Kornilov Affair, in which General Kornilov, in August 1917, attempted to overthrow the Russian Provisional Government and undertake counterrevolutionary actions against leftists in Petrograd.

ODESSA 1919

And there was November 3/16.

The Cain of Russia, with the joyously mad frenzy of one who had given his soul to be trampled on by the devil for thirty pieces of silver, triumphed in full splendor.

Moscow, having been defended for a full week by a handful of cadets, burned constantly and shook from cannonade.

Everything quieted down. All the barriers, all the divine and human gates fell. With wild abandon the conquerors freely took control of the city, each of its streets, each of its dwellings. They immediately hoisted their banner over its stronghold and sacred place, the Kremlin. In my entire life there has never been a day more terrible than that one—God be my witness, it is true!

After a week of being held captive by four walls, without air, almost without sleep or food, behind barricaded windows and walls, I walked out of the house on unsteady feet. No sooner had I flung open the door when a gang of "warriors for a bright future" rushed in, no less than three times. Looking for enemies and weapons, they were completely crazed by victory, booze, and the most animal-like hatred. They had parched lips and savage looks; and ever faithful to the tradition of all "great revolutions," they carried all kinds of weapons with an almost carnival-like grotesquerie.

Ravens cawed hoarsely in the evening of that short, dark, icy, and rainy day of late autumn. Moscow, pitiful, dirty, disgraced, resigned, and riddled with bullets, took on a battered look.

Cabbies made their way; the triumphant Moscow mob poured through the streets. A filthy old woman with spitefully green eyes and raised veins on her neck stood and croaked out for the whole street to hear: "Comrades, dear ones! Beat them, punish them, burn them!"

I stood for a while, looked around—and then wandered home. But at night, being alone, and though by nature extremely disinclined to tears,[5] I suddenly burst out crying with terrible and copious tears even beyond my imagination.

5. This is wishful thinking on Bunin's part.

I also cried during Holy Week—not alone this time, but with the many, many others who had gathered in the dark evenings, in dark churches dimly lit with the red lights of candles, amidst dark Moscow with its hermetically sealed Kremlin, and who cried when they sang the now terrible hymn: "By a sea wave . . . of the persecutor, the tormentor hidden under the wave. . . ."[6]

How many people there were then in these churches who had never been in them before, who had never cried as they did now!

I again cried tears of cruel grief and sickly delight when I left behind Russia and my entire former life, when I crossed the new Russian border, the border at Orsha. At that time I raced from that boiling sea of screaming savages who were terrible and unhappy; who screamed with violence and hysterical passion; and who had lost all vestige of humanity. They set fire to literally every train station, beginning from Moscow itself right up to Orsha, stations at which all the platforms and paths were literally covered with vomit and defecation. . . .

June 13 / 26, 1919
Yes, peace has been signed. Even now, will those in the West not think about Russia? How true the words: "Fight, those of you who believe in God!" Tens of millions of Russian souls cry out in a frenzy for help. Will they really not intervene in our "internal affairs"? Will they finally not rush into our unhappy home where a ravenous gorilla has literally been swallowing our blood?

June 15 / 28, 1919
The newspapers have been carrying on in an especially frenzied way: "A pirate's band has seized Germany by the throat![7] To arms! One minute more—and the volcano will explode, the banner of

6. "By a Sea Wave" is one of the most popular hymns of the Holy Week liturgy.
7. A reference to the harsh terms imposed by the Allies in the Treaty of Versailles, which the Germans signed in Paris on June 28, 1919.

communism will unfold and glow red throughout the entire world! The moment is a serious one. . . . Let the alarm sound! Now is not the time *to sit around and talk!*"

The *Communist*, published in Kiev,[8] has a marvelous speech by Bubnov about the "unprecedented, panic-stricken, and shameless flight of the Red Army from Denikin."

June 16 / 29, 1919
"Kharkov has fallen under the avalanche of the tsarist hangman Denikin. . . . Denikin has moved on to Kharkov with a horde of officer Huns, savage and drunk. This wild horde is moving like locusts through this tormented land, destroying everything that the blood of our best warriors had won for our bright future. The underlings and lackeys of the imperialist gang of the world are bringing to the gallows the laboring folk, executioners, policemen, hard labor, and continual slavery. . . ."

Strictly speaking, what are the distinguishing features of *all* our revolutionary "literature"? But the hell with them. I'm so glad that I'm an old man. . . .[9]

The "liquidation of Grigoriev's bands" still continues.[1]

June 17 / 30, 1919
Deribasovskaya Street has a new poster: pulp-art of a peasant and a worker with axes who are angrily bashing away at the bald head of an extremely bowlegged and chubby general, struck through with the bayonet of a running Red Army soldier. Under it is the inscription: "Beat 'em lads, good and hard!" Again the work of the

8. The *Communist* (*Kommunist*) was the official newspaper of the Ukrainian Communist party and was published from March 20, 1919, to August 18, 1921.
9. Bunin was forty-nine years old at this time.
1. Grigoriev's rebellion had been crushed by the Bolsheviks by late May 1919, though for the next two months Soviet troops were still engaged in defeating the remnants of his forces. Grigoriev himself would be murdered by Makhno's men on July 27, 1919, their fear being that Grigoriev would set himself up as a rival to their leader.

Political Administration.[2] I ran into S[emyon] Yushkevich who was just coming out of the building where this "administration" was; he *impassively* told me that the Bolsheviks have taken back Kharkov.[3]

I walked home, as if drunk.

Nighttime, the same day

I've calmed down a little. Everyone assures me that it's nonsense to say that Kharkov has been taken back by the Bolsheviks. Moreover, people are saying that Denikin has taken Ekaterinoslav[4] and Poltava, that the Bolsheviks are evacuating Kursk and Voronezh, that Kolchak has broken through the front and is moving toward Tsarytsin, and that Sevastopol' is in the hands of the English (a landing that involved forty thousand troops).[5]

This evening I was out on the main thoroughfare. At first I sat with S. I. Varshavsky's wife and daughter. The daughter was reading. She is a girl scout. She answered my questions hurriedly, curtly, and sharply, like girls of her age often do. The rose-colored crescent of a young moon in the delicate sunset behind Vorontsov Palace; the pale, gentle, almost greenish sky; and the sight of a dear, sweet girl avidly reading a book, and the repulsing of the Bolshevik rumors about Kharkov—all these touched me in a sickly type of way.

People told me this story: Last year, when the Germans came to Odessa, "friends" asked them for permission to have a ball that would last until morning. The German commandant shrugged his

2. The Political Administration of the Revolutionary Military Soviet (*Politicheskii Otdel Revoliutsionnogo Voennogo Soveta*) was founded in March 1919 and organized party propaganda for the army.

3. This was not true. The Whites held Kharkov until December 12, 1919.

4. The Whites had, in fact, taken Ekaterinoslav.

5. Voronezh is a major city in Russia, situated approximately three hundred miles southeast of Moscow. Ekaterinoslav is now known as Dnepropetrovsk. Kursk is a small city in the Ukraine, roughly seventy-five miles northwest of Kharkov. White forces under Denikin did in fact take control of Sevastopol', but with assistance from the English. Sevastopol' was recaptured by the Red Army on November 15, 1920.

shoulders with contempt: "Russia is such a surprising country," he said. "Why is everyone so eager to have a good time?!"

June 18 / July 1, 1919
"The final desperate fight! Everyone, take up positions! The dark clouds are getting thicker and thicker, the cawing of the ravens is getting louder and louder!"—and so forth, and so forth.

In Kiev Rakovsky delivers a lecture about the international situation: "Revolution has seized the entire world. . . . The plunderers are fighting over the catch. . . . We must drown the counterrevolution in Hungary in blood!"[6] Later on he adds: "For shame! In Kharkov *four* of Denikin's men have caused an indescribable panic among our *numerous echelons!*" And the crowning glory: "The fall of Kursk[7] will spell the end of the world revolution!"

I was just at the market. A tramp was running along with a newspaper "extra" in his hands and crying out: "We've just retaken Belgorod, Kharkov, and Lozovaya!"[8]—it literally got so dark before my eyes that I almost fell.

June 19 / July 2, 1919
Yesterday, for several minutes at the market I felt as though I was going to fall. That has never happened to me before. Then I felt lethargy, a revulsion for everything, and a complete loss for the taste of life. After dinner I went to visit the Shchepkins. Kaufman and Lur'e were there. Fel'dman insists that no one believes the telegram that Ispolkom ordered to be published. I bought a copy of this telegram so as to weigh every bit of it. Every word cuts like

6. Hungary was declared a "soviet" republic on March 21, 1919 with Bela Kun as leader. Kun's "red terror," though, so antagonized the population that he paved the way for a dictatorship under Miklos Horthy that came into being on August 1, 1919. Kun fled Budapest three days later.

7. Kursk was occupied by Denikin's men on September 20, 1919, but liberated by the Red Army two months later.

8. Lozovaya is a small city about seventy-five miles directly south of Kharkov. The rumor is not true.

a knife and turns the soul upside down: "A News Bulletin from the Odes. Sov. Wrkers., Peas., and Red Arm. Deputies. The Red forces have taken back Kharkov, Lozovaya, and Belgorod. On June 18th at 1:35, there was this joyous news from Kiev: 'Kharkov, Lozovaya, and Belgorod have been cleansed of White Guard bands, which are fleeing in panic. Denikin's fate has been decided! The proletariat is rejoicing in Kursk. The mobilization is going on at an unheard-of pace. The enthusiasm in Poltava is high.' . . ."

Simply put, instant victory over an expanse of five hundred miles. But if there's "enthusiasm in Poltava," that must mean that the city is safe and sound. But there are also rumors that say something completely different: our forces have taken Kamyshin, Romodan, and Nikopol'.[9]

This morning I still got up at seven and bought newspapers which all said one and the same thing: "Circulating rumors that we have taken back Kharkov, Lozovaya, and Belgorod have not been confirmed. . . ." I did not believe my eyes from joy.

We visited the Rozenbergs just before dinner. It was a very strange evening! They were completely calm — "Why get upset," they said, "the rumors have so far not been confirmed." So things are splendid. . . .

June 20 / July 3, 1919
"Waves of revolution are battering the West. . . . Denikin brings the chains of starvation and slavery. . . . An insane, inhuman terror is bearing down upon the White Guard bands at a frenzied rate. . . . The helpless proletariat has been looted by savage gangs. . . . Our calloused hands must mercilessly crush the counterrevolutionary *reptiles*, both at the front and at home. . . . We must wage a merciless terror against the bourgeois as well as against White Guard bastards, traitors, conspirators, spies, cowards, and self-seekers. . . .

---

9. Kamyshin is a city on the Volga River, about one hundred miles northeast of Volgograd. Romodan is a small town approximately one hundred miles west of Kiev. Nikopol' is a minor urban center roughly two hundred miles southwest of Kharkov.

ODESSA 1919

We must strip the bourgeois of clothes and whatever extra money they have, we must also take hostages!"

All this, including the "calloused hands" that must "crush the *reptile*," is not from the newspapers but rather from the appeals by the People's Commissars of the Ukrainian Socialist Soviet Republic.

All the walls of the city buildings are covered with such appeals. And these appeals, along with what is being written in the newspapers, are rife with savagery and give witness to the terrible horror of these creatures.

"We have abandoned Konstantinograd. . . . A wandering band has seized Kharkov. . . . The taking of Kharkov did not give Denikin the desired results. . . . We have given up Korocha. . . . We have surrendered Liski.[1] . . . The enemy has driven us back farther west of Tsaritsyn. . . . We are chasing Kolchak, who is fleeing in a panic. . . . The Rumanian government is writhing in predeath agony.[2] . . . The revolution is in full swing in Germany.[3] . . . The revolution in Denmark has taken on threatening dimensions.[4] . . . Northern Russia is eating oats and moss. . . .

1. Konstantinograd (renamed Krasnograd in 1922) is a city roughly fifty miles southwest of Kharkov. Korocha is a small town, also about fifty miles from Kharkov, but to the northwest, and Liski is a small hamlet, approximately eighty miles directly west of Korocha.

2. Rumania suffered greatly from the devastation of the world war as well as from the onerous terms imposed by the Allies. For example, the country had to pay more than 5,000 million francs in gold on the grounds that it was liable for part of the debts of the Austro-Hungarian state. Worker strikes also had grown in such number and intensity that the government declared a state of emergency and assumed control of industry. Rumania, though, was still strong enough to put down a "worker-peasant" revolt in Transylvania in December 1918 and to intervene successfully in Hungarian affairs.

3. Throughout the winter and spring of 1919 Germany experienced the establishment of short-lived "soviet republics" in Bremen and Bavaria, as well as strikes and revolts in such cities as Berlin and in such areas as Saxony and the Ruhr region. Such events, however, occurred without a "revolutionary" plan or leadership. In fact, the constitution that would end the Germany monarchy and establish the Weimar Republic was promulgated on July 31, 1919.

4. After the war, unemployment in Denmark increased, prices soared,

Pieces of clothing and snatches of rags are being found in the stomachs of workers who are falling and dying on the streets. . . . To the rescue! The final hour has come! We are not plunderers, we are not imperialists, we give no significance to the fact that we are surrendering territory to the enemy. . . ."

Izvestia has published this verse:

Comrades, the ring has already closed!
Take to arms, those who bear our name!
The house is burning, burning!
Brothers, the house is all aflame,
Toss out the dinner pot, comrades,
Can you think about gorging now?
Our native haunts are perishing.
Sound the alarm, blow the whistle,
Shoot the canon from the bow!

As regards the "dinner pot," things are not good. At the very least our heads keep spinning from the lack of food. At the market, entire crowds sell old things. They sit right on the rocks, and even on the manure. Small piles of rotten vegetables and potatoes are the only things around. This year the harvest around Odessa has been truly biblical. But the peasants do not want to bring anything in. They pour the milk into troughs for the pigs, they visit the taverns, but they don't bring any food with them. . . .

We again went to the archbishop's garden. We often go there now because it is the only clean and quiet place in the city. From there, though, the view is unusually sad—an entirely dead land. Was it all that long ago that the port was bursting with riches and people? Now it is empty, completely empty. Everything that still lies around the docks looks pitiful; everything is rust-covered, peeling, and stripped bare. The protruding smokestacks of the factories

---

strikes were common, and workers often clashed with police. The country also suffered from the effects of the blockade of Germany, resulting in a financial deficit, a severe shortage of goods, and rampant inflation.

over at Peresyp[5] have long died out. But it is still marvelous and quiet and solitary in the garden. We often also drop in at the church there; and each time we are seized by an ecstasy that borders on tears when we observe the singing, the bowings of the priests, the incensing of the church; when we come into contact with all that is grand and decent, with the world of all that is good and merciful; and where all earthly suffering is lightened and assuaged with such comfort, tenderness, and relief. Just think that formerly people of the circle to which I partially belonged went to church only for funerals! Only when a member of an editorial board, the head of a statistics department, a university friend, or someone in exile had died. . . . And once we were in church, we had only one thought, one dream: to go out on the porch and have a smoke. And the deceased? Good Lord, what possibly could have been the tie between his former life and the funeral prayers and the ribbon[6] that he wore on his lemon-colored forehead!

P.S. My Odessa notes break off here. The pages that once followed them I buried so well in a spot in the ground that when we fled from Odessa at the end of January 1920 I could not find them.

5. Peresyp is a suburb of Odessa.
6. Bunin is referring to the *venchik*, a paper band placed on the forehead of the deceased.

CODA

September 25 / October 8, 1919

It has been almost a thousand days and a thousand nights.

I remember the summer of '17 as the beginning of some terrible illness. I felt that I was mortally ill. My head burned, my thoughts were confused, and my surroundings took on a new and terrifying air. But I managed to stay on my legs and waited for something to happen. I waited with feverish tension, with the very last of my physical and spiritual powers.

At the end of that summer I opened the morning newspaper with hands that would not stop shaking; and I suddenly felt I was going pale, and that my mind was going blank as if I were about to faint. A hysterical appeal written in large letters struck me in the eye. "To one and all!"—a cry from Kerensky *urbi et orbi,* to the city and to the world, that Kornilov was a "rebel, a traitor of the homeland." Kerensky did not understand what he himself had brought about,[1] nor did he know that henceforth his own name would be cursed throughout Russia to the *n*th degree. . . .

I have had to listen to thousands of dispatches and bulletins

1. With the failure of the Kornilov Revolt, Kerensky assumed near-dictatorial powers and appointed himself supreme commander of the Russian armed forces. As a result, the last remnants of military discipline collapsed, and Russian soldiers began deserting the front. See Lincoln, *Red Victory,* 42–43.

issuing forth from what was once *our* Russia, news items that have chilled my bones and soul. And I have often said to myself: "Perish the day I was born and the night I was conceived!"[2] If God extends my time on this earth, then perhaps my soul, having been charred by this evil fire, will again look from the heights and see all that is earthly, sordid, and soiled, all that is bloody and base in a different way from the very sickly manner in which I live life now. . . .

Truly, Job's terrible story has become our own. . . . For truly we are "without a home" and outside of human existence. We live on the ashes of a great burned-out edifice, on a garbage heap on the outskirts of the city, beyond the pale of everything where I once drew breath, and outside the walls of a destroyed and profaned Zion.

On this day I lack the words to express all I have endured. But they are not necessary, for my torments can be understood without them.

May your warlike path be blessed, O Hope of Russia.

October 20/November 12, 1919

NOTES

Pogroms against the Jews have resumed. Before the Revolution they were rare, exceptional events.[3] For the past two years,

---

2. Bunin is quoting from Job 3:3.

3. Bunin is sadly mistaken here. The Russian Empire, especially the Ukraine, had a long tradition of pogroms. (In fact, "pogrom" is among one of very few Russian words to enter the English language.) The last tsars masterfully joined anti-Semitism to the rampant xenophobia of the folk and to the schemes of politicians looking for scapegoats for their nation's ills. Government officials and supporters of the tsar often depicted revolutionary leaders as foreigners and grossly exaggerated the numbers of Jews in their ranks.

As a result, Russian statesmen closed their eyes to the pogroms that occurred after the 1881 assassination of Alexander II. The fury continued sporadically for the next two decades. At the beginning of the twentieth century, no Jew could pass a crowd of lower-class Ukrainians or Russians without fear of hearing the terrible cry, "*Bei zhidov!*" or "Beat the kikes!" In the revolutionary events of 1905, local populations staged nearly seven hundred pogroms against the Jews,

CODA

though, they have become a common, nearly everyday occurrence.[4]

This is intolerable. Always to be at the mercy of an unbridled human beast, a human pig; always to be dependent upon this pig's kindness or wrath; always to live in fear for one's home, one's honor, and one's personal life, as well as for the honor and life of one's relatives and close ones; always to live in an atmosphere of fatal catastrophe, of bloody injury and theft; always to be fated to perish without any defense, and for no reason at all, and on the whim of a scoundrel or a brigand—this is an unspeakable horror which we all know now, too well.[5]

Those of us who have already endured three years of the "great Russian Revolution" have this common duty: we must constantly rise up against the perfidy of pogroms; we must constantly keep this wrongdoing in the public consciousness; and we must

---

more than eight of every ten occurring in the Ukraine or nearby Bessarabia. Predictably, Jews suffered greatly in the years immediately after 1917, since they were blamed for the miseries of the Great War.

4. Most of the Jews in the new Soviet state lived in the Ukraine, where they made up more than 60 percent of the 2.6 million inhabitants. Compared to what would follow, the Jews in the Ukraine passed relatively unharmed during the early stages of the civil war. With the departure of the Germans from the area, though, they became frequent victims of pogroms. Indeed, before Hitler the greatest mass murder of the Jews occurred in the Ukraine during the Russian civil war. Estimates range from between 35,000 deaths to more than 100,000. If one includes individuals raped, wounded, orphaned, or stricken with disease, more than a million Jews suffered at the hands of their enemies in the years 1918 and 1919. All participants in the conflict were guilty of murdering Jews, even Bolsheviks. It was, however, the soldiers, Cossacks, and peasants of Denikin's White Volunteer army who committed the greatest number of atrocities.

5. It should be noted that at this time Bunin was one of very few individuals who spoke in the Jews' defense. Indeed, almost no one dared repeat Gorky's bold statement that anti-Semitism was a "disgrace to Russian culture" and that the Jews "were the old, strong leaven of humanity who exalted its spirit and brought noble ideals to the world." Rather, as one observer noted, people preferred "to remain silent and to wash their hands." See Lincoln, *Red Victory*, 323.

Bunin also resisted pressure to join such anti-Semitic groups as the Union of the Russian People (*Soiuz russkogo naroda*), even though such resistance potentially endangered his life. See Muromtseva-Bunina's diary excerpt of September 5/18, 1919, in Grin, *Ustami*, 313–314.

speak out constantly against what everyone knows is going on. . . . For, simply put, we cannot go on living like this.

The time has come for certain groups to think seriously about what they have been doing . . . revolutionaries, Russians, and Jews; people who plot murders with abandon; and all those who for so long now—either individually or in collusion with others—advocate hatred, malice, and seizures of all kinds . . . or yell "death, death!" on highways and byways.

Such groups arouse the beast in man. They set one person against another, class against class; they hoist red banners and fly black flags with white skulls. . . .

Yes, Trotsky is a Jew,[6] but Lenin is not. Biographers write that Lenin's father was "a Volga peasant who . . . became superintendent of schools in that region."[7] . . .

It is wrong that cathedrals have become movie houses and are named after "Comrade Sverdlov." It is monstrous and base to kill a thousand absolutely innocent people to retaliate for the murder of one Uritsky. And it is equally heinous to blame a trampled-on Jew for desecrating churches[8] or for plotting Uritsky's end. After all, that deed was accomplished by Russian sailors, Red Army soldiers, Latvians, and Chinese.[9]

One cannot live without divine and human law, without a sys-

6. Anti-Semites in the Ukraine never tired of pointing out that prominent Bolshevik leaders were Jewish, i.e., Trotsky (whose real name was Bronstein), Zinoviev (Radomyslsky), Kamenev (Rozenfield), Litvinov (Meyer Wallach), Gusev (Drabkin), Sokolnikov, Sverdlov, Uristky, Slutsky, and others.

7. This is not true. Ilya Nikolaevich Ulyanov was not a peasant but a highly educated *intelligent* who, like many idealistic youth of his time, renounced the opportunity for a brilliant career to devote himself to the needs of public education.

8. A common charge in the Russian and Ukrainian anti-Semitism of the time was that "Jew-Communists had changed our holy houses of God into stables." See Lincoln, *Red Victory*, 320.

9. Moisei Uritsky, head of the Cheka in Petersburg, was killed by a poet turned assassin named Leonid Kannegiser. Ironically Uritsky, the son of devoutly Orthodox Jews from the Ukraine, was one of the few Bolsheviks who opposed Lenin's summons to terror, since he feared that it only would deepen the hatred that had begun to consume Russians in the civil war. Uritsky's murder, together with an attempt on Lenin's life on the evening of that same day, triggered a new

CODA

tem of authority and protection to restrain self-willed individuals.[1]
Leo Tolstoy once remarked: "It is a terrible thing to say, but most
people are animals." But one must rise up against the animal in
man and curb it in every possible way; and to do this one must include all peoples—those who are near and far, Russians, Jews,
French, and Japanese. . . .

"Everyone is equal before the law," General Denikin has said.
His government is for conscience, not fear. . . . It seeks to struggle
against everything that brings pain and grief to all the citizens of
Russia, regardless of nationality or class.[2] . . . The pogroms against
the Jews are not the fault of Denikin's government. The fault lies

---

wave of terror in which many innocent people died in the slaughter. See Lincoln, *Red Victory*, 156–160.

1. The Ukrainian Cheka disagreed. They wrote in one of their newspapers:
"For us, there do not, and cannot, exist the old systems of morality and 'humanity.' . . . To us, all is permitted. . . ." See Lincoln, *Red Victory*, 389.

2. Bunin is sadly and shamefully mistaken here: Denikin was an unabashed
anti-Semite. He once told a group of Jews: "Gentlemen, I will be honest with
you. I don't like you Jews. But my attitude toward you is based on humanity. But
I, as commander-in-chief [of the Volunteer Army], will take steps to prevent
pogroms and other acts of lawlessness and will punish severely those who are
guilty. I cannot guarantee, though, that there will be no excesses in the future."
Denikin believed and proclaimed that bolshevism and Judaism were essentially
the same, that Jews were his enemies, and that all Jewry was responsible for Bolshevik "crimes." Denikin deplored the pogroms as "acts of barbarism"; but he also
believed that the folk had good reason to hate the Jews. He thus refused Jewish
requests to condemn and stop the pogroms, or to punish instigators and participants of the violence. Such actions, he believed, would increase hostility toward
his regime, exacerbate the already considerable dissension in his ranks, and nur-
ture suspicions that he had sold out to the "enemy."

Bunin, though, continued to regard Denikin as a hero. Seven years later,
when both men were emigrés in Paris, Bunin gifted the Russian general with a
copy of his works, inscribed with these effusive words: "To Anton Ivanovich
Denikin, in remembrance of the most beautiful day of my life—September 25,
1919, in Odessa—when I would have unhesitatingly and gladly died for him!"
Bunin was referring to the occasion of Denikin's arrival in Odessa after its liberation from the Bolsheviks, and of the delirious welcome given to him by the city's
citizens, including Bunin. (The date, however, is wrong; Odessa was liberated in
August, not September.) See Kenez, *Civil War*, 166–177; Lincoln, *Red Victory*,
318–323; and, Lehovich, *White Against Red*, 424, 524.

with those Russians . . . who wage all kinds of fratricidal strife and
indulge in all kinds of bestial behavior. . . .

The pogroms against the Jews have been going on for such a
long time now that one must call attention . . . to what the ill-fated
Jewish population has had to suffer not only throughout the
Ukraine but throughout all of Poland and the regions in the southwest. . . . Streams of Jewish blood have merged with the rivers of
blood pouring forth from all the fronts of our civil war, a conflict
that grows increasingly terrible and absurd. It is the elemental
anger of the Russian people . . . that rages on with such terrible
force.

What can [Denikin's] government do about this unhappy
state of affairs? One can only hope . . . that it will staunchly . . .
with harsh and just punishment, put an end to all that is criminal,
base, and unacceptable in the community of humankind. . . .

Our revolutionaries are completely justified when they express their indignation at pogroms and at the Russian extermina-
tion of the Jews. . . . But, good God, how cruelly and regularly did
these revolutionaries also hurl their spears at me . . . when I spoke
about the dark and bestial aspects of my people . . . or when I de-
cried all the wrongdoing that passed under the name of revolution,
or when I waited for Europe to intervene in the savage and absurd
villainy that has been taking place on our Christian soil for the
past two and a half years!

In December of last year, when the French entered Odessa
. . . and promised to return us to some minimal level of humanity
. . . I wrote:

And pain and shame—and joy. . . .
But let it all be so.
Hail to you, Varangian.[3]

3. The Varangians were Norman warriors who served the Byzantine emperors. In Russian sources they are first mentioned in the *Primary Chronicle* in
which, according to legend, they were invited to rule the Russian land. During
the ninth and eleventh centuries Varangian warrior-bodyguards served Russian
princes, and Varangian merchants conducted trade from Scandinavia to Byzan-

CODA

Kill the enemy, destroy the foe!
In the name of God and humankind.
Stop the bloody killing,
Subdue the filthy hog,
Tear down the bloody flag,
Oust the demagogue![4]

But how did our revolutionaries answer me? *Odessa News* wrote that my political views were "repulsive" and sought to lecture me by saying that "revolution is something more complex than Mr. Bunin thinks it is." *Southern Worker* addressed these ironic ditties to me:

Fearful, you wasted no time
To revere the Varangian as your god,
And with shameful, abject praise
Proclaimed yourself his slave, his rod. . . .

I am encountering the same hostility even now. How many pages did Pavel Yushkevich fill when he calculated the number of Jews who were killed in pogroms? How many criminal acts did he register, how many cruel words did he utter as regards Russian savagery? . . . But just look at how this very same Yushkevich mocks me for my lecture on the Russian people and the Russian Revolution, how passionately he stands up for the very folk [which he himself has judged so harshly], how he fulminates against me, how he censures me. "Bunin's judgments are boring and bilious," he says.

---

tium along Russian rivers. Also, the Kievan princes Vladimir Svyatoslavich and Yaroslav the Wise often invited hired detachments of Varangians to participate in internecine wars and struggles against neighboring countries and peoples. Varangian warriors and merchants, though, did not play a substantial role in the development of the Russian state, and were rapidly assimilated into Russian society.

4. The final stanza of this poem reads: "Enough of the tears that villain has caused/ Under his banner of 'equality and joy'/ Enough of these leaders of the streets/ And of sham power of the 'people,' of the hoi polloi." See O. Il'nitskaia, "V *Okaiannye Dni*," *Neva*, No. 3 (1991), 182.

Indeed, as far as Yushkevich and these other gentlemen are concerned, all the suffering, all the pain of our country's great torments are only bile!

"Most honorable academician Bunin," these rebels tell me, "one cannot approach the Revolution with the outlook and understanding of a *criminal reporter. . . .*"

These same revolutionaries continue: "Hegel talked about the rationality of all existence . . . and the Russian Revolution has this rationality, a sense of purpose." . . .

I respond: "O, you extremely wise Hegelians . . . if you insist that rationality and sense exist when the skulls of landowners, merchants, and officers are being split open . . . then God knows what kind of conclusions you can come up with! . . .

October 25 / November 7, 1919

NOTES

On October 25, 1917, the Winter Palace fell. It had been the meeting place for the so-called Provisional Government, a group of lawyers, doctors, and journalists who would peacefully sing student songs and hoist beers to Stenka's "cliff."

Why is this date so important? Precisely what happened on this day? This day brought to a climax six months of revolutionary chaos in Russia, events that took place under the exalted leadership of a second-class lawyer, who, as one of the ministers of this Provisional Government, I. M. Kishkin, told me, could not live an hour without cocaine.[5]

5. Kishkin's first initial is "N" (Nikolai), not "I," as Bunin asserts. Although there is no truth to Kishkin's charge, Kerensky's frenzied oratory seemed to suggest that he had questionable sources for his inspiration. Milyukov recalled: "By the expression of [Kerensky's] eyes, the tense gesturing of his hands, the intonations of his voice, which first rose to a scream . . . and then to a tragic whisper, by his measured phrases and calculated pauses, this man wanted to instill fear and to create an impression of power and force. The actual effect was pitiful." See Lehovich, *White Against Red,* 121.

CODA

The supporters of the Revolution defend the "great Russian happening" by saying that "events of these days were just like those that took place during the great French Revolution." One can only thank them for such a defense. Yes, yes, it was exactly the same. First, the vanguard was a group of dreamers and idealists who were shortsighted and flighty; who lacked an understanding of real life; who, even if they had been seized by noble goals, did not think them out to the end; and who, in the final analysis, were chatterboxes, phrasemongers, and power-hungry types. Then authority grew weak and confused. . . . Next the folk became increasingly savage and insane. Growing numbers of riffraff and scum—innate murderers, robbers, and scoundrels—screamed that they represented the "people." Finally there arose from this folk a gang of the most select villains and beasts, genuine leaders of any genuine revolution, individuals who yelled "in the name of the people" and "freedom, brotherhood, and equality" in a frenzied, pompous, and theatrical way.

One must always remember that repulsive theatrics are one of the key features of any revolution. Indeed, this gang of thugs orchestrated a puppet show which was so bloody, a comedy which was so vile and base, that even a hundred years from now the world community will be stunned when it recalls how base and bloodthirsty the human heart can be . . . that it is the most evil and sordid of all the hearts beating on this earth.

Yes, the French Revolution was indeed monstrously loathsome and bloody, but how can one bloody and loathsome event justify another? . . .

This "great Russian Revolution," though, differs from its great French counterpart in that it is more absurd, base, vulgar, and inane, and that it has brought about greater wickedness, destruction, shame, cold, hunger, and wholesale slaughter. The "great Russian Revolution" is a thousand times more bestial, filthy, and stupid than the vile original which it claims to copy, because it exceeds—step by step, item for item, and in a horribly shameless and explicit way—the bloody melodrama that had played itself out in France. The "great Russian Revolution" is worse than the "great French Revolution" because it is taking place on the Russian stage, amidst idiots from Poshekhon'ya[6] and half-savages from the forest and the steppe; because it is being sustained by German merce-naries at the bidding of their government; and, because, I repeat, it is a vile and bloody puppet show, one that is beyond all human description.

October 25, 1917, was the beginning of a folk spectacle. Be-fore that the violins had only been tuning up, even though Russia had already been destroyed, disgraced, and forever debased by the Kerenskys of all shapes, colors, and sizes . . . as well as by *tens of thousands* of the most bloody and insane petty tyrants, savages from the folk who, from March through August, had begun to register— only begun to register, mind you—with this very same Provisional Government.

I believe that from now on that date will be cursed by almost all the Russian presses that exist in places occupied by the White Army, by forces which are gradually destroying the blood-soaked stage where this spectacle plays out.

But I also know well that there still exist people who will joy-ously cry "Long live [the Revolution]," for they do not want to un-derstand—or simply cannot understand—that one "cannot keep the rumble going after the drum has been beaten." And part of the press here in Odessa will go along with such individuals, heart and soul.

But was it all that long ago that when the "people's revolu-tionary army" marched triumphantly into Odessa, almost a third of the population, including many die-hard supporters of the Rev-olution, went into absolute panic, ran wherever their eyes could

6. Bunin is referring to Saltykov-Shchedrin's fictionalized autobiography, *Old Days in Poshekhonie* (*Poshekhonskaia starina*, 1887–1889), in which the writer censures the landed gentry of his youth.

CODA

follow, and carried on worse than our ancestors did at the sight of the Polovetsian Hordes at the gates of their cities?[7]

Was it all that long ago that revolutionary ribbons and bows glowed like fire so pervasively on all Odessa "comrades" and even on cabbies' horses, that the sight of red still oppresses the heart in such a sickly and nauseous way?

Was it all that long ago that red flags and glass stars, Medusa-like, hovered above the streets, the police stations, and theaters and clubs with the names of "Trotsky," "Sverdlov," and "Lenin"; and that the reflections from these flags and stars shone forth like streams of blood on the sidewalks, during those cursed wretched evenings when it was still light out but the clocks showed something mocking and absurd?

Was it all that long ago that "comrade" aristocracies and "warriors for socialism" declared "peace to the huts and war on the palaces" but then immediately took up living in these very same palaces?

Was it all that long ago that the streets were filled with pickpockets, criminal thieves, and sailors sporting automatic pistols and shiny boots?

Was it all that long ago that clean-shaven dandies tried as hard as they could to imitate the fops of the "old regime" whom they so hated? Was it all that long ago that they showed their gold teeth, their huge, cocaine-filled eyes, and their dandyish shoes, service jackets, and most repulsive looking riding breeches with the inevitable spurs? . . .

Was it all that long ago that these dandies and their hookers rushed through the strangely empty but still lighted streets in cars

---

7. The Polovtsy were a primarily Mongol- and Turkic-speaking people who, sometime in the eleventh century, migrated from the Trans-Volga region to the steppes north of the Black Sea. Originally nomadic herdsmen, they turned to various crafts and made shoes, saddles, weapons, and clothes. The Polovtsy clashed with the Russians from 1054 until the 1180s. In time they were absorbed into the Golden Horde or moved to Hungary, where they settled and were hired for military service.

and smart-looking cabs to attend their own theaters and to applaud their own peasant actors?

Was it all that long ago that truck drivers parked alongside police stations and revved up their motors at night so that no one could hear the rifle shots and the cries of victims who were being tortured and killed, and sometimes even literally being stripped of their skins[8]—and all for the glory of the European "socialist proletariat," who, to this very day, furiously demand that other countries stay out of these "internal affairs" of Russia?

Was it all that long ago that all kinds of "proletcults" flowered alongside the hellish receptacles of endless crimes, and that all kinds of young scoundrels created savagely boorish posters using the slogans of the Futurists, i.e., people of the future?

Was it all that long ago that artists hustled about, worrying about how to decorate and string lights over a city which, forsaken by God, had become a veritable place of execution, and that these artists did this to celebrate the joyous First of May and to entertain that very "revolutionary proletariat" who strolled about and looked at their "art" while munching sunflower seeds, having their socialist legs clothed with the trousers of murdered and robbed "counterrevolutionaries"? . . .

Was it all that long ago that these very same democrats who . . . protested so fearlessly when the Volunteers were here, taking them to task for the "repression of the free word," "the interference with the democratic congress," and the "arbitrary execution" of dozens of scoundrels, were so quiet and took cover when the

---

8. This was true. The Cheka not only skinned people alive but had other ways of torturing its victims. In Voronezh, for instance, the Cheka rolled its prisoners around in a barrel into which nails had been driven; their counterparts in Kharkov used scalping as a preferred form of torture. In other cities Chekhists used a "death wreath" which applied increasing pressure to prisoners' skulls; or they separated prisoners' joints by sawing through their bones; or they poured molten wax on prisoners' faces, arms, and necks. Chekhists in Kiev were the most sadistic of all. There the police placed rats in pieces of pipe that had been closed at one end, and placed the open end against prisoners' stomachs. They then heated the pipes until the rodents, maddened by the heat, tried to escape by gnawing their way into the victims' intestines. See Lincoln, *Red Victory*, 383–385.

CODA

"workers and peasants" returned and immediately snuffed out any human word, when they screamed . . . "Death, death!" . . . and when they began "arbitrarily" to execute and torture hundreds of thousands? . . .

Was it all that long ago that such events took place? And just how should these events be understood? . . . Simply put, such happenings are the stuff of all revolutions, not just that upheaval which calls itself bolshevism.

But bolshevism is a revolution, that very same revolution that is the inexpressible joy of all those people who dream of starting everything from the beginning and who, lacking a present, see the past as "cursed" and the future as "bright." . . .

Yes, yes, my dear rebels, go on defending revolutions not only in Russia but throughout the world. Yes, yes, go on insisting that revolutions are "elemental" phenomena and that there are "reasons" for everything that happens. Are not earthquakes more "elemental" [than revolutions]? Are there not "reasons" for cholera and plague? But who rejoices over any of these? Yes, yes, go on fantasizing that a heavenly garden will grow from where thistle has been planted, and that "the doglike face of a generation" will bring to God's world a new human countenance more splendid than any before now.

November 7 / 20, 1919[9]

NOTES

I have been leafing through the writings of Tolstoy, through pages I have read many, many times.

"There is no enlightenment other than the Christian one; our world is filled with scholarly savages. . . ." ("Thoughts").[1]

"Your Imperial Majesty, I am a weak, insignificant, and sin-

9. Bunin wrote this article on the ninth anniversary of Tolstoy's death.

1. Tolstoy's "Thoughts" ("*Mysli*") was a compilation of excerpts taken from his diary and other works, and was published in *Sochineniia grafa L. N. Tolstogo* (Moscow, 1911), vol. 20. This citation is found on 167.

ful soul, who is writing to advise you as regards the most complex and burdensome events ever to occur [in our land]. . . .

"Your father, that Russian tsar, who had accomplished so much good and always wished the people well, was a kind man who was brutally murdered in the name of a common good.[2] You now stand in his place and face the same enemies who wish to kill you also, in the name of that same bogus common good [that ended the life of your father]. I cannot imagine a worse situation than yours. . . .

"I know how far our present world is from the sacred truths handed down to us by Jesus Christ. . . . I know that I'm a worthless nobody who is subject to temptations that are a thousand times more trifling than those that surround you. And I know that I am being impudent and insane when I appeal to you to show a strength of spirit that is without precedent or example: to do good to enemies that wish you ill. . . .

"But truth will always be the truth. There are two plans of action you can follow, two pieces of advice you can pursue. You can put down evil with evil, or you can be 'liberal' and look the other way. Both these ways have been tried previously and lead nowhere. . . . But there is yet another new way—the way of Christian resignation to God's will. . . . Your Majesty! Follow this way. . . . 'Love your enemies' " ("Letter to Alexander III").[3]

"The Marxes, the Jaureses, the Kautskys, and other theoreticians have written tons of books on how human society must be. . . . But no one talks about how to end the most immediate and potent cause of evil—the violence that workers commit against themselves. Just the reverse, everyone agrees to the necessity of the

2. During his reign, Alexander II implemented a series of reforms which included the abolition of serfdom, the establishment of *zemstva* or "district assemblies," and changes in the judicial, municipal, and military systems. On March 1, 1881, in Saint Petersburg, Alexander was assassinated by a member of the terrorist group "The People's Will."

3. Tolstoy wrote "Letter to Alexander III" (*"Pis'mo Aleksandru III"*) on March 8–15, 1881.

very violence that brings about enslavement. . . ." ("To the Revolutionary").[4]

"To allow the Russian people to follow upon the path traveled by peoples of the West means consciously to commit acts of violence, i.e., to rob, to burn, to destroy, to kill, and to wage internecine war. . . . This error is at the root of all the chaos in the past, present, and even future lives of Christian peoples. . . . People have grown so accustomed to see force as the only way of influencing others that they do not see the contradiction in using violence to achieve equality and brotherhood. They do not see that equality, in its very essence, negates both power and subservience, that freedom is incompatible with force, that there can be no brotherhood between oppressors and oppressed. Indeed, this error gives rise to all the horrors of a terror. Furthermore this contradiction, which so coarsely and clearly expressed itself in the great French Revolution, is very much in evidence now. . . . And it will continue to make itself manifest in the ideas of the most progressive socialists and revolutionaries. . . .

"Revolutionaries say: 'It is through murder that one brings about the ideas of a common good!'

"The great French Revolution was that *enfant terrible* which, in its most undisguised form, showed the absolute absurdity of that contradiction which humankind struggled for then and continues to struggle for now, i.e., 'Freedom, brotherhood, equality—and death!'

"Revolutions have happened and continue to happen in France, Spain, and South America, and now in Russia; but whether these revolutions are successes or failures, their aftermaths have risen up like suppressed waves and have returned their countries to the very same situation as before, and sometimes to some-

4. Tolstoy wrote "To the Revolutionary" ("K *revoliutsioneru*") on January 20–26, 1909.

thing even worse. . . . Forms change, but the essence of human re-
lationships does not. . . . ("One Thing Do We Need").[5]

"The people of the great French Revolution wished to achieve
equality; but they erred when they thought this equality could be
attained through violence. They should have realized that such a
cause and effort could never be the case, since violence, in and of
itself, is the sharpest manifestation of *inequality*. Neither can the
freedom that is the goal of the present revolution[6] be achieved by
force. Yet the people who are waging revolution in Russia think
that if they do everything that is part and parcel of European
revolutions—solemn funerals, brilliant speeches, constituent assemblies, an end to prisons, and so forth—they will reach their
goal! . . .

"Cromwell, that very great hypocrite and monster, executed
another hypocrite, Charles I; furthermore he mercilessly sent millions of people to their ruin and destroyed the very freedom he was
supposedly fighting for. . . ."[7]

"Louis[8] was executed, and the Marats and Robespierres immediately seized power and committed crimes greater than the
crown had ever been accused of. They destroyed not only people
but also the truth that these people were proclaiming at this
time. . . ."

"Therefore speak to me about your interests and not about
[those of] the people. Do not lie when you speak about the folk.
Wage war with the government if you cannot help doing so; but
know that you are fighting for yourself, not for the people; that this
violent struggle embraces nothing noble or good; and that it is also
very harmful and stupid, and most importantly, immoral. . . ."

5. Tolstoy wrote "One Thing Do We Need" ("*Edinoe na potrebu*") on
March 25, 1905.

6. Tolstoy is of course referring to the Revolution of 1905.

7. Bunin is referring to the English civil wars as well as to the Irish and
Scottish campaigns in the mid-seventeenth century. Charles I was executed on
January 30, 1649.

8. Louis XVI, last king of France.

CODA

"For the people to improve their lot, they themselves must improve. . . ."

"In times of revolution, public morality keeps declining, and the most immoral people become the heroes of the period. . . ."

"Try to lighten the people's burdens as much as possible, but if you cannot help them, then, at the very least, do not confuse or torment them. . . ."

"The people in Russia who are now fighting the government—liberal gentry, doctors, lawyers, writers, and students, together with several thousand workers who have had no contact with the folk but who have come under the sway of propaganda— consider themselves the representatives of the people, but they have no right to do so. . . . *In the name of the people*, these individuals demand that the government proclaim freedom of the press, freedom of conscience, freedom of assembly, the separation of church and state, and so forth. But ask the people, the 100 million peasants, their view of these demands, and one will find that folk are not interested in them at all. The liberal and revolutionary activists who draft these manifestos and programs . . . are out only for themselves. . . ." (From various articles).

Having cited these excerpts from Tolstoy's writings, and having dwelled on the genuine essence of his teachings, I think I have done something that he would warmly approve of. . . . Indeed, even *Tolstoy* often has to be defended these days, since many of the individuals whom he has reproached in these excerpts either blaspheme his name or cite passages from his writings out of context, or maliciously distort his ideas to suit their own ends.

I repeat: Tolstoy is being routinely vilified and misrepresented by people who are covered with blood from head to toe, by monsters who are without precedent in the world, who have been ruling Russia in the name of the Russian people for two years already, yet who, louder than anyone else in the entire universe, cry out about the human good.

Some people now say that Tolstoy did a great deal of harm by destroying the authority and prestige of the government and by reprimanding Russian rulers and the upper strata of Russian society. But they forget that Tolstoy was like all great teachers of humankind in that he spoke for all time, not a specific moment in history. These individuals forget that when they rebuke Tolstoy, they also rebuke Christ and the Buddha.

By contrast, others rejoice that Tolstoy destroyed and reprimanded higher-ups. But these forget that he wished to destroy not only Russian authority but authority in general, and that he censured not only Catherine [the Great], Peter [the Great], and Nicholas II but, with his last words, also accused himself of being a very great criminal.

November 8 / 21, 1919

NOTES

There was, and thank God there still exists, an intelligent and talented Russian writer who has been neither tortured nor murdered, who is neither dead from a heart attack nor from sorrow and pain for his homeland, or from shame at being a human being. He is a rare type of writer not only because intelligence and talent are, generally speaking, rare things these days, but also because he has not lost his intelligence and talent amidst all the various types of vileness that have flowered so lavishly in Russian literature over the past few decades. This writer is Iv. F. Nazhivin.

Nazhivin is a peasant by birth, who has endured much to develop himself and to become an educated person. He lived in Europe for a long time where he was both a leftist and a disciple of Tolstoy. When he returned to the homeland and during the Revolution,[9] he lived for two years amidst his native villagers as well as those intellectuals with whom he shared scholarly and spiritual

---

9. Nazhivin visited the Bunins in late December 1918. The meeting, though, was bittersweet, since Nazhivin acknowledged the accuracy of Bunin's dire predictions for his homeland. "I used to hate you, Ivan Alexeevich," Nazhivin told the writer. "I could not bear to hear your name because of the way you depicted the folk in your novels. Now I bow low before you. . . . I, a peasant, did

interests. Throughout this period he saw and suffered much; he pondered and reevaluated many things in life.

Nazhivin summed up his experiences in a remarkable book entitled *What Really Should We Do?*[1] The work is valuable because it is talented and sincere: its facts, observations, and pictures of Russian life are authentic, not invented; its feelings, sentiments, and fundamental knowledge [of Russian life] are things that have been lacking in our literature, and, to our detriment, even more so now.

Because of his book, though, Nazhivin is beginning to be persecuted in a malicious, coarse, and most obscene type of way.

Why?

For the simple reason that he dared to say things that violated the credo of the left.

It would seem that one could simply say to Nazhivin: "In our view, you have made a mistake because of this thing or that."

One could express himself even more strongly and say: "It is not good that you have said this or that"—if the person really deserves such a remark.

But when reviewers begin mocking this outstanding Russian person and writer, when they start slandering him with all kinds of clichés, as leftists are often wont to do, when they say that Nazhivin's inner being is "bald" (whatever that means!) . . . that he has a "small and wrinkled soul with the devastated spirit of a frightened and repentant intellectual"[2] (as if we truly have nothing to fear or atone for amidst the hellish ferocity and vileness of our revolution) . . . [when these reviewers also assert] that Nazhivin "recites anxious lyrics and sheds democratic tears on the waistcoat of

---

not see what you, a *barin*, saw. You alone were right." See Muromtseva-Bunina's diary excerpt, written on January 12, 1919, in Grin, *Ustami*, 205.

    1. Nazhivin wrote *What Really Should We Do? (Chto zhe nam delat'?)* in 1919.

    2. Throughout his time in Russia, critics leveled the same charge against Bunin. See, for instance, Iu. Aikhenval'd, "Literaturnye nabroski. Ivan Bunin. Sukhodol," *Rech'* (November 6, 1912), 2.

officers in police stations"... that he changes his mind, even though this is nothing to be ashamed of ... since many great ... people have done so (after all, it was Tolstoy who said that only fools and dummies grow rigid, refuse to change, and do not mature with age and experience) ... and finally, when these reviewers tell shameful lies about Nazhivin and distort his book at every turn ... [such people] treat contemporary Russian literature with the greatest rudeness. And I ... hardly the newest person in this literature ... decisively protest their actions and hope that my views will be shared by many of my colleague writers. ...

I repeat: one may or may not agree with Nazhivin. One may argue with him, refute him, or regret that he is no longer a socialist and a revolutionary but a constitutional monarchist (as he has begun openly to call himself). One may shrug one's shoulders when Nazhivin suggests that Jews should be declared foreign nationals—if that is what he truly thinks—but to rebuke him ... in an indecent way ... or to rush off in a frenzy and seek to silence a great Russian individual and writer—such actions are not "liberal," nor should they be tolerated or allowed.

Dear God, what is going on? One dare not say anything these days! One can't "haul off and let someone have it" even in one's own home! Is it so terrible for Nazhivin to think that his homeland, as he knows and understands it, would be better off as constitutional monarchy, not a socialist republic? What's the big deal about that? Especially when given the fact that Nazhivin regularly makes the rounds of Muscovite cathedrals where, in his words, "all our history" unfolds before him: where, in his view, "the soul of Russia flickers under ancient arches, like the icon lamp before Tsar Ivan the Terrible's tomb";[3] and where he so deeply feels the past of our old, albeit somber and dark, native home.

Has Nazhivin committed such a terrible crime, and are his feelings so depraved that they reveal a "longing for Ivan the Terri-

---

3. Ivan the Terrible is buried in the Cathedral of the Archangel (*Arkhangel'-skii sobor*) inside the Kremlin.

CODA

ble," as his critics insist. . . . Let Russia be our common home, and let all its peoples have equal rights in it. . . .

November 12 / 25, 1919

NOTES

An Eastern proverb says, "If dogs are barking, that means we must be moving!"

But I know another Eastern poem:

Somebody once asked Saadi: "Where're you off to so fast?"
"To chase a drunken camel," Saadi said.
"But why bother about this? You're no camel, after all!"
"Well, dear, the bazaar's beyond your head:
There one can shout: 'Saadi's a drunken camel!'
And people will believe it and kill me dead."

In Odessa, after my lecture on the Russian Revolution[4] and two or three of my articles in the paper, people began to persecute me. They purposely distorted my words, even added things that I had never said.

The people of the Odessa bazaar will not succeed in turning me into a camel, but they are attempting to do so with singular inventiveness. . . . Indeed, they slander me with an abandon that is usually possible only when one lies about the deceased. . . .

For instance, in my recent "Notes on Nazhivin," I truly did not say a single word in defense of Nazhivin's beliefs, nor did I object to the possibility or to the charge that he had erred, or said an untruth, or uttered an infelicitous word in his writing. Rather, I only protested the rudeness, intolerance, fierce narrow-mindedness, liberal vulgarity, and bad writing [that greeted his works] and that has already caused so much harm in Russia. . . .

[A newspaper] responded . . . with a small article entitled

---

4. Bunin is referring to his lecture "The Great Narcotic," which appears in subsequent pages.

"Time to Mourn," which says that I myself am a camel, that I have been killed, and that I am also dead in Russian literature. . . .

Indeed, people have not only invented a story that I am among the deceased, but they also have begun to wail on the streets: "Time to mourn, time to mourn."

And in all probability, there have been passersby who have stopped and thought: "Well, there's no smoke without fire, and one can't cry like that without a reason . . . so, perhaps, if Bunin's not dead yet but still alive, he's probably on his last legs." Then *Odessa News* verifies the rumor, and everyone starts writing [obituaries]. In light of everything that had been said above, and also taking into account the wisdom of Saadi, I do not consider it superfluous to inform my readers that "rumors of my death are greatly exaggerated."

All joking aside, I do have this to say. I know that it is not good to get mixed up with the bazaar. And I repeat: [what has happened to me] is not a random or a personal occurrence but something that is typical, and by its very essence more remarkable than it seems at first sight. [What has happened to me] is something that is very, very stupid and sad, especially when one takes into account these terrible times which are far from over for us.

These days it is routine for our political rivals . . . to spread lies about us . . . to discredit us and shut our mouths. This is a bolshevism of a special type. As one of our writers for this newspaper said so well: "What's the point of talking? All means [to ends] are good, and the best of them is to take your enemies to the wall and shoot them"!

I am not for the left or the right. I have been, am, and will be an implacable enemy of everything that is stupid and divorced from life, of all that is evil, false, dishonest, and harmful, whatever its source.

I also do not fear Russians, despite the fact that I have had the courage to say many harsh words about my people—words which not only reality but *even L. N. Tolstoy* have verified so terribly. . . .

CODA

Indeed, even though the critics have reproached me for citing Tolstoy, it was his own lips that uttered literally the following in 1909 (to Bulgakov):

"If I have cited Russian peasants as harborers of some especially attractive features, I regret what I have done, and I am ready to retract my words."[5]

Furthermore, I am not afraid of Germans and the English. Nor do I fear Rumanians and the Jews. And I think that attempts to label me as favoring either right or left are stupid, malicious, and politically motivated.

I do acknowledge, however, that I have an acute sense for certain distinctive and distasteful traits that mark various nationalities. And, generally speaking, I do not have a high opinion of people, especially now, after all that God has caused me to see over the past few years.

I believed in people a bit more in the past than I do now—I was a supporter of the republics;[6] but at present I have begun to have doubts about them. (Do not trouble yourself to look at me with menacing eyes—you do not frighten me.) And I am not so proud as those Odessa journalists who imagine that what satisfies English constitutional monarchists will not suit our idiots who lose their way in broad daylight and who gnaw at each other's throats to the delight of Satan himself.

Even now I sometimes think: "In an ideal world, all these direct, equal, secret, and open elections would be a wonderful idea." And, generally speaking, "government by the people" also seems quite plausible. But, as I am no shy ten-year-old, I will say openly and without any fear: I am convinced that all these Pilas and Sysoikas[7] don't give a damn about these open and secret elections,

---

5. Bunin is again quoting from Bulgakov's memoirs of Tolstoy.
6. After the Revolution, Finland, Estonia, Lithuania, Poland, Belorussia, and the Ukraine pursued a policy of "self-determination" apart from the new Soviet state.
7. Pila and Sysoika were poverty-stricken peasants in Fyodor Reshetnikov's *The People of Podlipovnoye (Podlipovtsy)*, published in 1864.

and that this Russian "government by the people" will once more perpetuate the most vile and bloody nonsense. We have seen and continue to see what our "government by the people" has shown itself to be!

I gasp from shame and pain when I think about this "government by the people" as well as about the reign of both the "Provisional Government" and of "Worker-Peasant Power." I do not believe in something better or different either. I really don't. Convince me [of the contrary]; I will be only too happy if you would.

I have still one more thing to say. . . . [for] I have no intention of hiding my emotions. . . . I have a genuinely savage hatred and a genuinely savage contempt for revolutions. [And I believe] that one cannot help but have these emotions in these days when one must have a steadfast heart to talk at length . . . especially when the republics are experiencing new extremes of internecine slaughter in the trenches and on the fronts, when they are standing on the very edge of the hellish abyss into which Russia has fallen, and when hundreds of thousands of beings—still living—suffer in unheard-of ways, when they perish in tears, grief, darkness, cold, and hunger, when they endure torture, shootings, bloody outrages, and constant insults and abuse, and when they groan under the heel of exultant scoundrels, monsters, and boars!

There, I've said it. This is what I *personally* feel and think *at the present moment*. What I will think and feel tomorrow, I do not know. But I will be the first one to rejoice should life lessen my pessimism. Now I'm saying what I'm saying: "I do not suggest anything, I do not propose anything, I am only stating how I think and feel."

CODA

November 17 / 30, 1919

FROM "THE GREAT NARCOTIC"[8]

[I recall] the summer of 1917. . . . My head had become muddled from reading newspapers all day long, from the speeches, appeals, and exclamations from all those ludicrous and abominable Kerenskys. And I thought: "No, these Bolsheviks are a bit smarter. Not for nothing do they go on being impudent and arrogant. They know their public!". . . .

[I also recall] a grey, nasty day at the end of October that year. Having made my way down along a dirty village street, I entered a hut. An old lady was lying on the stove;[9] and a soldier's wife, her daughter-in-law, was sleeping on a bunk bed. An old man was sitting on a wooden horse and making bast shoes. It was twilight. There was a terrible stench, and the wet and rotting straw on the floor made smacking sounds under our feet. It all was so humdrum, so backward and still, that I seemed to be living in the sixteenth century, not in the stormy epoch of the "great Russian Revolution," on the eve of elections for the Constituent Assembly. I sat down on a bench, lit a cigarette, and said in a joking way:

"Well, old lady, are you getting ready to vote? After all, the election campaigns have already begun."

She answered me in a rather bad-tempered way:

"What elections? What campaigns?"

8. Bunin delivered his lecture "The Great Narcotic" on September 21 and October 3, 1919. What follows are three excerpts from his speech.

After the first reading of his lecture, Muromtseva-Bunina wrote on September 21, 1919: "Ian became completely hoarse after the lecture. He never imagined how hard it would be to read it through. Also, he got so carried away that he forgot to take a break. He held the public's attention for three hours; not one person left the hall. When he finished, everyone rose and applauded him for a long time. Everyone was very excited. . . . One said, 'Ivan Alexeevich is the greatest of all writers—what courage, what truth! It is remarkable! What an historic day!' He had tears in his eyes, and I was deeply touched." Two weeks later she added: "Ian read his 'The Great Narcotic' a second time. Even more people came out to hear him." See Grin, *Ustami*, 315, 316.

9. Russian stoves are huge affairs with bunks for people to lie on top.

"This is the tenth time I've told you about them. You know, the election campaigns that are going on all over the place." She first fell silent and then spoke in a manner that was firm, unbending, and, because of our long-standing friendship, wantonly coarse:

"I know you're joking. No village woman would take part in such a shameful thing—only stupid, curious girls, perhaps, but who would also object to getting all gussied up for such an event. May lightning strike them, all these elections. It's fugitive soldiers and brash masters like you that's shoved the tsar off his throne— now you'll see what's gonna happen. It's all right now, but wait 'till you see what's gonna happen, what's yet to come!"

"And how about you, old man?" I asked.

But he too answered very firmly:

"Master, you couldn't tie me up and drag me to such a place. Why, they'd crack my skull if I didn't vote the way they wanted me to. Russia has perished, master, you mark my words, it's perished! We can't have this voting thing." . . .

"What do you mean—'We can't have this voting thing'?"

"We can't have any freedom. Take me, for example. Don't you see how quiet and submissive I am? I'm good and kind so long as I don't have freedom. But if someone would give it to me, I'd be the first to rob, pillage, and destroy. Not for nothing do we have the proverb: 'Freedom is worse than no freedom.' No, master, I ain't going to any elections, I'll die first."

At that moment the soldier's wife woke up. She opened her clear eyes, still filled with sleep. Then, with a slight smile, she stretched and saw that I was looking at her.

"And what about you? Are you going?" I asked.

"You bet I am! Sure as I'm lying here! I'm not afraid of any old Kabelek." . . .

You're probably asking: "Who's this Kabelek? What kind of person is he?"

Kabelek was one of those fugitive soldiers the old lady had spoken of, who had stormed through our village throughout the summer and fall of '17. For days on end he would run about drunk. This Kabelek once saw the people of the village gathering in the churchyard to meet the two young women who had just arrived from the city to conduct a census. . . . He immediately rushed off to where everyone was; and once he got there he sent the registry table flying to the devil, waved his fists at the women and the peasants, and yelled in a frenzied voice: "Down with all of you! Get the hell out of here! I will not allow this to go on. Don't you know what you're signing your names to? To bring back serfdom, that's what! I'll kill everyone here first! All of you get out of my sight!"

And so it went all summer and fall. He kept chasing everyone away. He even chased away the laymen and clergy who had come to the church to vote. "Down with you all! Get the hell out of here!" he would say. "My brother is coming home from the front—he'll give you something to pray about!"

The village gathered together five times that summer to "trim Kabelek's wings"—but to no avail. They were afraid he would burn down their homes.

November 24 / December 7, 1919

FROM "THE GREAT NARCOTIC"

Last year, on the First of May, there appeared in Moscow, in so-called "Soviet" Russia . . . the first issue of the *Communist International.*[1] The cover of this journal had the usual cheap popular print: a most vulgar picture of a hastily drawn earthly sphere, surrounded with iron chains, and the figure of a worker who is smashing these chains with a hammer. Not unexpectedly, the worker is naked, wearing only a leather apron; and, equally unsurprising, he flexes muscles like those of Hercules.

Opening the issue, one first reads Gorky's shockingly shame-

---

1. The *Communist International* (*Kommunistcheskii Internatsional*) was a journal published from 1919 to 1945.

less proclamation to the "proletariat of the entire world" that Russia "is now performing a great, planetary deed." Next come lines that lacerate the soul with their coarseness and vulgarity:

"One surmises that the old rulers of the Kremlin, the tsars and the priests, never suspected that its grey walls would embrace representatives from the most revolutionary group of contemporary humankind. But such a thing has happened. The mole of history has not done a half-bad job in burrowing under the Kremlin wall."

These lines were penned by one of the most important representatives of "worker-peasant power" now reigning in the Kremlin. Good God, what a hundredfold absurdity this "worker-peasant" power is! What a supremely mocking laughter it has for a Russia that, narcoticized, had sold its soul to the devil! These lines were written by Trotsky; and, as you can see, they have a very confident ring about them. Trotsky, though, is right only in this: a mole is a beast that is blind and base, cunning and sharp-clawed; it has truly "not done a half-bad job" in burrowing into the Kremlin, but only because the ground under the wall is so soft. In everything else Trotsky is wrong. The old rulers of the Kremlin—its legitimate masters, its native fathers and children, the builders and champions of the Russian land—would turn over in their graves if they heard what Trotsky had said, and if they knew what his followers had done to Russia. Indescribable would be their pain at the sight of what is going on on either side of the Kremlin walls, where today's Moscow poets joyfully proclaim:

Blood, blood rushes forth
Like water in a bathhouse
From an overturned bucket.[2]

Inexpressible horror would seize these tsars and "priests" at the sight of the enormous and bloody carnival that Russia has become. But it also seems to me that these individuals not only could

2. Bunin is quoting from the poem "October" ("*Oktiabr'*") by Anatoly Mariengof, published in the almanac *Reality* (*Yav'*) in 1919.

CODA

have—but also should have—foreseen the misfortunes and disgraces that strike their unhappy land. They knew and remembered that Rus' had been host to terrible and constant periods of sedition, internecine strife, "boilings over," and absurdities." They knew and remembered the words of the chronicler who might have been speaking of our own days when he wrote that "the earth was sewn with the seeds of internal strife and produced their bitter fruit," that "the voice of the tiller was seldom heard, but that the ravens often cawed over the land, dividing the corpses among them," and that "one brother said to another: 'This is mine, and this is also mine,' while pagans fell on them from all sides, winning victory after victory, and Kiev groaned under the infidel's yoke, and Chernigov wailed under his blows. . . ."

The tsars and the "priests" could have foreseen much, for they knew and recalled the chronicles of Rus' as well as the fickle hearts and fitful minds of their people. They knew and remembered their nation's proclivity for "savagery" and tears, its boundless steppes, its impenetrable forests, its impassable swamps, their historical destinies, its neighbors "so greedy, cunning, and merciless," its immaturity before their neighbors, its endless backwaters, and, finally, its fatal peculiarity of always moving forward in circles.

In a word, they knew and remembered everything that had safeguarded Russia's "tsars and priests," its prelates and ascetics in Moscow, Radonezh . . . and Solovetsk;[3] everything that had made Ivan the Terrible exclaim—"I am a beast, but I reign over beasts!" In a word, they knew and remembered everything that has changed but little right down to our present day, and in truth could not change, as if by magic, in our steppes and forests and bogs, during that very short period of time in which a genuine Russian state came into being.

"The tsars and priests!" But we also truly did not foresee what

---

3. Radonezh was an old Russian city situated roughly fifty miles northeast of Moscow; Solovetsk is located on an island in the White Sea, some four hundred miles northeast of Saint Petersburg.

had to happen. What has happened—what has happened again—
is that same Pushkin rebellion[4] which, "senseless and cruel," we
are only beginning to recall and reflect upon now. What has happened is merely what has happened before. Many people, though,
still do not understand this, since they are thrown off by that new
and vulgarly absurd word "bolshevism." They believe that "something" singular has occurred, "something" without equal or precedent. And they believe this "something" is connected with the
changing psychology of the world and with the emergence of that
Europeanized proletariat which presents the world with a new and
beautiful religion of the highest humanitarian ideals but which, at
the same time, demands the "noninterference" [of the European
powers] in the endless and basest criminality going on in the very
light of day, in the Christian Europe of the twentieth century.

History repeats itself; but nowhere, it seems, does it repeat itself as it does with us. And its dynamics have given us God knows
how many grounds for rosy hopes. But, consciously or unconsciously, we have forgotten these grounds. . . . Do you not know the
first page of our history? "Our land is great and plentiful, but there
is no order in it. . . . Pull us apart or we shall cut each other's
throats. . . . Bring peace into our midst—for we are unbelievably
cruel, despite our starry-eyed idealism and faintheartedness. . . .
Lead us to the shafts of the plow and force us to dig the furrows;
otherwise our land, which is the richest in the world, will become
overgrown with weeds, for we are lazy by temperament, despite our
beastlike capacity for work. . . .

"In short, [we asked the Varangians] to come and rule over
us, for everything with us is unstable and disorganized. . . . We
are greedy and careless, capable of things which are most beautiful and noble—and also the lowest and most base. We approach
life with a diabolical mistrust; but we can also be ensnared by the

---

4. Bunin is referring to Pushkin's study *The History of Pugachev* (*Istoriia Pu-
gacheva*, 1833) and his novel *The Captain's Daughter* (*Kapitanskaia dochka*,
1833–1836), both of which deal with the revolt of Pugachev.

CODA

most absurd and crude lies, and be led, very easily, into any trap. . . ."[5]

That typifies our beginnings, and after that? We have Vas'ka Buslaev, who, in his old age, bitterly weeps and repents the crimes of his youth, i.e., he had "murdered and robbed" without end.[6] . . . Next are the "great Russian revolutions": the constant struggles among the principalities before the rise of Moscow, the equally endless internal strife in Moscow itself, and the false leaders and pretenders to the throne who hailed from the ranks of the lowest scoundrels and scum, individuals before whom we first groveled on our knees to frenzied shouts of joy and the pealing of bells, and then mocked their mutilated bodies with similar frenzy and repulsiveness. . . . Then came the ubiquitous savagery and massacres in the Ukraine, the bloody khan Razin who was literally worshiped by entire generations of the Russian intelligentsia, who passionately desired Razin's second coming, that blessed time when "the people would awake. . . ."

And so, I repeat, our history has been one and the same thing: we vacillated in mind and heart, we swung from side to side, seeking self-destruction and ruin. We murdered and robbed, we caroused in taverns, and we gulped down fiery poisons which rose like a high tide in which crazed men and women literally drowned or "choked to death." But on the following day we expressed our terrible hangovers in bouts of frenzied sentimentality, shedding repentant tears before the sacred churches we had cursed only the day before, and "parading" in front of the Red Staircase inside the

5. Bunin is here paraphrasing from the Russian Primary Chronicle (*Povest' vremennykh let*), the highly standardized account of early Russian history from its legendary origins to about 1110 A.D.

6. Vasily (Vas'ka) Buslaev is a prominent figure in the so-called Novgorodian cycle of Russian *byliny* or "epic folktales." Buslaev was indeed a brawler. In fact, he and his colleagues would have slain all the men of Novgorod had his mother not wrapped him in her sable cloak and carried him off to her manor. Buslaev perished on a return trip from the Holy Land where he had sought to atone for his youthful sins.

Kremlin,[7] bearing the bloody heads of decapitated false tsars and atamans. Remember, remember this, you, "the most revolutionary people of humankind," who now sit in the Kremlin!

Having endured, however unwillingly, events that took place yesterday and that are still taking place today in the Ukraine, in the cradle of the Slavic soul, I, also involuntarily, recall Khmelnitsky and his followers. Who were they? What did they do? Again read from our history about things which have become normal for us:

"The serfs gathered in bands, completely destroying the homes of both rich and poor, and razing entire villages to the ground. They pillaged and burned and murdered and mocked the dead and those victims they had impaled on sticks—victims from whose backs they had torn the skin, whom they had sawed in two, roasted on coals, or scalded with boiling water. But their most savage frenzy they had reserved for the Jews. They danced and drank vodka on the Jews' holy books, they tore the intestines from Jewish children, and, showing these to the parents, asked with ribald laughter: 'Hey kike, is this kosher or not?'

"All of this is true.[8] But we go and blame all these pogroms on the tsar and his 'satraps and stooges.' "

And what about Khmel'nitsky? "First he fasted and prayed, then he drank himself into a stupor. Next he sobbed on his knees before the icon, and finally sang songs that he himself had written. He was first very tearful and mild, then suddenly savage and haughty. . . ." How many times did Khmel'nitsky change his "worldview"! How many times did he violate oaths and kissings of the cross! How many times did he betray his allies and friends!

---

7. The Red Staircase, or more accurately the Golden-Red Staircase (*Zolotaia-krasnaia lestnista*), was attached to one of the sidewalls of the Granovitaia Palace inside the Kremlin. It no longer exists.

8. Kenez writes: "The seventeenth-century Cossacks of Ataman Bogdan Khmel'nitsky, when rising against Polish rule, carried out massacres of Jews which would have no parallel until our own times." Indeed, some 200,000 Jews died at this time. See Lincoln, *Red Victory*, 304–305, and Kenez, *Civil War*, 166.

CODA

Then there was Emel'ka [Pugachev] and Sten'ka [Razin], whose rebellions we are beginning to compare with what is taking place today—though we still dare not draw the obvious conclusions. Open your history books and read again what perhaps you read inattentively the first time around:

"And Sten'ka's revolt spread throughout all of Russia. . . . And everything that was pagan rose up and made its appearance. . . ."

Yes, yes, let all the Trotskys and Gorkys stop boasting about their "red" Bashkiria,[9] about the "planetary deeds" that had been accomplished long before the founding of the "Third International"!

Continue reading: "And there rose up the Zyrians and Mordovians, and the Chuvash, and the Cheremis, and the Bashkirs, and they murdered and rioted, themselves not knowing why. . . ."

And throughout the entire Muscovite realm, right up to the shores of the White Sea, there circulated Sten'ka's "charming" letters, in which he declared that "he had come to destroy all *boyars*, nobles, and officials, to sweep away all power and authority, and to establish equality for all. . . ."

All the cities that Sten'ka had captured were turned over to the Cossacks, all the property of these places was "divided" among Sten'ka's warriors. But each day Sten'ka himself would get drunk and condemn to death anyone who had the misfortune of not winning favor with the "people."

Read on: "Sten'ka's followers drowned some, hacked others to pieces, chopped off the arms and legs of still others and forced them to crawl about in their blood. They raped innocent maidens; and, imitating Sten'ka, they not only ate meat on fast days but also forced everyone else to do the same thing. . . ."

Sten'ka himself was a "self-willed and unstable individual. He was alternately somber and severe, then violent and insane. He

---

9. Bashkiria is the home of the Bashkirs and is located in the area between the middle Volga River and the Ural Mountains. In the thirteenth century Bashkiria was ruled by the Mongolian Golden Horde, but beginning in 1557 it was gradually assimilated into the Russian state.

would often make a pilgrimage on foot to the far-off Solovetsky monastery;[1] but then he would mock the fasts, reject the sacred teachings, defile churches, and murder priests with his own hand. . . . Bloodthirsty and cruel, Sten'ka hated law, society, and religion—anything that restrained personal desires. . . . Suffering, honor, and humanity were unknown to him because envy and revenge penetrated his very being. . . ."

Sten'ka's entire "army" consisted of fugitives, thieves, and sluggards—riffraff that called themselves "Cossacks," although genuine Cossacks despised them as "fake Cossacks." To all the bastards and scum whom Sten'ka captured in his net of promises, he vowed to give complete freedom and complete equality; but in reality he brought them into bondage, enslaving them all. The slightest disobedience was punished by the torture of the lash. He called them brothers, but he forced them to crawl on their knees before him. . . .[2]

Good God! What a striking similarity there is between the time of Sten'ka and the pillaging that is going on today in the name of the "Third International"; but there are differences. Sten'ka's authority was a thousand times more genuine than today's "worker-peasant power," the most unnatural and absurd "absurdity" in Russia's history. His government—menials like Vas'ka Us . . . was also a hundred times better than the "worker-peasant" government now sitting in the Kremlin and the Hotel Metropole![3]

1. The Solovetsky Monastery, one of the most important monasteries of the Orthodox church in the Russian state, was founded during the late 1420s and early 1430s on the shoreline of Solovetsky Island in the White Sea.
2. Bunin is drawing his information about Razin, Pugachev, and Khmelnitsky from his earlier readings of such Russian historians as Kostomarov, Solovyov, and Tatishchev.
3. The Metropole hotel, built in 1899–1903, is not only one of the best-known hotels in Moscow but has figured prominently in the early history of the Soviet state. Revolutionary troops battled to occupy the building in November 1917, and Lenin frequently spoke from the assembly hall of the building.

CODA

FROM "THE GREAT NARCOTIC"

The course of human affairs has been greatly affected by human limitations and mental poverty, by faulty thinking, observation, and logic, and by weak and unfocused thoughts which often cannot bring anything to a conclusion. Indeed, as we Russians are a deeply emotional people, we are particularly paralyzed by this last shortcoming.

But there are also . . . several other grievous sins that can be ascribed to all those people who, freely or otherwise, have contributed to the bloody outrages and horrors that we have already endured for three years.

These sins include estrangement from genuine life, ignorance of existence, and even an *unwillingness* to understand reality.

Herzen said: "If one does not know the people, one can conquer and oppress them, but one cannot liberate them." The Russian folk have this ancient proverb: "We are like a piece of wood. From us come both the icon and the club." But in our stupidity and flightiness, did we not ourselves desire this club? And together with this, did we not also want to see only an icon in the folk?

People took from literature and life only the things that were grist for the revolutionary mill; everything else whizzed by their ears or was passed over in silence.

Take Gleb Uspensky, for example. How cruelly he indicted the folk in his writings! "No, my memories [of the people] do not speak about human virtue," he said. "Everyone in the village is unhappy, insane, mean, and base. . . . At first the peasant is strong, gentle, intelligent, and spiritually alive; but then he comes into possession of the land. . . .

"At one time priests and monks brought light to places where savagery reigned . . . but now there remains only Karataev[4] and the

---

4. Platon Karataev is the "hero" peasant in Tolstoy's *War and Peace*.

predator. . . . I have often been asked why I depict only horrors in the village? But I do so . . . because they hold sway there. . . .

"Consider, for instance, the village kulak who runs a brothel. Everyone is impressed by what he has done. People say, 'Way to go! He's really raking it in!' Or they bow before him and exclaim with joy: 'He's a better man than I. I'm a bum who'll never amount to anything!'

"Also consider the young man in the village. What deep hatred, what inborn bloodthirstiness he harbors for his fellow peasants! Such an individual even likes to watch animals suffer and die. He once incinerated a whole bunch of puppies in an oven—and was very happy that he did it. . . .

"All of the village's talent and intelligence belongs to the kulaks; and *schadenfreude* forms the basis of all their activity. No one values either himself or others. . . . All that people say is: 'There's no good stick to beat our brother!' "

This is what Uspensky wrote. But people saw [in him also] only what they wanted to see. . . . They had recast Russian peasants as socialists and republicans, and used Uspensky to attack me. . . .

It was only five years ago . . . that I came across some socialist peasants from Oryol who talked seriously about a mare that was twenty miles long and had fallen from the clouds and landed somewhere on the banks of the Volga. Why would our peasant revolutionaries even concern themselves about such an event? How could they spend time talking about such a thing?

About me these same revolutionaries have said: "Yes, of course, Bunin is an artistic talent who writes about this and that; what he writes is true but also not true. After all, he is not a peasant, and only a peasant can speak truthfully about other peasants."

Yes, they have said even more ignorant things about me, completely forgetting that to write *King Lear*, for example, one does not necessarily have to be king. I could even ask my critics: "How can you who are not kings criticize *King Lear*?"

Last July in Odessa I came across a Red Army soldier teach-

CODA

ing his comrades. He was on guard duty, sitting in a velvet arm-chair, toying with the lock on his gun, and intimidating the "citi-zens" who passed by. His face was vacuous-looking, his cap was perched way on the back of his head, and his greasy hair covered his dark, sleepy, hostile eyes! . . .

How we praised this very soldier, even though we had to tie hay to his left hand and straw to his right, so that during the first weeks of boot camp he could tell one from the other. . . . How we exclaimed and continue to exclaim to the entire world that this Red Army soldier is an ardent and willing participant in the "world socialist revolution"! . . .

I am writing all this not because I want to be funny, or be-cause I am touched by such ideas personally, or because I want to settle accounts with my readers. After all, these are social matters which are tightly bound to the very disaster affecting all of Russia.

I have touched upon literature, its practitioners, its connois-seurs, as well as writers who depict the folk, because all of them bear responsibility for what has happened. Indeed, whether they know it or not, most of them are contributing to the chaos even now by nurturing their ideas and image of the folk precisely with huge doses of literature. And the literature over the past few decades has been terrible. Our grandfathers and fathers launched Russian literature on its course of fame; despite what people write about them today, not all our literary forefathers went to "warm waters," "sought out the company of dogs rather than people," walked with Parny's books,[5] or strolled in their "parks, amidst arti-ficial grottos and statues with smashed noses." No, our grandfathers and fathers knew the people. Indeed, they could not help but know them, if only because they lived on such close terms with them. They were flesh of flesh, bone of bone with the people, and they did not have to worry about money or other constraints in their

---

5. For instance, Parny's *Poésie érotiques* (1778) were quasi-erotic elegies on the vicissitudes of love.

pictures of the folk. This was all made manifest by Pushkin, Lermontov, Tolstoy, and many other writers. But what happened then?

Writers began to encounter *nonfreedom* because they believed their writing had to serve a definite idea. They also began to separate themselves from the people, since they had left the country for the city. Their knowledge of the folk began to weaken, and studies of the people were not successful. Kireevsky and Rybnikov wrote down a thing or two. Yakushkin visited the folk once or twice; but once when he was in the village, he had too much to drink and got into a fight with a local policeman. That was the end of his trips there.[6]

Then came the *raznochintsy*,[7] who were much less talented than their predecessors, and who were bitter and mournful drunks with a grudge against the world. Just read, for example, all those Levitovs, Reshetnikovs, Orfanovs, and Nikolai Uspenskys. They were extremely tendentious, despite their noble goals, as well as completely dependent on fashion, on the ideology of their circle and the bias of the journals they wrote for. Gleb Uspensky, for example, had an abundance of nobility and talent; but he was also a man with a broken heart.

Uspensky and others were followed by an ever-growing group of so-called professional writers, who were not innate artists per se but who had pretensions to talent in their fiction. Readers were treated to highly polished puff pieces, liberal lying, and the inevitable love for the folk.

Clichés abounded. A horse became a . . . "sly outrunner." A peasant riding in a cart was invariably "a serf-chik" who kept bending over to flog his "outrunner." A provincial town had to have geraniums on the windowsills and pigs playing in the mud in the

6. Bunin is referring to the attempts of all three men to collect folk sayings and songs in the mid-nineteenth century. He is also being unfair as Kireevsky, Rybnikov, and Yakushkin published their findings in many volumes.

7. Beginning with the reign of Alexander II (1855–1881), the *raznochintsy* were identified with radical revolutionary youth who aligned themselves with the folk and wished to transform both state and society.

CODA

middle of the square. A landowner had to be a reactionary die-hard, a local leader of the Black Hundreds, and a breeder of hunting dogs. The table in his home had to have "a brightly polished samovar, yellow cream, and rich cookies personally baked by some Marfa Polikarpovna." A village was the site for "disheveled little huts that leaned up against one another, and that looked fearfully at passersby."

Good God, how many legends did these writers concoct about the cruelties of serfdom and the virtues of Sten'ka Razin! And always when their characters were out hunting! "With my dog and my gun, I happened to wander into the dense Volga forests," they began. "And I roamed about for quite some time, looking for fowl. But meanwhile the day had come to an end, the rain had gotten heavier, and I had to start thinking seriously about a place to spend the night . . ."—where, of course, the hunter had to hear the legend about Razin.

What next? Literature became really poor with all kinds of stupid, false, and pulp-fiction stuff. Then there . . . was Gorky, that very same Gorky who, in my twenty-year acquaintance with him . . . literally did not spend a single day in the village. Having returned to Russia after eight years in Capri, he never ventured any farther than Moscow; but he nevertheless wrote heroically about the Russian people, insulting reviewers and readers alike with his sham inspiration and his "vivid" images and ideas. . . .

Writers like Gorky lied about the people on cue, to conform to tradition and thus not to appear reactionary. Their fiction about the folk was false, ignorant, crude, and illiterate; but it was also a depository of information for intellectuals who knew absolutely nothing about the people. Literature about the village included such images as "ear-laden millet," "flowering wormwood," "pigeons sitting in birch trees," and flowers that "ripened" in the garden. Tolstoy often regarded such writing as absolute fraud, as "caricatures liberally sprinkled with stupidity," and a "complete falsification of art." . . .

Once, in the spring of 1915, I was walking in the Moscow

Zoological Garden and saw a guard . . . beating a swan with his boot and smashing ducks' heads with the heel of his shoe. When I got home I found V. Ivanov waiting for me. I had to listen to a turgid speech about Russia's "Christ-like image," and about how, once Russia proved victorious over Germany, this Christ-like Russia would accomplish another great "task," i.e., it would spiritually enlighten India—no less a country than India, mind you, which, as regards enlightenment, is three thousand years older than we are![8]

What could I have said to him after what I had seen the guard do to the swan? We have "images" around here all right: that of a swan crushed by a boot. . . .

How did our intellectuals get their knowledge about the people? Besides literature, they also had conversations with the folk, for example:

Once late at night, a *barin*, returning home from some party or meeting and traveling along the streets of Moscow or Petersburg in an old rickety cab, asked the driver in a yawn:

"Hey, driver, are you afraid of death?"

But the driver mechanically replied to the stupid *barin*:

"Death? Why should I be afraid of death? There's nothing to be afraid of."

"And do you think we can beat the Germans?"

"How can we not beat them? We've got to beat them!"

"You're right, old boy, we've just got to. . . . But here's our problem. . . . Our tsaritsa is a German.[9] . . . And our tsar—what kind of a Russian is he really?"[1]

---

8. For the influence of India on Bunin's work, see T. Marullo, *If You See the Buddha: Studies in the Fiction of Ivan Bunin* (Northwestern University Press, forthcoming)

9. The Empress Alexandra was a granddaughter of Queen Victoria and the daughter of Louis IV, grand duke of Hesse-Darmstadt. In the last years of Alexandra's reign, she was widely but erroneously believed to be a German agent.

1. The mother of Nicholas II, Maria Fyodorovna, was the daughter of King Christian IV of Denmark. Nicholas was also a first cousin to George V of England.

CODA

The cabbie nodded in a restrained type of way:
"That's true, all right. I once had this boss who was a German. He charged me from fifty kopecks to a ruble every time my cow damaged the crops. A real son of a bitch he was. . . ."

From such a conversation one can rest fully assured that the "peasant has a wise attitude toward death," and that he has not a shadow of a doubt as regards Russia's triumph over Germany. One is also confident that the peasant is a potential wonder-working *bogatyr*,[2] a "religious pilgrim," and a "simplehearted lover of Christ," if only "he would not drink and be kept in chains."

In early March '17 everyone, with childlike excitement, thought and affirmed that a "miracle, a great miracle" had occurred, that there had been a "bloodless revolution," and that "all that was old and rotten had been destroyed—forever!"

Will someone please explain to me what all this means? The peasant as a "religious peasant"? The revolution as a "miracle"— and a "bloodless" one at that?"

Let me see if I have this straight. A sober "religious pilgrim" has created a bloodless miracle which eclipses all other miracles. But the views of this miracle are . . . monstrous . . . shallow, flighty . . . and mistaken about the past. The "pilgrim" was not sober when he accomplished this miracle but in a drunken frame of mind. Also, the past has not been destroyed but has only repeated itself in almost every iota. Indeed, the only thing that has changed is the degree of unprecedented absurdity, bloodiness, lying, and vulgarity that is currently going on. No, "ancient Rus' has not passed on"! I stubbornly affirmed this years ago, and I do so now; and, alas, with more right to so do than before.

Everywhere people say: "A great change has occurred in the Russian people. They are maturing not by the day but by the hour. Russia is engaged in a great new war, but just look at how the folk rose up in their struggle with German militarism! The greatest revolution in the world has come into being—and without a drop of

2. A *bogatyr'* is a hero in Russian folklore and epics.

blood! Long live this new war! Let it continue to its victorious end! Long live the liberated soldier-citizen!"

So now we had "change" and "risings up" and "not a drop of blood" and the "soldier-citizen" who was liberated by Order No. 1,[3] whose authors—again, what terrible stupidity!—were some Steklov-Nakhamis and also a lawyer named Sokolov. This Sokolov was also a war commissar who, when he arrived at the front roughly two months later, was hit on the head by a pail—the doings of a soldier who, the newspapers said, "was covered with blood below his waist. . . ." God forgive me, but I recall that when I came across this story in the newspaper, I wrote "Read with pleasure!" in the margin. . . .

We could have predicted this atrocity; but we did not, nor did we want to.

When our English allies were fighting the Germans, there appeared in England several books about the Russian soul. They even bore such titles as *The Soul of Russia*. So at a time when the English thought the Revolution would sprinkle living water on Russia, and that it would redouble our efforts to vanquish the enemy, I happened to see an English journal with this picture of Russian life:

There was a great deal of snow. In the background was a small cottage, and in the front was a little girl who was walking toward it, dressed in a fur coat and with a bunch of schoolbooks in her hand. Upon close inspection this cottage turned out to be a Rus-

---

3. Order No. 1 was an instruction issued by the Petrograd Soviet of Workers' and Soldiers' Deputies on March 1, 1917—the same day the Provisional Government was being formed, and twenty-four hours before the abdication of Nicholas II. Essentially Order No. 1 equalized the rights of officers and soldiers, and placed all servicemen under the command of the Soviet. In so doing its authors sought to discredit military officers who had not joined in the February revolution and who conceivably could have halted its progress. The members of the Provisional Government, unsure both of themselves and of the loyalty of the troops in the city, accepted the order but hoped that nothing would come of it. They were wrong, though, and Order No. 1 contributed greatly to the dissolution of the Russian Army. For more on Order No. 1 see Lehovich, *White Against Red*, 75, 92–93; and Swettenham, *Allied Intervention*, 17–18.

sian village school; the little girl was a student there, and, as the inscription under the picture announced, she had an extremely strange first name: *Petrovna*.[4]

Not long after that I happened to run into Kokoshkin. This Kokoshkin is now dead, having been murdered so brutally and absurdly, and with the same bestial indifference that I had often emphasized in my own pictures of killing by Russians—pictures which, incidentally, had so upset almost all my readers at that time, and which everyone had thought were fabrications. Anyhow, Kokoshkin and I were discussing the Russian people when he suddenly said to me with his customary politeness but also with an unusual sharpness:

"Let's change the topic. Your views on the folk have always seemed—you will excuse me, too bizarre, if you know what I mean. . . ."

Having returned home after this conversation, I recalled with great surprise and even almost horror:

"What is going on? How can this 'Petrovna' be any better [than what I have said about the folk]? The English can, of course, be forgiven for their 'Petrovna,' but what about us? What childish ignorance or unwillingness there is to know our own people, a people who only recently had been destined to take part in the fate of Europe, and whose conscious, passionate readiness to do so was something that all the Kokoshkins of this world, together with hundreds of others, had affirmed in words that were greatly insincere, and also erroneous and simply deceptive! No, this [treachery] will come back to haunt us."

And I was right. It did. Moscow caught fire because of a one-kopeck candle. And it is particularly dangerous to play with fire in houses made of wood and covered with straw. . . .

I find it very difficult to say all that I have said . . . for I no less than others have sought and continue to seek the Kingdom of God on this earth. But I am well aware of the cruel world of the

4. Petrovna is not a first or last name but a patronymic, meaning "daughter of Pyotr."

"lords of San-Francisco"[5] . . . as well as everything else on this evil and pitiful planet. . . . I know that what is impossible cannot become possible . . . (even though we sometimes are silent about this). . . . I know that the peasant who beat the swan with his shoe in the Moscow Zoo will not be a good socialist. . . . And I know that neither this ancient earth nor ancient Rus' "has passed on."

5. A reference to the hero in Bunin's story "The Gentleman from San Francisco," written in 1915.

PROMINENT INDIVIDUALS
MENTIONED IN THE TEXT

Adrianov, Alexander Alexandrovich (1862–1918), White general and town governor of Moscow from February 1908 to May 1915.

Akhmatova, Anna Andreevna (1888–1966), poet.

Aksakov, Ivan Sergeevich (1823–1886), prominent Slavophile, publicist, and poet.

Aldanov-Landau, Mark Alexandrovich (1886–1957), writer.

Alexeev, Gleb Vasilievich (1892–1938), author and journalist.

Alexeev, Mikhail Vasilievich (1857–1918), military commander and one of the early leaders of the anti-Bolshevik White forces.

Andreev, Leonid Nikolaevich (1871–1919), writer.

Anna Ivanovna (1693–1740), empress of Russia from 1730 to 1740.

Antonov-Ovseenko, Vladimir Alexandrovich (1884–1939), revolutionary, party, and state leader, and commander of Red Army units in the Ukraine.

Auslender, Sergei Abramovich (1886–1937), writer and Soviet party and government figure.

Bagritsky (pseudonym of Dryubin, Eduard Georgievich) (1897–1934), poet.

Bakh, Alexei Nikolaevich (1857–1946), academician, biochemist, member of the pre-Revolutionary terrorist group "The People's Will."

Balabanova, Anzhelika Isaakovna (1878–1965), writer, political figure, and international social activist.

Bal'mont, Konstantin Dmitrievich (1867–1942), Symbolist poet.

Barmash, Vladimir (dates unknown), agronomist.

Batyushkov, Konstantin Nikolaevich (1787–1855), poet.

Bely, Andrei (pseudonym of Bugaev, Boris Nikolaevich) (1880–1934), poet and writer.

Beranger, Pierre (1780–1857), French poet.

Biron, Ernst Johann (1690–1772), prominent favorite of Empress Anna Ivanovna.

Blok, Alexander Alexandrovich (1880–1921), Symbolist poet.

Bogdanov, Boris Osipovich (1884–1956), Menshevik and prominent revolutionary activist.

Breshko-Breshkovskaya, Ekaterina Dmitrievna (1844–1934), one of the leaders of the Social Revolutionary party, also known as the "grandmother of the Russian Revolution."

Bronstein. See Trotsky.

Bryusov, Valery Yakovlevich (1873–1924), poet.

Bubnov, Andrei Sergeevich (1884–1940), member of the Politburo and chief of the Revolutionary and Executive committees of the soviet at Kiev.

Budberg, Alexei Pavlovich (1869–1945), White officer.

Bukovetsky, Evgeny Osipovich (1866–1948), genre painter.

Bulgakov, Mikhail Afanasievich (1891–1940), writer and playright.

Bulgakov, Valentin Fyodorovich (1886–1966), writer, memoirist, and secretary to Leo Tolstoy in 1910.

Bunin, Yuly Alexeevich (1857–1921), journalist and brother of Ivan Bunin.

Catherine II, the "Great" (1729–1796), empress of Russia from 1762 to 1796.

Chaliapin (Russian: Shaliapin), Fyodor Ivanovich (1873–1938), bass singer, best known for his role of Tsar Boris in Mussorgsky's opera *Boris Godunov*.

Charles I (1600–1649), king of Great Britain and Ireland.

PROMINENT INDIVIDUALS

Chekhov, Anton Pavlovich (1860–1904), playwright and short-story writer.

Chermenykh, Mikhail Mikhailovich (1890–1962), graphic artist.

Chernov, Viktor Mikhailovich (1873–1952), Social Revolutionary, leader, and theoretician, and minister of agriculture in 1917.

Chicherin, Georgy Vasilievich (1872–1936), Soviet comissar for foreign affairs.

Chirikov, Evgeny Nikolaevich (1864–1932), writer and poet.

Chukovsky, Kornei (pseudonym of Korneichukov, Kornei Ivanovich) (1882–1969), writer, children's poet, critic, and literary scholar, translator, and editor.

Clemençeau, Georges (1841–1929), minister-premier of France.

Couthon, Georges-Auguste (1755–1794), Jacobin and member of the Committee of Public Safety in France.

Cromwell, Oliver (1599–1658), English soldier, statesman, and leader of the Puritan revolution.

Denikin, Anton Ivanovich (1872–1947), White general.

Derman, Abram Borisovich (1880–1952), literary critic.

Derzhinsky, Feliks Edmundovich (1877–1926), Bolshevik and first head of the Soviet secret police.

Diaghilev, Sergei Pavlovich (1872–1929), Russian ballet impresario.

Dombrovsky, Vitaly Markovich (?–1921), mayor of Odessa.

Dostoevsky, Fyodor Mikhailovich (1821–1881), novelist.

Dragomanov, Mikhail Petrovich (1841–1895), Ukrainian historian, folklorist, and public figure.

Dybenko, Pavel Efimovich (1889–1938), military commander and leader of the Crimean Army in the Russian civil war.

Egorov, Pyotr Valentinovich (1871–1933), journalist.

Ehrenburg, Ilya Grigorevich (1891–1967), writer, journalist, and memoirist.

Eisenstein, Sergei Mikhailovich (1898–1948), film director.

Esenin, Sergei Alexandrovich (1895–1925), poet.

Fel'dman, S. (dates unknown), secretary of the Odessa soviet.

Ferdinand I (1865–1927), king of Rumania from 1914 to 1927.

Fet, Afanasy Afansievich (1820–1892), poet.

Figner, Vera Nikolaevna (1852–1942), revolutionary, member of the pre-Revolutionary terrorist group "The People's Will."

PROMINENT INDIVIDUALS

Fioletov, Anatoly Vasilievich (1897–1918), poet.

Fondaminsky-Bunakov, Il'ia Isidorovich (1879–1942), publicist and leader of the Social Revolutionary party.

Friche, Vladimir Maximovich (1870–1929), literary critic and commissar for foreign affairs in Moscow.

Fyodorov, Alexander Mitrofanovich (1868–1949), poet, dramatist, and novelist.

Gal'bershtadt, Lev Isaevich (1878–?), journalist.

Gallen (Gallen-Kallela), Axel (1865–1931), Finnish painter.

Gandhi, Mohandas Karamchand (Mahatma) (1869–1948), Indian nationalist leader.

Gel'tser, Ekaterina Vasilievna (1876–1962), ballerina with the Bolshoi Theater.

George V (1865–1936), king of England 1910–1936, and first cousin of Nicholas II.

Gide, André (1869–1951), French writer.

Gimmer-Sukhanov, Nikolai Nikolaevich (1882–1940), revolutionary, economist, and publicist.

Ginzburg, Evgeniya Semyonovna (1896–1980), memoirist.

Gippius-Merezhkovskaya, Zinaida Nikolaevna (1867–1945), poet, critic, novelist, and memoirist.

Gnedich, Nikolai Ivanovich (1784–1833), poet and translator.

Gogol, Nikolai Vasilievich (1809–1852), novelist and short-story writer.

Golovin, Alexander Yakovlevich (1863–1930), painter.

Golubenko, Nikolai Vasilievich (1898–1937), military commander and commissar of the 45th Infantry Division in the Ukraine.

Goncharov, Ivan Alexandrovich (1812–1891), novelist.

Goncourt, Edward (1822–1896), French naturalist writer.

Goncourt, Jules (1830–1870), French naturalist writer and brother of Edward Goncourt.

Gontaryov, Ivan Grigorievich (dates unknown), journalist and editor.

Gorky-Peshkov, Alexei Maximovich (Maxim) (1868–1936), writer and social figure.

Griboyedov, Alexander Sergeevich (1795–1829), diplomat and dramatist.

Grigoriev, Nikolai Alexandrovich (1878–1919), ataman and temporary ally of the Bolsheviks.

Grigorovich, Dmitri Vasilievich (1822–1899), writer.

Grishin-Almazov, Alexei Nikolaevich (1880–1918), White lieutenant colonel and war minister of the Siberian government.

Grossman, Leonid Petrovich (1888–1965), writer and literary critic.

Gruzinsky, Alexei Evgenievich (1858–1930), literary scholar.

Grzhebin, Zinovy Isaevich (1877–1929), publisher.

Guchkov, Alexander Ivanovich (1862–1936), leader of the Octobrist party, head of the Third Duma, and minister of the army and navy for the Provisional Government.

Gurko, Vasily Iosifovich (1864–1937), White general.

Gusev, Sergei Ivanovich (pseudonym of Drabkin, Yakov Davidovich) (1874–1933), party and government figure.

Gvozdev, Kuz'ma Alexandrovich (1873–1937?), minister in the Provisional Government.

Hegel, Georg Wilhelm Friedrich (1770–1831), German idealist philosopher.

Herzen, Alexander Ivanovich (1812–1870), writer and philosopher.

Hindenburg (von Hindenburg), Paul (1847–1934), leader of the German advance into Russia, later president of the Weimar Republic.

Hoffmann, Max (1869–1927), German general.

Hohenzollern. See William II.

Horthy (Horthy de Nagybanya), Miklos (1868–1957), regent of Hungary from 1920 to 1944.

Huxley, Aldous Leonard (1894–1963), British novelist.

Ibsen, Henrik (1828–1906), Norwegian dramatist and poet.

Inber, Vera Mikhailovna (1890–1972), poet.

Ioann (Ivan) of Tambov (1800?–1850?), hermit and monk.

Ioffe, Adol'f Abramovich (1883–1927), revolutionary and diplomat.

Ivan VI (1740–1764), nominal emperor of Russia from 1740 to 1741.

Ivanov, Vyacheslav Ivanovich (1866–1949), poet, critic, and scholar.

Ivanyukov, Ivan Ivanovich (1844–1912), historian, economist, and publicist.

Jaures, Jean (1859–1914), historian and figure in the French and international socialist movement who fought against militarism and war.

Kachalov, Vasily Ivanovich (1875–1948), actor.

PROMINENT INDIVIDUALS

Kaledin, Alexei Maximovich (1861–1918), ataman-chief of the Don Army, leader of an anti-Soviet revolt in October 1917.

Kamenev, Lev Borisovich (1883–1936), revolutionary, Communist party official, and editor of *Pravda*.

Kamenev, Nikolai Mikhailovich (1862–1918), general.

Kamenskaya, O. A. (dates unknown), wife of Anatoly Kamensky.

Kamensky, Anatoly Pavlovich (1876–1941), writer.

Karakhan, Lev Mikhailovich (pseudonym of Rozenfeld, Lev Borisovich) (1889–1937), professional revolutionary, lawyer, journalist, and diplomat.

Kasabov, Blagoi Markov (1898–1925), Bulgarian Communist.

Kataev, Valentin Petrovich (1897–1986), writer.

Kaufman, Alexander Arkadievich (1864–1919), economist, statistician, professor, and one of the leaders of the Kadet party.

Kautsky, Karl (1854–1938), leader and theoretician of the German Social Democratic movement and the Second International.

Kazi-Mullah (pseudonym of Gazi-Magomed) (1775–1832), mountain leader during the Russian campaigns in the Caucasus in the 1820s and 1830s.

Kemal, Mustafa (1881–1938), Turkish statesman, and founder and first president of the Republic of Turkey.

Kerensky, Alexander Fyodorovich (1881–1970), head of the Provisional Government in Russia and commander-in-chief of the Russian army until October 1917.

Khemnitser, Ivan Ivanovich (1745–1784), fabulist and writer.

Khudyakov, Nikolai Akimovich (1890–1939), Soviet army leader.

Khudyakova, Klavdia Yakovlevna (dates unknown), wife of Sergei Khudyakov.

Kipen, Alexander Abramovich (1870–1938), writer.

Kireevsky, Pyotr Vasilevich (1808–1856), Slavophile and ethnographer.

Kishkin, Nikolai Mikhailovich (1864–1930), minister of welfare in the Provisional Government.

Klestov-Angarsky, Nikolai Semyonovich (1879–1943), writer.

Klyuchevsky, Vasily Osipovich (1841–1911), historian.

Klyuev, Nikolai Alexeevich (1887–1937), poet.

Knipper-Chekhova, Olga Leonardovna (1868–1958), actress with the Moscow Art Theater and Chekhov's wife.

PROMINENT INDIVIDUALS

Kogan, Pyotr Semyonovich (1872–1932), literary critic.

Koiransky, Alexander (Sasha) Arnol'dovich (1884–1968), writer.

Kokoshkin, Fyodor Fyodorovich (1871–1918), lawyer, publicist, member of the Provisional Government, and a leader of the Kadet party.

Kolchak, Alexander Vasilievich (1873–1920), admiral and the nominal head of the Whites in the Russian civil war.

Kollontai, Alexandra Mikhailovna (1872–1952), revolutionary and prominent Soviet party and diplomatic figure.

Kondakov, Nikodim Pavlovich (1844–1925), historian of Byzantine and ancient Russian art.

Kornilov, Lavr Georgievich (1870–1918), military commander and leader of the opposition against the Russian Provisional Government in 1918.

Korolenko, Vladimir Galaktionovich (1853–1921), writer, critic, publicist, translator, and social activist.

Kosciusko, Thaddeus (1746–1817), leader in the Polish insurrection of 1774, and prominent figure during the American War for Independence.

Kostomarov, Nikolai Ivanovich (1817–1885), Ukrainian historian, ethnographer, and writer.

Kropotkin, Pyotr Alexeevich (1842–1921), prince, revolutionary, and anarchist.

Krupskaya, Nadezhda Konstantinova (1869–1939), revolutionary and wife of Vladimir Lenin.

Krylov, Ivan Andreevich (1769–1844), journalist, playwright, and fabulist.

Kshesinskaya, Matil'da (Maria) Felixovna (1872–1971), ballerina.

Kun, Bela (1886–1939), Hungarian political leader, and head of the short-lived first Hungarian Communist republic (March–July 1919).

Kuprin, Alexander Ivanovich (1870–1939), novelist and short-story writer.

Kurbsky, Andrei Mikhailovich (1528–1583), Russian prince, writer, publicist, and a political and military figure during the reign of Ivan IV.

Kuskova, Ekaterina Dmitrievna (1869–1958), political figure, social worker, and publicist.

Kutuzov, Mikhail Illarionovich (1745–1813), Russian general and commander-in-chief of the Russian forces during the French invasion of Russia in 1812.

Kuz'min, Mikhail Alexeevich (1875–1936), writer, playwright, and critic.

Lavrov, Pyotr Lavrovich (1823–1900), populist, philosopher, and sociologist.

Lawrence, David Herbert (1885–1930), English novelist and poet.

Lazursky, Vladimir Fyodorovich (1869–1943), literary historian and professor.

Lenin, Vladimir Ilyich (pseudonym of Ul'yanov, Vladimir Ilyich) (1870–1924), revolutionary leader and writer.

Le Notre, L. L. T. Gosselin (1857–1935), historian and member of the French Academy.

Lermontov, Mikhail Yurievich (1814–1841), writer.

Levitan, Isaak Ilyich (1860–1900), artist.

Levitov, Alexander Ivanovich (1835–1877), writer.

Litvinov, Maxim Maximovich (pseudonym of Wallach, Meyer) (1876–1915), Soviet diplomat.

Lloyd George, David (1863–1945), British statesman and prime minister of England from 1916 to 1922.

Lombroso, Cesare (1836–1909), Italian criminologist.

Louis XVI (1754–1793), Bourbon monarch and last king of France.

Lunacharsky, Anatoly Vasilievich (1875–1933), Bolshevik and first Communist director of culture.

Lur'e, Semyon Vladimirovich (1867–1927), publicist.

Luxemburg, Rosa (1871–1919), a leading figure of the German, Polish, and international workers' movements.

Mackensen (von Mackensen), August (1849–1945), German general.

Makhno, Nestor Ivanovich (1889–1935), anarchist guerrilla leader in the southern Ukraine during the civil war.

Malinovskaya, Elena Konstantinova (1875–1942), director of the Bolshoi Theater from 1920 to 1924 and from 1930 to 1935.

Malinovsky, Pavel Petrovich (1869–1943), revolutionary and architect.

Malyantovich, Pavel Nikolaevich (1870–1942), lawyer and minister of justice in the Provisional Government.

Mamai (?–1380), Mongol-Tartar strongman who ruled over the largest portion of the Golden Horde in the 1360s and 1370s, and who was defeated by Grand Prince Dmitri Ivanovich Donskoi at the Battle of Kulikovo in 1380.

Mandelstam, Nadezhda Yakovlevna (1899–1980), memoirist and wife of the poet Osip Mandelstam.

Mandelstam, Osip Emilievich (1891–1938), poet and essayist.

Marat, Jean-Paul (1743–1793), French politician, radical, and journalist.

Mariengof, Anatoly Borisovich (1897–1962), poet and dramatist.

Marx, Karl (1818–1883), German socialist, revolutionary, and writer.

Mayakovsky, Vladimir Vladimirovich (1893–1930), poet.

Mel'gunov, Sergei Petrovich (1880–1957), editor, historian, and writer on public affairs.

Mikhailov, Mikhail Larionovich (1826–1865), revolutionary, poet, and translator.

Milyukov, Pavel Nikolaevich (1859–1943), historian and minister of foreign affairs in the Provisional Government.

Minor, Osip Solomonovich (1861–1932), writer, editor, Social Revolutionary, and member of the Constituent Assembly.

Mirbach (von Mirbach-Harff), Count Wilhelm (1871–1918), German ambassador to the Soviet government.

Mirolyubov, Viktor Sergeevich (1860–1939), writer and publisher.

Mishchenko, Pavel Ivanovich (1853–1919), White general and ataman-chief of the Don Army.

Mizikevich, Pavel Petrovich (1866–1919), mayor of Odessa.

Monomakh, Vladimir Vsevolodovich (1053–1125), Grand Prince of Kiev.

Munsch, Edvard (1863–1944), Norwegian painter.

Muralov, Nikolai Ivanovich (1886–1937), revolutionary and Red Army commander.

Muromtseva-Bunina, Vera Nikolaevna (1881–1961), third wife of Ivan Bunin.

Nansen, Fridtjof (1861–1930), Norwegian Arctic explorer and philanthropist.

Nazhivin, Ivan Fyodorovich (1874–1940), writer.

Nekrasov, Nikolai Alexeevich (1821–1878), poet, writer, and publisher.

Nemirovich-Danchenko, Vladimir Ivanovich (1858–1943), dramatist, director, and cofounder of the Moscow Art Theater in 1898.

Nemits, Alexander Vasilievich (1879–1967), vice-admiral and commander of the Black Sea Fleet.

Nevsky, Alexander Yaroslavich (1220?–1263), prince of Novgorod, Grand Prince of Vladimir, and national hero.

Nilus, Pyotr Alexandrovich (1869–1943), writer and artist.

Ogaryov, Nikolai Platonovich (1813–1877), poet and publicist.

Olesha, Yury Karlovich (1899–1960), novelist and short-story writer.

Orlov-Davydov, Nikolai Vasilievich (1848–1920), lawyer and writer.

Orwell, George (1903–1950), British novelist and satirist.

Osipovich, Naum Markovich (1870–1937), writer.

Ovsyaniko-Kulikovsky, Dmitry Nikolaevich (1853–1920), linguist, cultural historian, and literary critic.

Paleologos, Sophia (1449?–1503), second wife of Ivan III.

Paleologue, Maurice Georges (1859–1944), French ambassador to Russia from 1914 to 1917.

Parny, Evariste-Desire de Forges, Vicomte de (1753–1814), poet.

Pasternak, Boris Leonidovich (1890–1960), poet and prose writer.

Paustovsky, Konstantin Georgievich (1892–1968), prose writer and editor.

Peshekhonov, Alexei Vasilievich (1867–1933), statistician, publicist, social figure, and minister of foodstuffs in the Provisional Government.

Peshkova, Ekaterina Pavlova (1876–1965), writer, social worker, and wife of Maxim Gorky.

Petlyura, Simon Vasilievich (1879–1926), Ukrainian nationalist whose forces tried to secure autonomy for the Ukraine between 1917 and 1920.

Pisemsky, Alexei Feofilakotvich (1821–1881), writer.

Plekhanov, Georgy Valentinovich (1856–1918), revolutionary, historian, theoretician, and philosopher, generally acknowledged as the "father of Russian Marxism."

Pleshcheev, Alexei Nikolaevich (1825–1893), poet, writer, dramatist, and journalist.

Podbel'sky, Vadim Nikolaevich (1887–1920), Social Democrat, revolutionary, and commissar for post office and telegraphs.

Podvoisky, Nikolai Ilyich (1880–1948), party and military figure.

Polevitskaya, Elena Alexandrovna (1881–1973), actress.

Polezhaev, Alexander Ivanovich (1804–1838), poet.

Polonsky, Yakov Petrovich (1819–1898), poet.

Popov, Nikolai Nikolaevich (1890–1938), revolutionary and Communist historian.

Potyomkin, Grigory Alexandrovich (1739–1791), general, administrator, and favorite of Catherine the Great.

Potyomkin, Pyotr Petrovich (1886–1926), poet.

Premirov, Mikhail L'vovich (1878–after 1933), writer.

Pugachev, Emelyan (Emel'ka) Ivanovich (1742?–1775), leader of the massive uprising that threatened the government of Catherine the Great in 1773–1775.

Pusheshnikov, Nikolai Alexeevich (Kolya) (1882–1939), Bunin's nephew and a translator of Kipling, Galsworthy, and Jack London.

Pusheshnikova, Sofya Nikolaevna (?–1942), cousin of Ivan Bunin.

Pushkin, Alexander Sergeevich (1799–1837), writer and poet.

Radetsky, Ivan Markovich (1890–?), publicist.

Radonezhsky, Sergei (1321–1392), monk and social figure.

Rakovsky, Khristian Georgievich (1873–1941), Bulgarian, chairman of the Council of People's Commissars in the Ukraine.

Rasputin, Gregory Yefimovich (1871–1916), monk and adventurer.

Razin, Stepan (Sten'ka) Timofeevich (1630?–1671), Cossack leader of the massive popular uprising in 1667–1671.

Reginin, Vasily Alexandrovich (pseudonym of Rappoport, Vasily Alexandrovich) (1883–1952), writer and journalist.

Renan, Ernest Joseph (1823–1892), French philosopher, philologist, orientalist, and historian of religion.

Repin, Ilya Efimovich (1844–1930), painter.

Reshetnikov, Fyodor Mikhailovich (1841–1871), writer.

Rivkin, Nikolai Ivanovich (1877–1922), poet and revolutionary.

Robespierre, Maximilien (1758–1794), French revolutionary and radical Jacobin leader.

Rodzyanko, Mikhail Vladimirovich (1859–1924), statesman.

PROMINENT INDIVIDUALS

Romanov, Alexander II (1818–1881), tsar of Russia from 1855 to 1881.

Romanov, Alexander III (1845–1894), tsar of Russia from 1881 to 1894.

Romanov, Ivan III, the "Great" (1440–1505), tsar of Russia from 1462 to 1505.

Romanov, Ivan IV, the "Terrible" (1530–1584), tsar of Russia from 1533 to 1584.

Romanov, Ivan VI, nominal tsar of Russia from 1740 to 1741.

Romanov, Mikhail Alexandrovich (1878–1918), brother of Nicholas II.

Romanov, Nicholas I (1796–1855), tsar of Russia from 1825 to 1855.

Romanov, Nicholas II (1868–1918), tsar of Russia from 1894 to 1917.

Romanov, Peter I, "The Great" (1672–1725), tsar and first emperor of Russia from 1682 to 1725.

Rostovsky, Dmitry (1651–1709), church leader who supported most of the reforms of Peter the Great.

Rozenburg, Vladimir Alexandrovich (1860–1932), journalist.

Rudnyov, Vadim Vasilievich (1874–1940), political figure and editor.

Rybnikov, Pavel Nikolaevich (1831–1885), ethnographer.

Saadi (1184?–1291), Persian Sulfi poet.

Sablin, Yury (Yurka) Vladimirovich (1897–1937), Red Army officer.

Saint-Just, Louis-Antoine-Leon de (1767–1794), Jacobin and member of the Committee of Public Safety in France.

Salikovsky, Alexander Fomich (1866–1925), Ukrainian journalist, civic and political leader, and ally of Petlyura.

Saltychikha, Darya Nikolaevna (pseudonym of Saltykova, Darya Nikolaevna) (1730–1801), landowner infamous for her cruelty toward her serfs.

Saltykov-Shchedrin, Mikhail Evgrafovich (1826–1889), writer and satirist.

Samarin, Alexander Dmitrievich (1868–1932), church and political figure.

Santayana, George (1863–1952), philosopher.

Sats, Natalya Il'inichna (1903–1993), writer, actor, and director.

Savich, Sergei Sergeevich (1863–?), pre-Revolutionary general.

Savina, Mariya Gavrilovna (1854–1915), actress.

Savinkov, Boris Viktorovich (pseudonym of Ropshin, Boris Viktorovich) (1879–1925), writer, member of the Social Revolutionary party, and minister of war in the Provisional Government.

Scheidemann, Philip (1865–1939), leader of the Social Democratic party in Germany, and first chancellor of the Weimar Republic.

Serafimovich, Alexander (pseudonym of Popov, Alexander Serafimovich) (1863–1949), writer and journalist.

Severnyi. See Yuzefovich.

Severyanin, Igor (pseudonym of Lotaryov, Igor Vasilievich) (1887–1941), poet.

Shchadenko, Efim Afanasievich (1885–1951), military commander in the Ukraine.

Shcheglovitov, Ivan Grigorievich (1861–1918), minister of justice from 1906 to 1915, and president of the State Council.

Shchepkin, Evgeny Nikolaevich (1860–1920), historian, professor, and political activist.

Shchepkina-Kupernik, Tatiana L'vovna (1874–1952), writer, and translator of Shakespeare and Molière.

Shershenevich, Vadim Gavrielevich (1893–1942), poet, theoretician, translator, playwright, and screenwriter.

Shishkov, Nikolai Filippovich (dates unknown), friend of Ivan Bunin.

Shklovsky, Viktor Borisovich (1893–1984), literary scholar, essayist, and novelist.

Shklyar, Nikolai Grigorievich (1876–1952), writer.

Shmelyov, Ivan Sergeevich (1873–1950), novelist and short-story writer.

Shmelyov, Sergei Ivanovich (1896–1921), artillery officer.

Shmidt, Ivan Fyodorovich (?–1939), director of the theater of the Red Fleet, and husband of Elena Alexandrovna Polevitskaya.

Shpan (dates unknown), Soviet commissar of theater.

Shpital'nikov, David Lazarevich (pseudonym of Tal'nikov, David Lazarevich) (1882–1961), literary and theater critic.

Skabichevsky, Alexander Mikhailovich (1838–1911), literary historian and critic.

Skobolev, Matvei Ivanovich (1855–1939), Menshevik and first minister of labor in the Provisional Government.

Slutsky, Anton Iosifovich (1884–1918), Bolshevik activist.

Sobol', Andrei (pseudonym of Sobol', Yuly Mikhailovich) (1881–1926), journalist, writer, and commissar for the Provisional Government on the Northern Front.

PROMINENT INDIVIDUALS

Sokolnikov, Grigory Yakovlevich (1888–1938), revolutionary and party official.

Sokolov-Mikitov, Ivan Sergeevich (1830–1892), writer.

Solovyov, Sergei Mikhailovich (1820–1879), historian and professor.

Solzhenitsyn, Alexander Isaevich (1918–), novelist and writer.

Speransky, Nikolai Vasilievich (1861–1921), journalist.

Spiridonova, Maria Alexandrovna (1884–1941), revolutionary, terrorist, and leader of the Left Socialist Revolutionary party.

Stanislavsky, Konstantin Sergeevich (1863–1938), actor, director, co-founder of the Moscow Art Theater in 1898.

Starostin, Pyotr Ivanovich (1881–1918), head of the regional executive committee of the Odessa Soviet Republic.

Steinberg, Isaak Zakharovich (1888–1957), Soviet commissar of justice.

Steklov, Yury Mikhailovich (pseudonym of Nakhamkis, Yury Mikhailovich) (1873–1941), revolutionary, party, and government figure, historian, and publicist.

Stuchka, Pyotr Ivanovich (1865–1932), Latvian revolutionary, political figure, lawyer, and writer.

Sudeikin, Sergei Yurevich (1882–1946), painter and stage designer.

Surikov, Vasily Ivanovich (1848–1916), painter.

Sverdlov, Yakov Mikhailovich (1885–1919), Bolshevik leader and titular head of the Soviet government from 1917 to 1919.

Svyatopolk Izyaslavich (1050–1113), grand prince of Kiev.

Sytin, Ivan Dmitrievich (1851–1931), publisher.

Tatishchev, Vasily Nikolaevich (1686–1750), historian.

Teffi, Nadezhda (pseudonym of Buchinskaya, Nadezhda Alexandrovna) (1872–1952), writer and poet.

Teleshov, Nikolai Dmitrievich (1867–1957), writer.

Teslenko, Nikolai Vasilievich (1870–1942), lawyer.

Tikhon (secular name: Belavin, Vasily Ivanovich) (1865–1925), patriarch of Moscow in 1917.

Tikhonov, Alexander Nikolaevich (pseudonym of Serebrov, Alexander Nikolaevich) (1880–1956), editor and writer.

Tolstoy, Alexei (Alyoshka) Nikolaevich (1883–1945), Soviet writer.

Tolstoy, Alexei Konstantinovich (1817–1875), poet.

Tolstoy, Leo Nikolaevich (1828–1910), novelist.

Trenyov, Konstantin Andreevich (1876–1945), writer and dramatist.

PROMINENT INDIVIDUALS

Trotsky, Leon (pseudonym of Bronstein, Lev Davidovich) (1879–1940), revolutionary Marxist, Bolshevik leader, and Soviet official.

Trubetskoy, Prince Evgeny Nikolaevich (1863–1920), religious philosopher, lawyer, and social figure.

Tsakni, Anna Nikolaevna (1879–1963), Bunin's first wife.

Tseitlin, Mikhail Osipovich (1882–1945), poet and critic.

Tseitlina, Maria Samoilovna (1882–1976), wife of Mikhail Tseitlin.

Tsereteli, Irakly Georgievich (1882–1959), Menshevik and first minister of posts and telegraphs in the Provisional Government.

Turgenev, Ivan Sergeevich (1818–1883), writer.

Tyutchev, Fyodor Ivanovich (1803–1873), poet.

Ul'yanov, Alexander Ilyich (1866–1887), older brother of Vladimir Lenin.

Ul'yanov, il'ia Nikolaevich (1831–1886), father of Vladimir Lenin.

Uritsky, Moisei Solomonovich (1873–1918), revolutionary and party activist.

Us, Vasily Rodionovich (?–1671), Cossack follower of Sten'ka Razin.

Uspensky, Gleb Ivanovich (1843–1902), writer and journalist.

Uspensky, Nikolai Vasilievich (1837–1889), writer and cousin of Gleb Uspensky.

Varneke, Boris Vasilievich (1874–1944), philologist and historian of the Russian theater.

Varshavsky, Sergei Ivanovich (1879–?), journalist.

Vas'kovsky, A. V. (dates unknown), artist.

Vasnetsov, Apollon Mikhailovich (1856–1933), painter.

Verhaeren, Emile (1855–1916), Belgian critic, dramatist, and poet.

Vertinsky, Alexander Nikolaevich (1889–1957), poet, singer, actor, composer, and memoirist.

Veselovsky, Yuly Alexeevich (1872–1919), literary scholar and writer.

Vladimir Svyatoslavich (?–1015), also known as Saint Vladimir the Great, ruler of Kievan Rus'.

Voloshin, Maximilian Alexandrovich (1877–1932), poet.

Vyrubov, Vasily Vasilievich (?–1963), social figure.

Wilde, Oscar (1856–1900), Irish poet and dramatist.

William II (1859–1941), last Hohenzollern ruler of Germany, forced to abdicate in the German revolution of 1918.

Wilson, (Thomas) Woodrow (1856–1924), twenty-eighth president of the United States.

PROMINENT INDIVIDUALS

Wrangel, Pyotr Nikolaevich (1878–1928), White general.

Yablonovsky, Alexander Alexandrovich (1870–1934), journalist.

Yakushkin, Pavel Ivanovich (1822–1872), writer, ethnographer, and folklorist.

Yanovsky, Feofil Gavrilovich (1860–1928), clinical therapist and member of the Ukrainian Academy of Sciences.

Yanushkevich, Nikolai Nikolaevich (1868–1918), White general.

Yaroslav Vladimirovich, the Wise (978–1054), prince of Rostov, Novgorod, and Kiev.

Yavorskaya, Lidiya Borisovna (pseudonym of Gyubbenet, Lidiya Borisovna) (1871–1921), actress.

Yordansky, Nikolai Ivanovich (1876–1928), journalist.

Yushkevich, Pavel Solomonovich (1873–1945), Social Democrat, philosopher, and brother of Semyon Yushkevich.

Yushkevich, Semyon Solomonovich (1868–1927), writer and brother of Pavel Yushkevich.

Yuzefovich, Boris Samoilovich (dates unknown), head of the Cheka in Odessa in 1919.

Zagoskin, Mikhail Nikolaevich (1789–1852), historical novelist.

Zamyatin, Evgeny Ivanovich (1884–1927), writer, literary critic, dramatist, and editor.

Zeeler, Vladimir Feofilovich (1874–1954), lawyer.

Zelyonyi, Danylo (pseudonym of Terpylo, Danylo) (1883–1919), Ukrainian peasant warlord.

Zhemchuzhnikov, Alexei Mikhailovich (1821–1908), poet.

Zhemchuzhnikov, Vladimir Mikhailovich (1830–1884), poet and brother of Alexei Zhemchuzhnikov.

Ziber, Nikolai Ivanovich (1844–1888), economist and popularizer of Marxism in Russia.

Zinoviev, Grigory Evseevich (pseudonym of Radomyslsky, Ovsei) (1883–1936), revolutionary and party official.

Zubov, Konstantin Alexandrovich (1888–1956), actor.

BIBLIOGRAPHY

SELECTED TRANSLATIONS OF BUNIN'S WORKS

Robert Bowie, *Ivan Bunin. In a Far Distant Land: Selected Stories* (Tenafly, N.J., 1983).

John Cournos, *Grammar of Love and Other Stories* (Westport, Conn., 1977).

Bernard Guerney, *The Elagin Affair and Other Stories* (New York, 1968); *The Gentleman from San Francisco and Other Stories by Ivan Bunin* (New York, 1964).

Richard Hare, *Dark Avenues and Other Stories by Ivan Bunin* (London, 1984).

William Ransom, *The Gentleman from San Francisco and Other Stories* (London, 1975).

David Richard, *The Gentleman from San Francisco and Other Stories* (London, 1993).

Mark Scott, *Wolves and Other Stories* (Santa Barbara, Calif., 1980).

Olga Shartse, *Ivan Bunin, Shadowed Paths* (Moscow, 195- and 1979); *Light Breathing and Other Stories* (Moscow, 1988).

Andrew Baruch Wachtel, *The Life of Arsen'ev. Youth* (Evanston, Ill., 1994).

BIBLIOGRAPHY

CRITICAL WORKS

On Bunin:

Julian Connolly, *Ivan Bunin* (Boston, 1982).

Serge Kryzytski, *The Works of Ivan Bunin* (The Hague, 1961).

Thomas G. Marullo, *Ivan Bunin: Russian Requiem, 1885–1920* (Chicago, 1993); *Ivan Bunin: From the Other Shore, 1920–1933* (Chicago, 1995); *Ivan Bunin: The Twilight of "Emigré" Russia, 1934–1953* (Chicago, forthcoming); *If You See the Buddha: Studies in the Fiction of Ivan Bunin* (Evanston, Ill., forthcoming).

On the Russian Civil War:

J. Bradley, *Allied Intervention in Russia* (London, 1968).

G. Brinkley, *The Volunteer Army and Allied Intervention in South Russia, 1917–1921* (Notre Dame, 1966).

P. Kenez, *Civil War in South Russia, 1918* (Berkeley, 1971); *Civil War in South Russia, 1919–1920* (Berkeley, 1977).

D. Lehovich, *White Against Red: The Life of General Anton Denikin* (New York, 1974).

W. B. Lincoln, *Red Victory: A History of the Russian Civil War* (New York, 1989).

E. Mawdsley, *The Russian Civil War* (Boston, 1987).

J. Swettenham, *Allied Intervention in Russia, 1918–1919* (London, 1967).

INDEX

INDEX

INDEX

Kachalov, Vasily, 30n, 261
Kadets. *See* Cadets.
Kaledin, Alexei, 46n, 57, 61, 262
Kamenets, 174
Kamenev, Lev, 60, 140, 262
Kamenev, Nikolai, 46, 74, 216n, 262
Kamenskaya, O. A., 53, 262
Kamensky, Anatoly, 53, 262
Kamyshin, 206
Kannegiser, Leonid, 216n
Karakhan, Lev. *See* Rozenfeld, Lev.
Kasabov, Blagoi, 111, 262
Kataev, Valentin, 10, 11, 12, 13, 77, 129, 262
Kaufman, Alexander, 205, 262
Kautsky, Karl, 226, 262
Kazi-Mullah. *See* Gazi-Magomed.
Kemal, Mustafa, 175n, 262
Kerensky, Alexander, 11, 70n, 213, 220n, 222, 237, 262
Kharkov, 65, 83, 89n, 179, 204, 205, 206, 207
Khemnitser, Ivan, 126n, 262
Kherson, 83
Khmel'nitsky, Bogdan, 244
Khmelnytskyi, 173
Khudyakov, Nikolai, 262
Khudyakova, Klavdia, 170, 262
Kievan Thought, 187
Kipen, Alexander, 141, 262
Kireevsky, Pyotr, 250, 262
Kirovgrad, 142
Kishkin, Nikolai, 220n, 221, 262
Klestov-Angarsky, Nikolai, 49, 262
Klimov, Sergei, 163
Klyuchevsky, Vasily, 147, 262
Klyuev, Nikolai, 157, 262
Knipper-Chekhova, Olga, 11, 262
Kogan, Pyotr, 32, 50, 263

Koiransky, Alexander (Sasha), 30, 137, 263
Kokoshkin, Fyodor, 184, 255, 263
Kolchak, Alexander, 78n, 83, 94, 110, 111, 122, 135, 161, 204, 263; Belebey and, 157, 158; Entente and, 177; fleeing of, 207; joining with Denikin, 196, 197; Trotsky article about, 121; Ufa and, 175n
Kollontai, Alexandra, 122, 198, 263
Kondakov, Nikodim, 173, 263
Konstantinograd. *See* Krasnograd.
Korneichukov, Kornei. *See* Chukovsky, Kornei.
Kornilov, Lavr, 61, 62, 200, 213, 263; Volunteer Army and, 84n
Korocha, 207
Korolenko, Vladimir, 107, 263
Kosciusko, Thaddeus, 166, 263
Kostomarov, Nikolai, 148, 246n, 263
Krasnograd, 207
Kronkardi, 155
Kronstadt, 174
Kropotkin, Pyotr, 166, 263
Krupskaya, Nadezhda, 263; Lenin and, 263; mug shot of, 74n
Krylov, Ivan, 126, 263
Kshesinskaya, Matil'da (Maria), 119, 263
Kudinov, Adrian, 34
Kun, Bela, 205n, 263
Kuprin, Alexander, 8, 30n, 193n, 263
Kurbsky, Andrei, 153n, 263
Kursk, 204, 205, 206
Kuskova, Ekaterina, 45, 264
Kutuzov, Mikhail, 42, 264
Kuz'min, Mikhail, 63n, 264

INDEX

INDEX

INDEX

INDEX

INDEX

INDEX

INDEX

A NOTE ON THE EDITOR

Thomas Gaiton Marullo is associate professor of Russian and Russian Literature at the University of Notre Dame. He was born in Brooklyn, New York, and grew up on Long Island. He received a bachelor's degree from the College of the Holy Cross, and M.A. and Ph.D. degrees from Cornell University, and has held fellowships from the Lilly Endowment and the National Endowment for the Humanities. The first two volumes of his re-creation of Ivan Bunin's life through letters, diaries, and fiction, titled *Ivan Bunin: Russian Requiem, 1885–1920,* and *Ivan Bunin: From the Other Shore, 1920–1933,* have been widely acclaimed. His study of Bunin's fiction, *If You See the Buddha,* is forthcoming.